THE STATES AND THE NATION SERIES, of which this volume is a part, is designed to assist the American people in a serious look at the ideals they have espoused and the experiences they have undergone in the history of the nation. The content of every volume represents the scholarship, experience, and opinions of its author. The costs of writing and editing were met mainly by grants from the National Endowment for the Humanities, a federal agency. The project was administered by the American Association for State and Local History, a nonprofit learned society, working with an Editorial Board of distinguished editors, authors, and historians, whose names are listed below.

EDITORIAL ADVISORY BOARD

James Morton Smith, General Editor
Director, State Historical Society
of Wisconsin

William T. Alderson, Director
American Association for
State and Local History

Roscoe C. Born
Vice-Editor
The National Observer

Vernon Carstensen
Professor of History
University of Washington

Michael Kammen, Professor of
American History and Culture
Cornell University

Louis L. Tucker
President (1972–1974)
American Association for
State and Local History

Joan Paterson Kerr
Consulting Editor
American Heritage

Richard M. Ketchum
Editor and Author
Dorset, Vermont

A. Russell Mortensen
Assistant Director
National Park Service

Lawrence W. Towner
Director and Librarian
The Newberry Library

Richmond D. Williams
President (1974–1976)
American Association for
State and Local History

MANAGING EDITOR

Gerald George
American Association for
State and Local History

Texas

A Bicentennial History

Joe B. Frantz

W. W. Norton & Company, Inc.
New York

American Association for State and Local History
Nashville

Copyright © 1976 by
Joe B. Frantz
All rights reserved

Published and distributed by W. W. Norton & Co., Inc.
500 Fifth Avenue
New York, New York 10036

Library of Congress Cataloging in Publication Data

Frantz, Joe Bertram, 1917–
    Texas: a Bicentennial history.

    (The States and the Nation series)
    Bibliography: p.
    Includes index.
    1. Texas—History. I. Series.
F386.F72   976.4   76–23132
ISBN 0–393–05580–9

Printed in the United States of America
1 2 3 4 5 6 7 8 9 0

To Jolie and Lisa

Contents

Illustrations

Invitation to the Reader

IN 1807, former President John Adams argued that a complete history of the American Revolution could not be written until the history of change in each state was known, because the principles of the Revolution were as various as the states that went through it. Two hundred years after the Declaration of Independence, the American nation has spread over a continent and beyond. The states have grown in number from thirteen to fifty. And democratic principles have been interpreted differently in every one of them.

We therefore invite you to consider that the history of your state may have more to do with the bicentennial review of the American Revolution than does the story of Bunker Hill or Valley Forge. The Revolution has continued as Americans extended liberty and democracy over a vast territory. John Adams was right: the states are part of that story, and the story is incomplete without an account of their diversity.

The Declaration of Independence stressed life, liberty, and the pursuit of happiness; accordingly, it shattered the notion of holding new territories in the subordinate status of colonies. The Northwest Ordinance of 1787 set forth a procedure for new states to enter the Union on an equal footing with the old. The Federal Constitution shortly confirmed this novel means of building a nation out of equal states. The step-by-step process through which territories have achieved self-government and national representation is among the most important of the Founding Fathers' legacies.

The method of state-making reconciled the ancient conflict between liberty and empire, resulting in what Thomas Jefferson called an empire for liberty. The system has worked and remains unaltered, despite enormous changes that have taken

place in the nation. The country's extent and variety now sur-
pass anything the patriots of '76 could likely have imagined.
The United States has changed from an agrarian republic into a
highly industrial and urban democracy, from a fledgling nation
into a major world power. As Oliver Wendell Holmes remarked
in 1920, the creators of the nation could not have seen completely how it and its constitution and its states would develop.
Any meaningful review in the bicentennial era must consider
what the country has become, as well as what it was.

The new nation of equal states took as its motto *E Pluribus
Unum*—"out of many, one." But just as many peoples have
become Americans without complete loss of ethnic and cultural
identities, so have the states retained differences of character.
Some have been superficial, expressed in stereotyped images—
big, boastful Texas, "sophisticated" New York, "hillbilly"
Arkansas. Other differences have been more real, sometimes instructively, sometimes amusingly; democracy has embraced
Huey Long's Louisiana, bilingual New Mexico, unicameral Nebraska, and a Texas that once taxed fortunetellers and spawned
politicians called "Woodpecker Republicans" and "Skunk
Democrats." Some differences have been profound, as when
South Carolina secessionists led other states out of the Union in
opposition to abolitionists in Massachusetts and Ohio. The result was a bitter Civil War.

The Revolution's first shots may have sounded in Lexington
and Concord; but fights over what democracy should mean and
who should have independence have erupted from Pennsylvania's Gettysburg to the "Bleeding Kansas" of John Brown,
from the Alamo in Texas to the Indian battles at Montana's
Little Bighorn. Utah Mormons have known the strain of isola-
tion; Hawaiians at Pearl Harbor, the terror of attack; Georgians
during Sherman's march, the sadness of defeat and devastation.
Each state's experience differs instructively; each adds understanding to the whole.

The purpose of this series of books is to make that kind of understanding accessible, in a way that will last in value far
beyond the bicentennial fireworks. The series offers a volume
on every state, plus the District of Columbia—fifty-one, in all.

Each book contains, besides the text, a view of the state through eyes other than the author's—a "photographer's essay," in which a skilled photographer presents his own personal perceptions of the state's contemporary flavor.

We have asked authors not for comprehensive chronicles, nor for research monographs or new data for scholars. Bibliographies and footnotes are minimal. We have asked each author for a summing up—interpretive, sensitive, thoughtful, individual, even personal—of what seems significant about his or her state's history. What distinguishes it? What has mattered about it, to its own people and to the rest of the nation? What has it come to now?

To interpret the states in all their variety, we have sought a variety of backgrounds in authors themselves and have encouraged variety in the approaches they take. They have in common only these things: historical knowledge, writing skill, and strong personal feelings about a particular state. Each has wide latitude for the use of the short space. And if each succeeds, it will be by offering you, in your capacity as a *citizen* of a state *and* of a nation, stimulating insights to test against your own.

James Morton Smith
General Editor

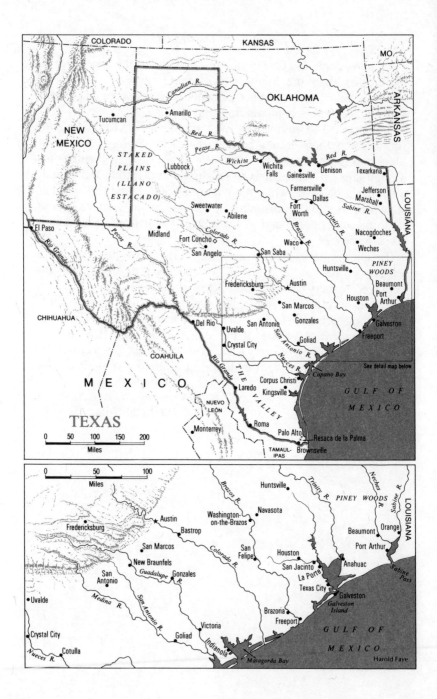

Harold Faye

Preface

WRITING a history of Texas with a short deadline, even a history more long on interpretation than loaded with fact, requires a carload of leaning on historians who have plowed ahead of me. In some instances I am reminded of Irvin S. Cobb, who once turned a phrase he liked and then admitted that he would have liked to have been its author but some clod plagiarized him before he had a chance to write it. A number of authors have already felt what I felt and said what I said, and I'll never know whether my interpretation is original or was shaded by them. Somewhere back there I read them and, since I have certain spongelike tendencies, I must have absorbed. But in the book ahead what I have tried to squeeze out are my own feelings, not theirs.

The three best factual books on Texas are Rupert N. Richardson, *Texas, the Lone Star State;* Seymour V. Connor, *Texas: A History;* and T. R. Fehrenbach, *Lone Star: A History of Texas and The Texans*. I have utilized Fehrenbach the least, for his is the fullest and most exciting, and I had space strictures. The most sophisticated book is by George Fuermann, *The Reluctant Empire,* but is like good Scotch to a connoisseur of fine whiskies—once you start sipping, there's no place to stop. And I have borrowed outrageously from myself, principally from articles in *The American West* and chapters in various books, notably John Francis McDermott, editor, *The Frontier Re-examined*. Finally, Walter Prescott Webb and H. Bailey Carroll's two-volume *Handbook of Texas* and the *Southwestern Historical Quarterly* have been staunch underwriters of my effort here.

In terms of personal support highest thanks go to Ruth C. Mathews, who has stayed a paragraph behind as we came roaring down the expressway like a two-ton truck with no brakes—I suppose I was the cab and she was the trailer, pushing as much as she was being pulled. Also, my gratitude goes to my wife,

Helen, who yielded that most precious commodity—time; to Gerald George of the American Association for State and Local History, who has been a rarity, an understanding and encouraging editor; to Russell Mortensen of the National Park Service, who persuaded me to undertake this task; to Eldon Branda, Arthur Mayer, and Susan Rubin, who checked and suggested; to the staff of the Texas Collection of The University of Texas at Austin, especially James C. Martin; to Colleen T. Kain, who cleared paths; to a much maligned institution, The University of Texas at Austin, which has always given me freedom to do what I wanted to do and seldom asks what I am doing with my time (when someone does inquire, he is usually a newcomer); and finally, to all those people who had to wait on my promises while I intruded this effort into my schedule.

I have enjoyed reliving the past of Texas. If I have one advantage, it is that I have suffered with the state most of my life, have lived away just enough to see it through outsiders' eyes, and perhaps can keep its foibles and failures, as well as its occasional triumphs, in perspective. Like the academic missionaries who move into the state, I sometimes think it is the most difficult, disappointing, overblown state in the Union—and then I visit Nebraska or Pennsylvania and rediscover that Texas has no exclusive contract on stupidity, obduracy, or bloody-mindedness. What really hurts about Texas lies in what it could be against what it is, and the fact that its leadership seldom reaches for top rungs. Its successive governors don't lead; they administer—comfortably.

Maybe in the pages ahead you can discern how Texas maneuvered itself into such a stalemate. My own feeling is that it was more enlightened, more sure of itself, more grasping for the right things in the period from 1890 to 1910 than it is now. But how do you reverse a backslide?

JOE B. FRANTZ

Austin, Texas

Texas

1

A Creature Called Texan

*F*OR nearly a century North Americans have fed on the
theory that from the time those first colonists moved
inland from Jamestown or Massachusetts Bay, they carried with them the elements of civilization—adapted to chang-
ing circumstances as they moved the frontier inland. This experience is supposed to explain the evolving democratic
institutions of the United States, a continuous development as
the cutting edge of civilization moved ever westward and sub-
dued the frontier and wilderness.

But the theory does not hold for the southwest in general or
for Texas in particular. When the Pilgrims landed at Plymouth
Rock, Texas had already known the European and the African
for more than nine-tenths of a century. By the time North Americans entered Texas the Mexicans had long since established
reasonably sophisticated political, social, and religious organizations and had even made educational progress. The same
holds true, of course, for Santa Fe and California. While Anglo-
Americans might delude themselves into believing that they
brought civilization to the frontier of Texas and points westward, the fact remains that they encountered an on-going civilization, couldn't quite adapt, and, as in other instances in which
solutions weren't easy, saw no choice but to take over. Unlike
their dilemma with aboriginal culture, however, they could not
adapt to the "Mexican problem" by exterminating their hosts.

3

In fact, some aspects of the Spanish-Mexican influence have been absolutely crucial to the settlement of Texas—most notably an understanding of ranginess, of thinking large. In New England, and in the European countries from which the New Englander came, a householder could subsist on eight acres and make a reasonable living selling his produce. In the west a steer would starve to death on eight acres, and an Indian or a Texan would get a sort of claustrophobia from such confinement. All need spaciousness.

Out of the large scale of thinking, and out of the clash between the Anglo and his Hispanic predecessors in Texas, has come a tendency to caricature the Texan. The Texan does it himself; but even more those who haven't quite come to terms with the fact of Texas's existence have resorted to it. The Texas man is expected to be tall, skinny, friendly, quick-tempered, charitable toward his friends and merciless toward his enemies, shy around good women, a hell-horse with more compliant ones, and possessor of a dozen other recognizable stereotypical attributes. Flamboyant, violent—the state and its citizens are expected to be bigger and tougher than life. In some ways he (or she—but the image is a very masculine one) is the epitome of the frontiersman; yet Texas became a sophisticated, stable government a good half-century before the frontier closed down and ranks chronologically ahead of such wild and woolly states as Michigan, Minnesota, and Kansas.

Not that Texans and Texas history evolved in a vacuum, with all characteristics theirs alone. They have their shared experiences. For instance, one factor that Texans share with the original thirteen states is the delay in finding mineral wealth, a delay that historical moralists tell us built perseverance, habits of hard work, and general good character. The English colonists arrived at Jamestown alive to the story of fabled wealth in the New World. The Spanish had gone into Hispañola and found some gold and then had moved on to Mexico and to Perú to extract unbelievable riches from beneath the soil. They had turned new money loose in the Old World, and a boom of unparalleled wealth lasting for five hundred years had ensued. Since the British did not believe that God was exclusively Spanish, they saw

no reason why He should not shower them with the same boun-
teous blessings when they began their colonization and exploration of their portion of the hemisphere. Instead, the British had
found land suitable chiefly for agriculture and for the slower
tempo of commerce. They had to cultivate patience, grow their
gold in the tobacco fields, and develop their wealth around the
rivers and harbors connecting the budding commercial towns.
Unlike the Spanish, they could not proceed into a new area, dig
deeply, carry out bags of precious metal, and lavish loot at
home and abroad. The British had to work and wait for their bo-
nanzas. They didn't even suffer the intermittent dreams and
disillusions of Cíbola.

Therefore, unlike the Spanish also, the British learned that organization and unceasing endeavor provided payoff, and although they probably never articulated the phrase, they also
learned to avoid the easy-come, easy-go attitude of the Spanish
colonials, as well as the Spanish Crown and its favored subjects
at home. The result was that the British created wealth, while
their utilization of organization continued. Not until more than
two centuries after it was settled did great mineral wealth come
to the United States, with the discovery of gold in California in
quantity. By then, the United States was strong enough and ma-
ture enough to take that windfall in its stride.

Similarly for Texas. The Seven Cities of Cíbola never allured
Texas, nor was there any Taxco or Potosí. No mountains of silver, no hills of gold to be loaded on the backs of the aborigines
and hauled to the central countinghouses. In fact, most of Texas
was geographically formidable in its refusal to cooperate with
the gathering of wealth. In the East and Southeast conditions ap-
proximated those of the Old South, and men could grow cotton
and fell trees and build towns around those activities that slowly
developed solidity. But "slowly" is the apposite word here.
Farther into Texas, the soil was inhospitable and the lack of rain
frequently disastrous. Irrigation projects had to be developed,
which takes time. At the end of its first fifty years as an Anglo-
American state and nation, Texas was settled only about one-
third of the way across its surface, just as the United States
required two hundred years to grow from Massachusetts Bay to

St. Louis. By the time Texas discovered at Spindletop its great pool of liquid gold that would set it on the road to undreamed-of riches, it had known two-thirds of a century as an organized area belonging to the have-not classification. As late as 1900, Texas was importing the bulk of its petroleum from Indian Territory. Texas had space, lots of square miles and heaps of acres and quarter-sections, but it anticipated slow ascent up the ladder of profusion.

Spindletop turned around that expectation and accelerated Texas growth until its expansion became one of the major commercial and productive influences in the nation based on something besides sheer spaciousness. But Texas, like the United States before it, had already learned to be patient, work hard, scan the skies, and pray for (but expect no) miracles. Texas's winning its lottery ticket somewhat late in its development parallels the story of the United States. The experience is important: though Texas has its share of immature tycoons grown affluent on exploiting resources and tireless in spreading their philosophical and political effluvia, most of its people remain workers who go steadily about their tasks. Texas was not spoiled in childhood, made unfit for honest labor, and forced to adjust to a world of windfalls. Instead, most pioneer Texans developed quiet character, not showy squandering, and somehow helped build a state with many prominent features. True, they did not always build wisely nor with consideration.

But right and wrong, mainstream and isolated, the Texan has remained an interesting, frequently implausible creature, alternatively exciting scorn, admiration, revulsion, consternation, fascination, and rejection—but always curiosity. And he has claimed his share of the continuing American drama.

2

The First Indians

ONCE Texas was a great empty land, a world of animals
and birds and insects and fish and Nature. And then, slowly,
people came into that land. They learned to bend copper and
bone into fishhooks, and they learned to chase and surround and
exhaust and stake out, and they learned to scavenge, and they
learned to live with the forests and the mountains and the
deserts and the prairies.

The first Texans spanned out over an area the size of modern
France. They didn't farm nor apartment-dwell in pueblos nor
cling to the sides of cliffs. They walked from bush to bush,
while basically pursuing a feral existence barely above the level
of carrion-eating animals. These Indians did not weave intricate
baskets or leave behind geometrically prized shards of pottery.
Instead, they left a huge sense of vacuum for the archaeologist,
who has had to piece together second-hand from those soldiers,
missionaries, explorers, and travelers who first came to Texas
most of what has been learned about the prehistoric Texan. To
reconstruct from the remains of the Indians in Texas would be
to build an anthill of knowledge in the presence of the mountain
of facts gathered from the other Indian groups who preceded the
coming of the European to the shores of North America. To the
Maya, Aztec, Hopi, Navajo, Iroquois, Pequot, Cherokee, the
Indians of Texas would have been simple and savage.

The earliest of these peoples, having long since learned to

7

make and use fire, to clothe himself, and to use some stone and maybe bone tools, showed up in Texas as the Llano man. He was a specialist in hunting an extinct species of elephant with a Clovis fluted point—a primitive flint spear or dart point. Although there has been some published evidence that a site near Lewisville in Denton County contains artifacts dating earlier than the 37,000-year range of radiocarbon dating, the generally accepted limit of the Llano civilization is about 12,000 years old.

Without attempting to write a millennium-by-millennium account of the progress of primal man in Texas, we can skip down quickly to a period when the Europeans arrived to find the Texas Indian, still a hunter, still aboriginal, still going his own elemental way, apparently untouched by and unreceptive to the cultural advancements of other Indians in Mexico, New Mexico, or the southeastern United States. Anthropologists agree that the reason must have been environment.

Anyway, the first Europeans found Texas a meeting ground for four distinctive cultural types, much as Texas today represents a crossroads for the Old South, the Spanish Southwest, and the Midwest. Along the coast and lapping across into northeastern Mexico were the Coahuiltecan and Karankawa tribes, living in their "cultural sink," so-called because anthropologists know so little about their original antecedents and because of the backwardness of the culture. They were a primitive people, somehow keeping starvation at arm's length while downing a bill of fare that included such exotic foods as berries (in season), animal dung, spiders, and an occasional—very occasional—deer, bison, or javelina which had given up its own chase or been encircled by fire. These two bands had any number of sub-bands with names known only to the specialist—the Payayas, the Katuhanos, the Capoques, and the Malaguites, to identify only an exotic quartet out of scores.

Theirs was largely a static culture, dedicated to supplying minimum needs. They did a little communal hunting, surrounding rabbits and an occasional bison; they dug pitfalls for javelinas, and they built traps of sharpened stakes, along which deer might impale themselves as they jumped the stakes. They also shot fish with bow and arrow and learned to seine. Evidently too they had discovered mescal, which mixed with ground red beans could make a poor man feel opulent. So could peyote, from which they obtained visions of well-being long before such hallucinating was fashionable.

In the center of Texas roamed the Tonkawas. Comparatively they were a superior people, hunting buffalo, sleeping in tee-pees, and otherwise behaving like uptown Plains Indians. Their name was derived from a Waco term meaning "they all stay together." The Tonkawas called themselves *tickanwatic,* which means "most human of people." As a group they were southern Plains Indians, closely similar to Lipan Apaches. Like other Plains Indians, they used dogs to pack buffalo hides. They also supposedly used poisoned arrows dipped in mistletoe on their opponents, who were not the last Texans to be poisoned by this omnipresent parasite.

Unlike the Karankawas, who were tall, they seem to have been ordinary sized, though quite slender and fleet. They tattooed, particularly the male torso, and the men wore extremely long breechclouts. About all the women wore were short skin skirts, and in warm weather the little children did not even wear that much. The men liked ornamentation, and the women too decorated their bodies with black stripes. Once the European arrived, they went downhill fast as a tribe, partly from introduced diseases. Unable to sustain themselves in an increasingly European world, they even resorted to requesting missions from the Spaniards, though the white man's religion was the least of their concerns. They wanted alliances, not Franciscan instruction.

In east and northeast Texas lived about two dozen tribes of Caddo Indians, who also spilled over into Louisiana, Arkansas, and Oklahoma and were really members of a southeast culture area. They tended to confederate, and the Kadohadacho and Hasinai confederacies undoubtedly provided the most advanced culture of all Texas Indians. Although, like the other early Indians, they were unable to sustain their culture into the era of Texas statehood, they were in today's term achievers. They practiced agriculture with some competence, probably the only aboriginal Texas group that did. Since they could be sure of food supply, they developed a relatively stable population and a cultural structure that is quite remarkable.

The Caddos would have been novel if for no other reason than they gave the state its name. The Hasinai confederation called each other *Tayshas*, a term that meant "allies" or "friends." When the Spanish came, the Hasinai let these wanderers know that they too were *Tayshas*, which the Spanish wrote as *Tejas* and which time has transformed into *Texas*.

Anthropologists believe that Caddo civilization may well stretch back a thousand years into prehistory, and that they may well have been going downhill in their civilization instead of forward when the white man encountered them. They had the good fortune, or the good sense, to live in the genteel part of Texas, the "piney woods" which support prime and hardwood forests (or did till the white exploiters began to clean out much of them), wild-plant foods, and black bear, deer, and buffalo. It was to the Hasinais that some of LaSalle's sad Texas explorers deserted because they were so much friendlier than fellow Frenchmen. But when shortly afterwards the Spanish moved into east Texas to establish missions among the Caddos, they found that the Tejanos were hostile to being taught what they didn't want to know. The result was that in March 1694 the viceroy of Mexico formally ordered abandonment of the province in Tejas. But at least the name of Tejas was beginning to stand up.

Some Caddos practiced artificial cranial deformation by making their heads taper toward the top, a practice tracing to prehistoric times. Like the Tonkawas, they also practiced a primitive form of tattooing. The men frequently tattooed plant and animal designs about their bodies, while the women placed tattooes at the corner of their eyes, not unlike today's well-turned out Texas lovely. When they met strangers, they wept and wailed. Both men and women practiced this public weeping, which required a bit of getting used to for Europeans. Both French and Spanish learned that Caddo women also wept in the face of impending death, so that if they caught a woman weeping, they wondered whether it was for their own imminent death that the tears were being shed.

When Henri de Tonti came looking for LaSalle's survivors, not only did the Caddos weep over him, but he ran into another avant-garde situation. The chief was a woman, whose husband had died at the hands of the Osages. To this extent the Caddos were more than three hundred years ahead of other Americans, though Texas with its Governor Ma Ferguson is not so much a sinner in this respect.

Even their religion provided a top role for a woman, instead of making her something of a tagalong in man's afterworld, the way that Christians and Jews and Mohammedans and Buddhists see the supernatural. Along with other southeastern Indians the Caddos believed in a deity who had created the universe and was omnipotent in directing its creatures. But unlike the Biblical statement that in the beginning was God, in the Caddo beginning there were first three women, a mother and two daughters.

The Caddos also showed certain other flourishes of modernity. They not only made two crops of corn each growing season, but they kept seed corn for at least two years ahead, they grew several varieties of beans, and wonder of wonders, the men worked alongside the women in the gardens, handling the heavier tasks. Only the leader was excused from productive labor.

Away out west, in trans-Pecos Texas, lived a fourth culture type of prehistoric Texan. Most commonly these people are known as Jumanos. Just as today the trans-Pecos is remote from the remainder of Texas, so are the Jumanos a remote people historically. Probably a part of the pueblo culture that wandered into Texas, the Jumanos have not been well delineated. They also disintegrated early enough following the European advent that anthropologists speak of them with more hesitation than of any other Texas group. They seem to have subdivided, one group living as settled gardeners, like their possible New Mexico cousins, in the valleys of the Rio Grande and the lower Rio Conchos. The other subgroup was comprised of hunters, in and beyond the Chisos and Davis mountains. Whether we are talking of two people, one nomadic and one sedentary, or whether we are talking of one people, some of whom were nomadic and some sedentary, is uncertain. But we do know that they were present when the first Spaniards came through and that they ranged from El Paso to the Pecos and even up the Rio Conchos in Chihuahua.

Where the Jumanos farmed, they raised good crops of corn, beans, squash, and possibly cotton. Beyond the range of the buffalo, they could only haul their dried meat from away off. They did seem to value buffalo hides. They owned some pottery, but Cabeza de Vaca noted that though the pottery could be used over fire, they still dropped heated rocks into pots to cook food. Why a people who owned pottery would cook by this method is another mystery.

What probably happened to the Jumanos was that they were caught up in time by the coming of the Spaniards. Theirs possibly had been a better civilization; but just as the Indians of another land abandoned great cities such as Tikal to move on to Chichén Itzá or Uxmal, to name the more obvious tourist visitations, or even as the cliff dwellers abandoned Mesa Verde, the Jumanos may have been caught by too many drouths, had been constricting for two hundred years when the Europeans arrived, and would have been gone from the area even if the Spanish had delayed their own arrival another century or two.

In their suffering from frequent drouth, the Jumanos strike a responsive chord with most old settlers of West Texas. Evidently the Indians had prolonged drouths over a period of three hundred years. West Texans have had prolonged drouths since they first pushed into the area in the latter part of the nineteenth century. They look for rain, and they pray for rain, and they even employ cloud seeders. But God answers prayers for rain only when the thunderheads are already building on the horizon. And how do you seed a cloud when you have no clouds? At times Texans feel that this country should be turned back to lizards and horny toads and scorpions and rattlesnakes—yes, and Jumanos—that if God had wanted human beings on the land, he would have invented rain. And undoubtedly like the Jumano many a Texan has migrated, his hopes seared and withered by the unending West Texas sun and his future clouded by eternally blue skies. Not all the Okies heading for California came from Oklahoma. In seeming ready to abandon the trans-Pecos to its steady heredity, the Jumanos were acting in the best Texas tradition.

These then are the principal people in Texas when the next wave of nationalities broke upon its shores. Other groups of Indians made their mark, some earlier, some later. To proceed doggedly from one native tribe to another—to include the Comanches, Kiowas, Wichitas, and Apakapans—could be justified, but basically they belong in a later time. The groups discussed here were the first Texans. Although less picturesque than other Indians scattered about the future United States, and although they left little mark on the road toward modern civilization, they were the best that Texas had to offer. Certainly other tribes in other areas influenced other future states to a greater degree. The first Texans did not even make the regional imprint that later Indians, such as the Comanches, left.

Nonetheless they *were* the first, the ones who gave the region a name, the ones who first wrestled with its vastness and its formidable geography and climate, the ones who first knew what Texas was all about. In them we discern the start of the Texas tradition.

Texas then has a strong Indian heritage from the standpoint of sheer chronology, one of the older within the continental United States. But Texas had almost no Indian tradition until the Spanish pushed their military-missionary activities after officials in Mexico and Madrid had been scared unreasonably by rumors that the French were about to take over the region. If LaSalle and his pathetic colony had never been blown off course onto the Texas coastline, the Indians might have been ignored until the Anglo-American thrust at the beginning of the nineteenth century. For all the tremendous conversion efforts back in Mexico proper and for all the exploitation of native labor in Montezuma's old empire, the Spanish treated the Texas Indian as if he did not exist and for nearly two centuries neither used nor abused him.

3

Sailors, Soldiers, and Pedestrians

*L*IKE so many others before and later, they were looking for a passage to the Orient. Acting under orders from the governor of Jamaica, they had hit the mainland shore at Vera Cruz in August 1519 only to find that the masterful Hernando Cortés had arrived there first, was in charge along the seacoast, and was on his way to taking charge of most of Mexico. So they had fled north, looking on Cortés not as a fellow countryman but as a rival who could strike like a Mexican serpent.

Thus came the first Europeans to Texas, four little ships and three hundred men commanded by Captain Alonso Alvarez de Pineda. Four thousand miles from where the center of western civilization was engulfed in a contest between established practice and revolutionary developments, these Spaniards laid eyes on the mouth of the Rio Grande, where they found naked Indians as friendly then as they would be to later arrivals, waiting to welcome them ashore and trade what little they had while each group peered curiously at the other. For forty days in the fall of 1519 Pineda remained while his men worked on the ships, explored inland, and decided that this river (which they christened Rio de las Palmas), while probably potentially important, provided no route to Cathay.

A year later the Indians could see another Spanish expedition,

14

again sent by the ambitious governor of Jamaica. This time the three ships that came over the horizon were under Diego de Camargo, and this time they came not because Cortés had chased them from down below but because they planned to counter the conquistador. They brought one hundred fifty soldiers, seven cavalrymen, masons, and materials with which to build. They sailed twenty miles up the river before coming to rest.

As before, the Texans were initially friendly. But whereas for forty days Pineda and his men had behaved themselves among their hosts, Camargo had come to take charge. Of how much, is not known; but by his heap of provisions and the presence of masons he undoubtedly intended to build a fort, and therefore to him the Indians were as inimical to his entry as was the presence of Cortés a vague hundred leagues to the south.

Whatever the provocation, the Indians turned on the invaders. The resulting battle cost Camargo eighteen men and his seven horses. The rest retreated to two of their ships and headed down-river with a fleet of canoes in pursuit. Other Indians lined the banks, threatening the ships with cries and stones and whatever else they could hurl. Since Camargo had not reconditioned his ships, he soon had to abandon another; ten days after the last crowded vessel reached Vera Cruz, it sank.

Three years later, still convinced that his future lay near the mouth of the Rio de las Palmas, Governor Francisco Garay brought his own expedition from Jamaica. He brought a bit of an armada: sixteen ships, two hundred guides, three hundred cannon, seven hundred fifty soldiers. Garay had laid out his plan of government before he had even left Jamaica. He seems to have expected to find one or two colonies from the two previous expeditions, and he probably wanted to set up rival claims to those of Cortés. From the mouth of the Rio de las Palmas, Garay sent one of his assistants up the river to find a site for a new city of Garay. When the official returned after four days with the report that he could find no suitable site, Garay decided that Texas should be left to Texans and took off toward Cortés—who did not exactly welcome him.

While Garay was imprisoned by Cortés, he commiserated

with Panfilo Narvaez, an involuntary houseguest of Cortés who had been sent by the governor of Cuba to arrest his host. From Garay, Narvaez learned of the Rio de las Palmas. When finally he could return to Spain, Narvaez petitioned for a chance at the Texas coast; in 1525 he was granted a new province of Panuco-Victoria Garayana, which was to run from the Atlantic to the Rio de las Palmas. With the naming of Narvaez as *adelanto* for this immense stretch of coastland, the story of modern Texas begins.

Narvaez and his four-hundred-man expedition embarked from Cuba for the Rio de las Palmas. Seven years passed before they were heard from again. The hapless band soon began to fall apart, and Narvaez eventually gave up all pretense of command. In late September 1528, the remaining men built five large rafts and set out on the Gulf of Mexico. They were no sailors, knowing only that they needed to go west. Some of the men starved, others died from drinking seawater; when they put ashore to forage, Indians drove them back to the gulf. The rafts became separated, and Narvaez himself vanished one night in a storm.

One man, Juan Ortiz, was eventually rescued back in Florida by de Soto. Of the others, only four emerged from their ordeal. The leader of the quartet was Alvar Nuñez Cabeza de Vaca, royally appointed treasurer of the proposed colony. The others were Captain Alonso de Castillo Maldonado and Andrés Dorantes de Carranza—both, like Cabeza de Vaca, Spaniards—and Carranza's slave, a black Moroccan named Estevanico.

Although Cabeza de Vaca should rate as one of the great adventurers in the history of the future United States, most Texans accept him as just another intriguing explorer. Almost nothing in Texas (nor the United States) commemorates his incredible career. He is the first white Texan who matters, but if he didn't have a name that rolls off the tongue and translates into "head of a cow," he probably would not be remembered by most Texas schoolboys.

His Texas story begins on November 6, 1528, on an elongated sandbar populated by perhaps one hundred curious Indians. The Spanish found the Indians friendly and in a pattern to be repeated innumerable times exchanged trinkets for fish and roots. When the Spaniards tried to sail away, however, they had bad luck; after two attempts, both their boats sank—bearing with them the Spaniards' clothes, which they had removed and stowed in the boats. Soaked to the skin and chilled by a norther, the Spaniards tried to find shelter in the lee of the dunes. Here the Indians found them and adopted the castaways, clothed them after a fashion, fed them, and danced around them all night. It must have been a performance that any Texan with an ounce of flamboyance could have enjoyed, though the Spaniards evidently were terrified that they might provide the Indians' next meal.

The Indians soon ran out of food, and the winter wind was too high and cold for fishing. Gradually the eighty Spaniards were reduced to fifteen, and half the Indians soon died as well. No wonder the Spaniards named the island Malhado—"bad luck."

When in the following spring the Spaniards divided into two groups, Cabeza was left behind because of illness. For two years he lived alone except for occasional Indian companions who treated him like a slave. But he began to develop a reputation as a trader between tribes, which gave him an opportunity to range inland and down the coast. After four years he ran across his three remaining comrades, Castillo, Carranza, and Estevanico—probably near the mouth of the Guadalupe River.

So now the three Spaniards and the black existed as slaves among a people who themselves existed on roots, spiders, worms, caterpillars, lizards, snakes, and ant eggs. Nonetheless, though Cabeza characterized his masters as thieves and drunkards, he recognized that they were a "merry people." In their wandering the Indians moved farther west into the prickly-pear country where in season they gorged themselves on tuna. Although life was difficult, Cabeza could see the possibilities of the land for grazing and cultivation. During the year he saw his first buffalo, which he mistook for cattle; his is the first written description of the American bison.

In October 1534 the four men finally escaped. They met, and for eight months lived with, a friendly group called the Avavares. Cabeza was impressed by the Indians' endurance of a difficult life; but the Indians were no less impressed by the Spanish. Ever since the early days at Malhado, they had attempted cures for ailing Indians, largely by laying on hands and intoning blessings. Castillo and Cabeza in particular were valued as medicine men, and they seem to have had incredibly good luck in their ministrations. When they moved on in the late spring of 1535 toward Mexico, their reputation preceded them. They straggled up the Rio Grande, guided by a belief that inland Indians were friendlier than those along the coast and by a forager's desire to discover riches which not even their continuing ordeal could quench. As they approached each new tribe, they were hailed like conquerors because of their powers, while each group they left wailed and lamented.

Along this meandering trail Cabeza did pull off a bit of a medical cure, which if there had been no other facet to his career would have left him memorialized: he performed perhaps the first recorded operation in North America when he removed an arrowhead from deep in an Indian's chest and, using a deer bone as a needle, sewed up the wound. The patient lived. From then on their procession was virtually triumphal, as the Indians treated them like gods. Discerning men, the Spaniards consciously built a distance between themselves and the Indians by seldom speaking to a tribesman. If words were necessary, "the Negro always spoke to them."

Finally, after six years in Texas, the Spaniards crossed the Rio Grande for the last time and continued across northern Mexico to the west coast. Not far from present Culiacán, in company with their latest escorts, they encountered the first fellow Christians they had seen in eight years. As the Christians were hunting slaves, and as Cabeza and his companions insisted that their Indian friends be treated as friends, the four men were at first in danger of being killed by their own countrymen. But the crisis passed, and the men eventually reached Mexico City, where the Viceroy and Cortés himself received them. Cabeza returned to Spain a hero, though eventually he fell into disfavor and died in obscurity. Castillo and Dorantes remained in Mexico uneventfully; Estevanico joined Fray Marcos de Niza's expedition as a guide and was killed by Pueblo Indians in New

Mexico in 1539. The trail on which he had led de Niza formed the route for Coronado within a year.

Thus the first European-African Texans. They had faced the worst that Texas had to offer, and they had endured.

4

The Thorn in the Heart
of America

*H*OW long the casual and haphazard exploration and settlement of Spanish Texas might have continued is incalculable, for Spain had problems in other parts of her empire. The spirit was going out of the Spanish striving for a worldwide conquest, and the Spanish had really reached their zenith before the 1580s. All they could do was rationalize that Texas was there for their convenience; like a lover with goodies stashed all over the place, the Spaniard could afford to wait until it suited him to make that call to the outskirts of empire.

But nothing activates like a new lover in town—particularly, in this era, when that suitor was French. In retrospect the intrusion seems inconsequential; but the earlier you dispose of a rival, the more likely he is to prove disposable. Thus the Spanish reaction to La Salle's landing on the coast of Texas in 1685.

The French could not have had a better representative than René Robert Cavelier, Sieur de La Salle. He knew the New World as few men knew it then or now: especially the great Mississippi Basin, for he had followed the Father of Waters from source to mouth. So when he set out from the port of La Rochelle on July 24, 1684, aboard the thirty-six-gun *Le Joly,* with three other ships, he was a man with a record for having been somewhere and for knowing how to get somewhere else.

Generally no organization succeeds in an atmosphere of mutual distrust; the spirit of discontent seems to have been evident from the day the ships embarked. The naval commander, Sieur de Beaujeu, and La Salle disliked each other, and their men could not help taking sides. Since La Salle did not want word of his destination to reach Spanish ears, he shared his plans as little as possible with his officers and men. In a day when most travelers had little idea where anything was, this might seem less serious than with today's general geographical sophistication. But crews and troops like to know where they're going; and if they don't, curiosity joins with imagination to predict all sorts of unlikely dangers.

En route, one ship was captured by Spanish privateers and one-fourth of the gear lost. But the expedition found itself after two months at Petit Gôave, Santo Domingo, on the opposite side of the island from where La Salle had wished to land but where Beaujeu chose to anchor his ships. After a wild night during which La Salle was deliriously ill, Beaujeu's sailors got deliriously drunk at a nearby tavern. Some even deserted to the pirates, having learned in the tavern that the mainland shores toward which they were evidently headed contained no bad women or other such civilized delights.

Finally the expedition, reduced again by one-fourth, left the Caribbean Islands for the Spanish waters known usually as the Gulf of Mexico. As frequently happened, the ships became separated, and La Salle, whose navigators had no accurate method of obtaining longitude, overshot the mouth of the Mississippi River by 400 miles. On January 20, 1685, the French colonists were put ashore at Matagorda Bay in Texas, with La Salle insisting that the lagoons that stood between him and the mainland were the receptacles for the outpourings of the Mississippi.

Before the colony could be planted, another disaster took place. One ship ran aground while attempting to land, and before it could be salvaged a winter storm took care of the cargo. La Salle suspected that the grounding was intentional, since he had been at odds with the ship's captain, Sieur d'Aigron. When the wind died, the company took stock to find that its principal products were dysentery and venereal disease, the latter an inheritance from Santo Domingo.

This was the colony which was to establish a French empire

half the size of Europe. But instead of swaggering heroes, they were reduced at the outset to a jungle detachment rotting away without even knowing where they were. Before he had left the New World to return to France and set up his expedition, La Salle had arranged for 15,000 Indian allies. What he had instead were two hundred not-very-friendly natives.

Six weeks after their landing La Salle's colonists tasted new humiliation. Spotting sails on the horizon, they knew that the Spanish were starting to invade. But if it was a Spanish vessel, it passed right by. The empire of New Biscay (Nueva Vizcaya, the Spanish called it) was not even worth noticing. In fact, to the Spanish this new settlement was little more than a rumor, probably to be discounted.

But on July 6 the Spanish suddenly became conscious of the French. Pirates, 750 of them, led by Michel de Grammont and the Dutch pirate Laurens de Graff (Lorencillo), struck at Campeche on the Yucatan peninsula. Another 550 pirates stood by on twenty-three ships in case they were needed. When the pirates ashore found no booty, they burned the fort, spiked its cannon, took Campeche, and conducted a seven-day orgy during which they hanged nine Spaniards.

Since they could find little treasure on Yucatan, the French corsairs decided to leave the peninsula, chased by 350 Yucatanese. On September 3 de Graff left Campeche to push northward along the coast. Chasing him was a small Spanish armada, but de Graff managed to slip beyond its reach. While the escape was successful, the pirates left behind a significant residue of information. From their interrogation of the 120 prisoners they had taken, the Spanish learned that La Salle had been in Texas establishing the French empire for more than a year.

This sort of news would not wait for action. If La Salle was permitted to succeed, other Frenchmen would pour in through the Matagorda funnel until Spain had a true threat in its back yard. Search must begin, and countermeasures be taken. As soon as they had executed the 120 pirates, they must extirpate this French threat, which the Spanish Council described as "the thorn which has been thrust into the heart of America."

The Spanish were not without knowledge, gained from a century and a half of exploration. They also had access to a small host of adventurers who would follow any flag that promised fortune. Notable among these was Diego de Peñalosa, a Peruvian who had served as governor of New Mexico from 1661 to 1664 and had explored other areas. After trying unsuccessfully to sell the King of England on conquering Santo Domingo and South America, he intrigued with Louis XIV for exploration of Quivira and Teguayo, the area between settled New Mexico and the Mississippi. Like other explorers before him, Peñalosa described Quivira as possessing great riches of silver and gold. Speculation persists to this day whether the French really intended to mount two expeditions to Nueva Vizcaya with Peñalosa following behind La Salle (who then must deliberately have landed 400 miles beyond the Mississippi). But Peñalosa does have his place in La Salle's history, for through his own freebooting expedition he gave away La Salle's secret of a new colony in the New World.

The Spanish wished to locate and to wipe out the colony they called Espíritu Santo as quickly and totally as possible. Accordingly, they sailed from Havana to make a survey of the coast from western Florida all the way to Tampico. If they failed to find La Salle, they would at least come home loaded with geographical information. They also authorized Admiral Gaspar de Palacios to start a land expedition northward from Tampico to see what it could learn from the Indians about the white settlement at Espíritu Santo bay. For the next four years this overland group, under the leadership of *sargento mayor* Alonso de León, would search for the French in Texas, and in the process become enduring figures on the Texas historic scene. Their quest for a chimerical Frenchman would teach the Spanish more about Texas than they had learned in the previous century and a half. Before they were through, they would have crossed muddy bayous and malarial jungles all the way to western Florida and Alabama, thereby improving their claim on this area, with effects that would be felt into the era of nineteenth-century territorial growth.

Travelers were prevaricating in Texas long before the name "Texas" had been entered upon the charts and maps. The Indians lied to Cabeza de Vaca about golden cities, Cabeza de Vaca lied to the viceroy almost on command, La Salle may have lied to his troops, and certainly de Graff lied to the Spaniards about the size of the French settlement. One pirate captain, Nicolás Brigaut, taken by the Spanish at St. Augustine, made La Salle's miserable station sound like a bustling city with half the French army and navy ringing around it. After listening to him, the commander at St. Augustine, Juan Márquez Cabrera, knew that the French must be swarming like termites and that, if undeterred, they would soon eat away the foundation of the Spanish Empire in the New World.

Accordingly, Cabrera gave vehement orders to one of his subordinates, Marcos Delgado, a Florida native who knew Indian dialects, to find that French metropolis and eliminate it. Delgado would keep careful if inexact records of his journey through canebrakes and bogs and bayous, and his observations provide the first effective Spanish reconnaissance of the old southwest. However, Delgado's party slogged their way only as far as southern Alabama where at the urging of the Indians, who argued that only death lay ahead for the Spaniards, they turned back.

Meanwhile reports of the size of the French domain had grown, helped along by the unlimiting fact that no one had actually seen it. Rumors held that as many as 1,000 people populated Fort St. Louis, and that five ships were at the ready. Obviously no hurry-up armada was going to root out this Gallic cancer. Any Spanish expedition should have size and good planning.

In Mexico the new viceroy, Conde de la Monclova, ordered Admiral Francisco de Navarro to assemble a small, heavily armed fleet to proceed to Espíritu Santo. The ships left Vera Cruz on Christmas day, 1686, with the holiday throngs turning out to see the crews embark. No sooner were the ships over the horizon than work resumed in the Vera Cruz shipyard, for this questing party had orders merely to locate the French settlement, map the harbor as best it could, note latitude, and return. Their discovery would be followed up with an *armada de barlovento,* a windward fleet of considerable size dedicated to destroying La Salle and his *compagnie*. Nearly six months later the probing expedition reached Havana, having seen no Fort St. Louis but having found a wreck of a French ship on the Texas coast and picked up two French survivors on the Florida shore. No question but what the French had been in the area. The only question was whether God had not worked a miracle, so that God had done for the Spanish and to the French what the Spaniards could not accomplish themselves.

Meanwhile La Salle had behaved like a true American, exploring westward from the fort as far as the Rio Grande, where he built another fort of no consequence. He was encouraged by learning that many Indians did not like the Spanish and that he probably could count on the Indians as allies whenever he was ready to liquidate his foes.

In April 1696, with twenty picked men, La Salle turned eastward toward the Mississippi. The expedition crossed the southeastern portion of Texas as far as the Neches River, not too far from the later Louisiana border. Here the Hasinai Indians welcomed the travelers, who remained several weeks while La Salle recovered from another of his fevers. While La Salle languished, his companions explored, probably as far as the Sabine River. After the leader's recovery, the men returned to Fort St. Louis, arriving there in August with only eight out of the twenty who had begun the journey. Four had deserted, one had been lost, an alligator took another one, while six had been left along the trail like so many worn-out strays in a later herd of trailing longhorns.

A third time, on the following January 12, 1687, La Salle began a land cruise eastward, reaching the vicinity of present-day Navasota when all his journeys ended. Henry Joutel indicates in his excellent journal of the expedition [1] that they crossed at least nineteen streams beyond the Brazos and may again have gone as far as the Neches, where presumably a cache of wheat and beans was hidden. If so, then La Salle was killed

1. Henri Joutel, *Journal of LaSalle's Last Voyage, 1684–7* (Albany, N.Y.: Joseph McDonough, 1906), pp. 54–137. The original French edition of Joutel's journal appeared in 1713, twenty-two years before Joutel's death, and there have been several editions in English.

in present Cherokee County, Texas, in an intraparty squabble over scarce food.

With La Salle dead, the survivors split, innocent and guilty alike striking off in two different directions. One party under Joutel walked northward for Fort St. Louis on the Illinois River and on to Canada, and finally returned to France in October 1688. Six others started back toward Fort St. Louis in Texas but never made it. In the Texas fort the straggling survivors could only wonder whether anyone would ever return. Early in 1689, two years after La Salle's death, most of the people at the fort quit wondering; the Karankawa attacked the fort, massacring with sticks and daggers everyone except a few children.

Texas has made a lot of the fleur-de-lis as one of the six flags flying over its vast domain. But the colony which gives credence to the claim of French sovereignty was at best a ragtag arrangement, foredoomed, eventually only smoldering ruins and rotting carcasses, and hardly a threat to Spanish possession. Nonetheless La Salle's Texas expedition must go down in history as a great public relations coup, for his tattered remnants gave France a basis to claim Texas and excited the Spanish into building a chain of mission forts in an area thitherto largely ignored. Still, the Spanish knew at last that they could relax. The threat of French settlement had been taken care of; Indians and alligators and smallpox and personal hatreds had undone a potential empire on lonely Garcitas Creek in faraway Texas.

Meanwhile Alonso de León had left in the summer of 1686 on his first expedition. He proceeded as far as the Rio Grande, where captured Indians told him of other white soldiers some distance across the river. De León explored the shore of the mouth of the Rio Bravo, found broken planking and pieces of mast timber, along with such other wreckage as cannon wheels, small boats, and a corked bottle of soured wine. While this was not definitive proof of the French occupation, it might be an indication.

In the next four years de León would make five trips to Texas. On April Fool's Day 1689 he crossed the Rio Grande with his fourth expedition, this time as determined to colonize as he was to find the French force. In his party were 115 men,

721 horses, 82 loads of flour, plus other supplies. Three weeks later he found the ruins of Fort St. Louis. Just a few weeks earlier and he might have saved the French and the fort from destruction by Indians. Instead he found emptiness and silence, plus whatever remains of Frenchmen the vultures had disdained.

Now indeed the search for La Salle was over. As a colonizing effort, however, de León's mission was a failure, because of the vagaries of Texas weather in the spring. But a year later de León returned to Fort St. Louis with a full complement of friars and soldiers, established two missions, and put what was left of the French Empire in Texas to the torch. From then on, French occupation would be a recurring rumor, enough to keep the Spanish from becoming too complacent, but never more than a rumor. Occasionally the French would wander in, as at the future (and misnamed) Spanish Fort in a bend of the Red River in north Texas, where in the eighteenth century the Taovaya Indians maintained a trading post for French trappers. A French flag flew over Spanish Fort at least from 1719 to 1778, but its presence never represented a real incursion by the official French. In this instance smallpox took care of both Taovaya and French.

Those Spaniards who thought about such things realized from the French experience that Texas had to be possessed and not just claimed. Back in Mexico City Governor de León told the viceroy that Texas was worth having. It had soil, it had grass, in some places it had trees, it had climate, and it had space. Its Indians might not be so advanced as the Aztecs had been prior to the coming of the Spanish, but generally they were friendly and receptive to missionary activity. This claim was backed up by the priests, particularly Fray Damian Massanet, a Majorcan who had visited Texas by way of Querétaro and La Caldera mission in Coahuila. The confused, perhaps insane Jean Henri, a French chieftain of obscure origins among the Indians, had told Father Damian about Texas, with the result that the priest had accompanied de León on his 1689 expedition. On his fifth *entrada* to Texas, de León had taken Massanet as his chief of missionary work, and the priest had responded by helping establish the mission of San Francisco de los Tejas, the first Spanish mission in east Texas, near present-day Weches. Although the mission was abandoned after three years, it was re-established in 1716 as Nuestro Padre San Francisco de los Tejas Mission and with interruptions remained in business until 1721, when it was moved to a new location.

Massanet returned to Texas with the expedition of Domingo Terán de los Rios in 1691, but that explorer—commissioned governor of Tejas, for whatever that was worth—dragged his feet, and the priest returned to his mission. Because the Spanish neglected it and failed to establish a presidio at the site, Massanet set fire to the mission on October 25, 1693, and returned to Coahuila. Lost forty days, his party finally reached Monclova on the following February 17. Soon word came from the viceroy asking Massanet to suggest new mission sites, but Father Damian replied that since he had made such suggestions before and had never received proper backing, he would no longer cooperate. As indicated, the mission at San Francisco had not been successful; and though Massanet was empowered to found seven new missions, he did not have the necessary supplies. But the Spaniards had made their way almost to the Red River and to French Louisiana, and their knowledge of Texas had been increased enormously.

In Coahuila, Father Francisco Hidalgo decided in 1711 that the slow movement of the Spanish brand of Christianity in Texas needed a tonic. So he sent the governor of Louisiana a letter suggesting that the French might help establish a mission for the Tejas. In response, in 1715 the governor of Louisiana sent a party under Louis Juchereau de St. Denis to the Spanish mission settlement on the Rio Grande, San Juan Bautista, ostensibly to open trade routes. The governor picked a good man, for St. Denis, Quebec-born, had worked from Hudson Bay all the way to France and down to Louisiana, and had learned to accommodate himself to the varying tasks and people at hand. At San Juan Bautista the French trader, then 38 years old, fell in love with Manuela Ramón, less than half his age—a precarious love affair since her grandfather had just arrested him.

In fact, St. Denis was a prisoner only because Spanish law demanded that any foreigner crossing the frontier into Spanish territory should be arrested and the viceroy notified. And St. Denis hadn't just crossed the frontier; he had crossed hundreds of miles of it from the Sabine to the Rio Grande. The imprisonment made a lasting mark on St. Denis. Manuela was evidently a beauty; and considering the fascination that foreigners always have in isolated communities, St. Denis's pursuit of Manuela's hand could only have been acceptable. The practical St. Denis also used his excursions with his beloved to gather information about the region.

But one day the melody of love turned into a dirge: word had come from Mexico City, and the men had come from Monclova to enforce the word, that St. Denis should be taken in chains to account to the viceroy, the Duke of Linares, for his unauthorized entry into Spanish territory.

Months went by, and at San Juan Bautista Manuela grieved and yearned for a man from whom she heard no word. Could he be in jail, maybe in a dungeon? Manuela must have wondered. Dead perhaps? Not St. Denis. He had told his story straightforwardly and winningly to the viceroy and other Spanish authorities, who then freed him to return to San Juan Bautista. Not just to return, but to return triumphantly as conductor of supplies for the Spanish at a salary equal to that of the *alférez,* commander of escorting soldiers, Domingo Ramón.

But true love does not follow a straight line, because others always get in the way. Legend holds that the grandfather, Don Diego, said that in order to win Manuela, St. Denis would have to prove himself by going into the Texas wilderness, finding a scattered band of Indians who had fled from the mission about six months before, and persuading them to return.

But glory be, grandfathers are not all meanness, and Diego Ramón himself found the runaways and brought them back. St. Denis was accepted into the bosom of the family. Thus the historic enmity of Spain and France was set aside by an affable Frenchman and a teen-age Spanish girl.

In 1717, as a result of his writing too explicitly about his plans, the Spanish imprisoned St. Denis. For the first six years of their marriage Manuela remained at San Juan Bautista and then finally joined her presumed beloved in 1721, by which time he was out of prison and commandant for the French fort at Natchitoches. Evidently he wanted to live at San Juan Bautista with Manuela and use the mission as depot for commercial activity. But with good reason the Spanish suspected that he could not resist expanding his trade back to French Louisiana, and they refused to let him stay. If he were to remain out of prison, he had to get out of the Texas territory. St. Denis could not have the best of both colonial worlds.

The Spanish had other concerns too in keeping St. Denis happy and busy. The time had come to settle Texas and to make the Spanish name stick. They had learned that merely claiming was insufficient and that sporadic settlement efforts were equally inadequate. For the Spanish to survive in Texas, pious missionary activity would not suffice; forts and civil settlements must be maintained.

Accordingly the Spanish hauled out Captain Domingo Ramón for another assignment in June 1716, sending him to Texas with seventy-five persons, including about twenty-five soldiers, a dozen missionaries, and the remainder families who would settle and work. As almost always, the Indians were pleasant and promising, and on July 3, 1716, the Mission Nuestro Padre San Francisco de los Tejas was founded east of the Neches River, not far from the old San Francisco mission which Father Hidalgo had founded a third of a century before. In fact, Father Hidalgo was placed in charge of this new mission.

Other missionary activity continued, and in May 1718 Don Martín de Alarcón established the *Villa de Bexar* and named the site of the nearby new mission San Antonio de Valero. Bexar would become the most important Spanish settlement in Texas, and as the city of San Antonio, now edging toward a million people, it still is thought of as Mexico's northernmost city even though it is 150 miles inside Texas.

The name of Texas as an official title was foreshadowed again when the Marqués de San Miguel de Aguayo of Coahuila was named governor and captain general of the provinces of Tejas and New Philippines and sent to drive out whatever French had spilled over from Louisiana into the eastern part of the province. Aguayo crossed Texas with 500 men, plus large herds of horses, mules, cattle, and sheep. In east Texas he met the commander at Natchitoches, that irrepressible gentleman St. Denis, who obligingly helped the Coahuilan set up. Aguayo reconstituted the abandoned Spanish missions, established a presidio at Los Adaes (nestled comfortably inside the Louisiana border), and left in charge more than a hundred soldiers, plus six brass field pieces and a good supply of ammunition.

Los Adaes became the Spanish capital for Texas. Its site was tantamount to placing the capital of the United States at Montreal inside Canada! Through St. Denis the French objected: Natchitoches, in Louisiana, was only fifteen miles to the east. But Los Adaes suggested something that St. Denis found persuasive—an opportunity for international trade, mostly in contraband, plus the usual diplomatic finagling over boundary disputes and other concerns between Spain and France. Los Adaes, with a setting rich in flora and fauna, might have become an important twentieth-century city, but diplomacy did it in. When the French ceded Louisiana to Spain in 1762, Los Adaes no longer served any purpose, and the community was abandoned. The Spanish ordered its inhabitants to move to San Antonio, more than 300 miles away. Instead, most of them eased over to Nacogdoches, about 30 miles inside today's Texas.

Altogether, on his return to Coahuila Aguayo left behind 268 soldiers and four presidios from San Antonio to Los Adaes, with responsibility for ten missions. The Spanish finally had made a Texas-size effort. But policy was made in Madrid and in Mexico City, and Philip V thought that his military post in the New World was costing too much. Consequently he sent an inspector, Pedro de Rivera, to look into the situation. Like any good cost accountant, Rivera recommended that the number of soldiers be reduced by more than half, a signal to the Indians that the Spanish were going to be less forthright in the colonization and defense of their Texas empire. The encouraged Apaches began to raid San Antonio with some success.

On the whole, however, Texas was a relatively quiet place during the remainder of the eighteenth century. The French antagonized the Spanish by frequent trade incursions, most of them successful, but the Spanish had a sufficient line of mis-

sion-fort settlements to discourage any claim by France to the
Texas region. Great pockets of land were still left unsupervised,
providing the Indians with refuge areas. By 1746 the Spanish
had decided that the Indian raids could no longer be tolerated,
and so they dispatched José de Escandón, an experienced Indian
fighter, to Texas.

Escandón left Querétaro with more than 3,000 soldiers and
settlers and added to his force as he marched northward. By the
time he was through in Texas, more than 6,000 colonists had
been dropped off at twenty-three settlements, largely between
Tampico and the San Antonio River.

But most of Escandón's colonizing activity was south of the
Rio Grande, and on the whole the Spanish work in Texas must
be accounted a failure. They never did accomplish a lasting conversion of the Indians, who came and went almost at will. They
would flirt with Christianity in the autumn, when cold weather
was coming on and food and shelter through the winter were
items for consideration. But with the first leafing out of the
mesquites and huisaches, the Indians would drop their Christianity and take to the wilderness again. In some instances, as at
San Sabá, where more than 200 women and children had been
settled along with the fathers and soldiers in 1757, the Indians
were actually hostile. In June of that first year, 3,000 Apaches
stopped over, en route south, which is not the direction to take
at the onset of summer in Texas. In fact San Sabá became a way
station for bands of Indians heading south, and the people
around the mission soon learned that they were fleeing from the
Comanches and their allies to the north. Finally in the spring of
1758 the Comanches and their associates, largely Wichita,
Tonkawa, Bidai, and even some Tejas, put the mission under
siege for four days and killed ten people. A year later they were
back, this time killing nineteen while driving away 750 horses.
When in the summer of 1759 the Spanish attacked the Comanches and Taovayas near Spanish Fort, the Indians drove
them back to San Sabá. The Spanish effort against the Indians
in Texas, whether in the name of the Cross or at the point of a
sword, was a repetitive humiliation for the proud Iberians.

5

Three Girls and a Dog
Named Galveston

N the Peace of Paris of 1763 ending the Seven Years' or
French and Indian War, Spain kept that portion of Louisiana already secretly ceded to her. But Louisiana was no
more profitable to the Spanish than Texas had been, and Spain
still had an empire which it had neither the inclination nor the
resources to develop. Furthermore, Spain had acquired a new
American neighbor to the northeast, the British, who from a
Spanish standpoint had the disadvantage of being more efficient
and aggressive than the French. Two decades later the situation
would worsen, for the new United States of America, an infant
suddenly thrust into maturity, brash, overconfident, and restless,
would make the English look like congenial *compadres* down at
the club. And in Mexico itself, that most profitable of colonies,
were distilling certain independent spirits, so that the Spanish
were beset on either side. Although the worry lies beyond our
story, the Spanish also were fearful of what the English and the
Russians might do to the Pacific slope of their empire.

The Spanish chose a strange (for them) path out of this
morass. They decided to reform. In Madrid Charles III, more
enlightened than most Spanish rulers, dispatched a field marshal
with the book-length name of the Marquis de Rubí, Cayetano
María Pignatellí Rubí Corbera y Saint Clement, baron of Llinas,

to inspect the northern outlying provinces of Mexico, running from Texas to California and to be known later as the Provincias Internas. Rubí set out for Texas by way of northwest Mexico, specifically Durango, in March 1766 and reached Texas through El Paso in August 1767. From there he turned east by southeast and made his way across the upper Nueces River to San Antonio and finally to Los Adaes. He returned by La Bahía and recrossed into Mexico in November of the same year. By the time he completed his inspection of the broad province he had traveled more than 7,000 miles.

In 1772, while the English colonists were girding for revolution, he published in Madrid his *Reglamento y Instrucción para los Presidos que se han de formar en la Línea de Frontera de la Nueva España*. Rubí's recommendation is nearly shorter than his title or the book's: Spain was spread too thin in the northern provinces, she had to distinguish between the possible and the impossible insofar as her dominions were concerned, and success in Texas depended on contracting the frontier and eliminating useless Texas missions. The King followed with a royal order, known as "New Regulations of the Presidios," which recommended abandoning all Texas missions and presidios except those at San Antonio and La Bahía, strengthening San Antonio, and a two-pronged Indian policy of friendliness toward the northern tribes and extermination of the Apache. All colonists were forbidden to re-settle nearer than one hundred leagues to Natchitoches.

In central Texas abandonment was no problem. Already the question there was whether the mission settlers should close down before the Comanches shut them down permanently. But in the east the situation was different. Settlers had dug in and begun a good life and were being moved simply to satisfy larger policies of the Crown. No hostile aborigines were forcing them out; only a piece of paper from Madrid. San Antonio, hundreds of miles away, meant nothing to them, and they were bitter. The Texas governor, Barón de Ripperdá, a native of Madrid, didn't even have the courtesy to live in Los Adaes but established his headquarters in San Antonio because, he said, Indian threats and other troubles precluded his going on to the designated capital in the east.

Ripperdá was not a gentle man. In the summer of 1773 he removed the more than 500 persons around Los Adaes, just as their crops were beginning to ripen. They had to abandon a year's work as well as a good bit of their livestock. Some people fled; others lost their will. The remainder refused to choose lands at San Antonio and announced they were going to settle in the east. Under the leadership of a Los Adaes native named Gil Antonio Ibarvo (or Ibarbo), they successfully petitioned to return as far east as the Trinity River, where they founded the town of Bucareli not too far from present-day Houston. That settlement didn't last long, and Ibarbo took his displaced persons farther east to rebuild the town of Nacogdoches. The signs of an independent spirit had appeared.

Pacifying the Indians was another problem. The eastern Indians refused to submit to the discipline of Christianity and mission life, while to the west missions of the Apaches and Comanches were useless. What success the Spanish did have in dealing with the Indians was due mainly to following a recommendation by Rubí that Frenchmen be employed to handle relationships. The most successful of these liaison men was Athanase de Mézières, who extended the historical shadow of St. Denis by marrying the latter's daughter in 1746 and who became lieutenant governor and also lieutenant colonel at Natchitoches. De Mézières summoned Indian chiefs to Natchitoches, traveled 300 miles into Indian country, and wrote classic reports of what he had seen and done that were almost a manual for care and governance in the region. Before he was through, he had made peace with the Taovayas and Wichitas, caused a treaty to be signed with some of the Comanches, and begun a plan to unite the northern tribes in a joint campaign with the Spaniards against the Apaches. For his success he was named acting governor in 1778 and the next year was named governor, but he died at San Antonio before taking office. On his death, pacification of the northern tribes ceased, as did plans for united campaigns against the Apaches.

Meanwhile both Comanche and Apache raids continued to harass the Spaniards as long as the Europeans remained in Texas. Rubí was right. The Spanish were strung too thin, seldom able to bring more than 200 troops to bear on the Indians, and these stretched between three or four presidios with duties other than fighting. When the massive effort of the Anglo-American troops with more modern weapons and communications to subdue these same tribes over a period of twenty-five years is considered, the Spanish effort is somewhat more impressive.

Still, nothing seemed to work. Military measures were insufficiently mounted. The Spanish tried to bribe the Indians with gifts; the Indians took the gifts and then attacked. The Spanish explored deeper into Indian territory, made treaties, and opened up trade routes. But still the Indian barrier endured. The only lasting accomplishment was that the Spaniards learned a whole lot more about Texas, troublesome though the information-gathering proved to be.

As if the Indians weren't enough, European diplomacy provided an impossible obstacle to the Spanish hold on Texas. First, Napoleon euchred Spain out of Louisiana, and the French were back. But to Spain's consternation Napoleon then sold Louisiana to the United States, and back home Texas was faced with the fact that once again it had a nettlesome neighbor. What to do? Colonize Texas, settle its boundaries with Louisiana hard and fast. Above all, repel Anglo-American intrusion.

First of all, the matter of boundary had to be settled. No great perception is required to see that the United States and Spain could not agree easily, and that the United States would ask for more than it deserved. The United States sent the so-called Freeman expedition up the Red River in 1806, and the Spanish stopped it near the western boundary of future Arkansas. The Spanish captured Zebulon Pike, who was nosing around in the northern reaches of the Rio Grande. The United States also sent troops into Louisiana, drove what were left of their neighbors out of Los Adaes, and generally acted as if they wished to make war on the border. But in the fall of 1806 General James Wilkinson, who may well be America's greatest rascal (an honor to be treasured, since the competition is severe), completed the Neutral Ground Treaty. Under it, the Spaniards were to remain west of the Sabine River, and basically that has been the eastern Texas border ever since.

The Texas penchant for massive unflattering publicity, frequently through no fault of its own, came to the fore about this time. What happened is reasonably clear, but what was contemplated is known only to General Wilkinson and Aaron Burr. All we can say with certainty is that Burr put together a filibuster expedition into the Southwest which may have had designs on Texas. Wilkinson, commander of the United States forces in that area, is implicated. Probably he was secretly in the pay of Spain. And to complete the mystery he made great public noises about preparing his defenses against attack from the unforbidding Burr. But nothing came of the scheme.

For more than a dozen years the boundary controversy continued. Neither Jefferson nor Madison, pro-French and anti-Spanish, could bring himself to treat equitably with the Spanish. In the summer of 1809 the Spanish Patriot Assembly sent Don Luis de Onís as its minister to the United States to work out a proper treaty. But the Madison administration delayed until December 1815—or more than six years—before Onís' credentials were accepted by the United States, and no real progress was made until late 1817, when John Quincy Adams became President James Monroe's secretary of state. Even then, negotiations lingered, were suspended temporarily, were transferred to Madrid, though they never left the forefront of the mind of either Adams or Onís. The two agreed that the definition of a boundary line between the United States and Spanish North America was required for settlement of issues between the two countries. Various lines were proposed by Onís, running westward from the Mississippi to Spain's ultimate, the Sabine. Adams started at the Texas Colorado River as a minimum westward limit of the United States. Onís, acting like his contemporary Talleyrand, agreed on the Colorado but argued that the only Colorado he knew was the Red River which cuts slaunchwise across Louisiana, passing near Natchitoches. Andrew Jackson even got into the act when to the consternation of the Monroe administration, he invaded Florida. Jackson's only official supporter was Adams, usually no man of war, who rightly felt that Jackson's precipitate move could only help his own strategy. If Jackson would occupy Spanish Florida, why would he not move into other Spanish territory? Adams was emboldened to suggest that perhaps the western boundary line of the United States should be the Pacific Ocean.

In January 1819 final negotiations began. Onís had instructions to agree to the Colorado if necessary and even to grant an extension to the Pacific. With those instructions he diplomatically offered the Sabine as the western limit, intending then to move his offers north and west. As much as Adams hated to surrender Texas, a region that he later abominated for other reasons, he figured wrongly that Onís had ceded all that he could. Also, Adams was winning on one major point—the first title by treaty of the United States to Pacific slopes. They signed the treaty on February 22, 1819. Two days later the United States Senate ratified the treaty unanimously. Intrigue in Spain delayed the treaty, which had provided that ratification should be exchanged within six months. Indeed, Spain delayed nearly twenty months before approving in October 1820. Ratifications were exchanged in Washington, again on Washington's birthday, in 1821.

Thus by the Adams-Onís Treaty of 1819 the United States received the Floridas and confirmed its domain east of the Mississippi. Spain retained title to Texas, a title heretofore believed in but never formally acknowledged by anyone else. Away off to the northwest Santa Fe was given a cushion of 360 miles between it and the new border, and farther northwest John Jacob Astor could be assured that the United States stretched legally from Maine to Oregon.

For Texas specifically the boundary with Louisiana ran along the west banks of the Sabine northward from its mouth to the thirty-second parallel, north to the Red River, along its south banks to the hundredth meridian, north to the Arkansas River, along its main branch to its source, and then northward to the forty-second parallel. Except for the northernmost portion and a later dispute with Oklahoma, the boundary would stand up through 1976 without change, a rather remarkable performance considering the inexactitude of geographical knowledge at the time of Adams and Onís.

So Spain knew where it was in Texas. It also knew—or should have—that its situation was still deteriorating there. Mission settlements had dropped off to three small groups, San Antonio de Bexar, Bahía del Espíritu Santo, and Nacogdoches, altogether maybe 4,000 halfway civilized people. While Spain had held Louisiana, it had permitted immigration from the United States there; but now it tried to prevent immigrants from moving into Texas. Since 1796 entrance had meant imprisonment. But with Louisiana now belonging to the United States, Spain was more than ever determined that any immigration would have to emerge from Mexico and not from the east. If some Spaniards wished to leave Louisiana for Texas, that could be considered. But Anglo-Americans, never!

One farseeing Spaniard, Bernardo Bonavía y Zapata, summed up the situation of Spain and Texas rather well. Bonavía, named governor of Texas as far back as 1788, had chosen not to serve. Later as military commander of Texas he had been ordered to meet with the governors of Nuevo León and Coahuila in Texas but again did not attend because he felt that he was needed in his position as governor-intendant of Durango, where he was trying to make the liberal reforms of Charles III work. Hoping to extend those reforms to Texas, he finally visited the province in 1809, requested all ranking officials to present written statements of their views on Texas's potential development, and then wrote his commandant-general that Texas must be strengthened *pronto* or the colonists would take their future into their own hands to the discomfiture of Spain. He saw Texas as the key to Spain's presence in America.

Bonavía felt that free trade and immigration were absolutely necessary and that direct communication by ship between Texas and Vera Cruz should be opened. The latter recommendation went against the suspicious official minds of Spain, which permitted only one legal port in Texas—at San Bernard in the Matagorda Bay area, which had no customhouse and no real facilities, so that ships wanting to do business with Texas landed anywhere along its shallow coastline and went inland without communicating with Spanish officials. In fact, not many captains violated the rules, for Texas had neither people to bring goods to nor obvious resources to take away.

So here was Spanish Texas, as big as Spain itself but with only a handful of people, and ripe for settlement. With a kinetic civilization beyond its eastern border, a people beginning to get a glimmer of Manifest Destiny, someone was going to colonize that area if the Spanish didn't. *Official* policy then became to settle, but *actual* policy became suspicion of all newcomers.

The governor of Texas after 1808, Manuel María de Salcedo, had lived in Louisiana as a boy, but after he was made governor of Texas by the Council of the Indies in April 1807, he ran an uneven antiforeigner administration. If foreigners arrived from either Mexico or Louisiana, he was inclined to be lenient toward them and to help them attain title to their land. But the retarding factor for settlement remained: how do you trust people whom you don't know? By the time the Spanish *cortes* finally decreed that all Spanish dominion should be opened to anyone who would respect the Constitution and laws of Spain, the year was 1820 and Spain was in the twilight of its experience in Texas. There never had been a high noon.

The Spanish were not without some justification for their suspicions. Those Anglo-Americans who filtered into Texas during the Spanish period largely had mischief on their mind. Best known of the intruders is Philip Nolan, a former employee of James Wilkinson. Nolan was a Texas resident around Nacogdoches most of the time from 1790 until his death. Though he carried legitimate Spanish passports, he covered too much Texas ground for the Spanish peace of mind, and after a decade they decided to arrest him. Nonetheless, he returned to Texas with a party of twenty-one men, penetrating as far as the Brazos in the autumn of 1800. His party gathered a herd of several hundred horses, visited with the Comanches on the Red River, and then built a fort near Nolan Creek in central Texas. The Spanish, trailing him, caught up with Nolan near present-day Waco and killed him on March 4, 1801.

Nolan's role is vague. He is reputed to be the first Anglo-

American to map Texas, which he covered personally as far as San Antonio. But was he an agent for General Wilkinson? Was he laying the groundwork for an invasion of Kentuckians to slice off a hunk of Texas? Were the Spanish correct in their suspicions that he was dangerous and therefore forbidden fruit?

He also left behind another heritage. When a century later Edward Everett Hale decided to write his paean to patriotism *The Man Without a Country,* he chose Nolan—with some historical liberties—for his anti-hero. Nolan lives on through literature, even though his historical importance is peripheral and transitory.

The fact that Nolan was killed, and his surviving colleagues were incarcerated in a Chihuahua prison for six years and then made to roll dice to see which one of them should be hanged, did not discourage all other filibusters. Texas was there, the Indian trade was there, the frontier was long and unguardable, and the profits and prospects of profits outweighed the risk of capture. The fact that from September 16, 1810, when Father Miguel Hidalgo de Costilla has issued his *grito*—his cry—for revolution, Mexico had been embarked on a career of chronic revolution, was also encouraging. Cut off from fiery speeches by a mountain-desert-distance barrier, the Texans remained loyal to the Spanish Crown at first and then lost interest in a fight that seemed so far away. But as the revolution spread from Dolores and Guanajuato into Guadalajara, Nuevo Santander, and Coahuila, the Texans became increasingly revolution-minded. In Bexar a revolt broke out in which the Texans seized Simón Herrera, the troop commander, and Governor Manuel María Salcedo. Any success was short-lived, but a revolution nearly always requires early losers. What the Texans needed was a leader who knew what he was doing.

The first applicant for that leadership post was José Bernardo Maximiliano Gutiérrez de Lara, a Tamaulipas native who had helped carry off the successful revolution in Nuevo Santander for Hidalgo. In 1811 Gutiérrez went to Washington to seek aid in establishing a republican government in Texas and in using Texas as a staging area to liberate Mexico from Spanish domination. Although he was not officially received, like other incipient revolutionists he was seen by a number of influential people from cabinet rank down and was given enough encouragement to go ahead with his plans. Back in Natchitoches he met with gathering agents who, with the optimism that always buoys revolutionaries, promised him that Texas would rise in revolt once the first shot was fired.

Enter here the Anglos in the person of Augustus William Magee, a not so proper young Bostonian barely old enough to vote. He too had received tutelage as a soldier under General James Wilkinson, the best one-man training academy anywhere for people with devious plans. Magee is said to have been handsome, and certainly he was one of the best-informed young officers in the United States Army. But when like Benedict Arnold he was passed over for promotion because of military politics, he began to feel that his career lay in some other direction than the United States Army. Consequently he joined with Gutiérrez in plans for taking Texas and began to raise his own army for the invasion. Gutiérrez was the propagandizer; Magee, the trained soldier.

Crossing the Sabine on August 8, 1812, with about 130 Anglo-Americans, leftover Frenchmen, Mexican revolutionists, and mischief-bent Indian allies, Magee swept the isolated frontier outposts before him. As the Spanish soldiers fled, the frontiersmen around Nacogdoches flocked to his assistance. The army, now numbering 700, marched deep into Texas to La Bahía (later to become a Texas shrine under the name of Goliad), meeting almost no opposition. There Magee holed up and was besieged by troops under Governor Salcedo from November until the following February. There too he did battle, died, and was succeeded by Samuel Kemper. Under Kemper the expedition broke the siege and pushed Salcedo back toward San Antonio, defeating a Royalist Army of 1,200 men under Simón Herrera and taking Bexar on April Fool's Day 1813.

Now Gutiérrez, who had remained nominal commander-in-chief of the expedition, began to reassert himself and reportedly sanctioned execution of fourteen Spanish leaders, including Herrera and Salcedo. For the Anglos, the questioning was immediate: this is liberal democracy? Or is it just an exchange of one form of Spanish tyranny and blood lust for another? A disillusioned Kemper decided to lead more than one hundred of his troops back to Louisiana on "furlough."

For the next several months intrigue among the revolutionists was the order of the day, with the result that a presumed Gutiérrez confederate, José Álvarez de Toledo, moved in on San Antonio, convinced the Americans that he was the leader they needed, and maneuvered Gutiérrez out of command. On August 15, 1813, the Battle of the Medina River took place with Toledo's troops facing a Spanish Royalist force under Joaquín de Arredondo. Toledo walked into an ambush, and in a battle lasting several hours the Royalists prevailed as three hundred American survivors fled back toward the security of Louisiana.

In the midst of all of this the revolutionists had declared the independence of the State of Texas with a rather liberal document, but had drawn up an illiberal constitution. Gutiérrez had made it clear that he was fighting for Texas to be liberated as part of Mexico but not for a Texas that would become an extension of the United States. This self-proclaimed free Mexican State of Texas lasted only about four months, none of them progressive.

The Spanish knew that their worst fears about foreigners in Texas had been realized. Consequently as a leader of the victors Arredondo had a clearcut challenge, which he responded to with vigor. He not only cleared Texas of insurgents and potential troublemakers, he cleared Texas. The only good Spaniard, he seemed to believe, was one who was not in Texas. By the time he had finished his scouring, San Antonio was the only real settlement left. So thorough was Arredondo that his constitution provided for more offices than he had office holders to fill. Texas had become a sort of lonely country club with membership limited to those who could pass Arredondo's stern loyalty test. But the fact of Texas would not go away.

One of the men who looked on Texas with approbation was a Frenchman named Charles François Antoine Lallemand, who had served both Napoleon and Louis XVIII with some distinction before fleeing to the Tombigbee region in Mississippi Territory. To him, Texas was a potential French military colony which might assist Joseph Bonaparte in becoming King of Mexico, or at least give French refugees a sanctuary in the New World. The French were back to worry a harried Spain.

Lallemand put together 150 men who embarked from Philadelphia and arrived at Galveston on January 14, 1818. Trouble dogged the expedition, for another renegade Frenchman, Jean Laffite, planned to betray the expedition to the Spanish. But Lallemand, running a little behind his first group, recruited around New Orleans with the assistance of Laffite. About 120 settlers moved from Galveston in small boats up the Trinity River to Atascosito, where they built two small forts. By then the Spanish were alert and the latest governor, Antonio María Martínez, sent an attacking force to the French settlement, now named Champ d'Asile. Its inhabitants fled back to Galveston, where the party fell apart.

For the Spanish in Texas life was becoming just one crisis after another. A year after the Lallemand colony had been dispatched, out of Natchez arose an even more serious threat to Hispanic serenity. James Long had been a surgeon for Andrew Jackson in the War of 1812, and after the Battle of New Orleans moved to Natchez. There he met and soon married seventeen-year-old Jane Wilkinson. As it turned out he had taken himself quite a wife, a girl who had the determination and drive that has cast her in the role of "Mother of Texas."

The couple had been married just four years when John Quincy Adams signed the Adams-Onís Treaty. The treaty was being damned in every tavern from Natchez-under-the-hill to Natchez-upon-the-bluff to Port Gibson and to anywhere else that Mississippian males gathered to talk. Adams had let Texas be stolen right under the eyes of Mississippi and the remainder of the southwestern United States. This treachery required something more than just bravado and fist-shaking.

Consequently about $500,000, an almost incredible sum, was subscribed, and recruits were gathered with impossible promises. Among other inducements, every soldier was to receive one league of Texas land. On June 8, 1819, an advance force of 120 men crossed the Sabine into Texas and walked on to Nacogdoches. Long as head of the expedition followed less than two weeks behind. The citizens of Nacogdoches welcomed the freebooters at a place appropriately called Camp Freeman, organized a provisional government, declared an independent republic, and elected Long as chief.

Now the price went up. The ruling Supreme Council voted ten sections of land (6,400 acres) to each private and provided for selling the rich bottom lands of the Red River at fifty cents an acre downward. Long soon had more than 300 men wanting to share in this material blessing of liberty. Any tinge of greed was disguised because it was all given under the revolutionary fervor of liberty.

Soon Long had traveled to Galveston to solicit the assistance of Jean Laffite and his buccaneers, who also always seemed willing to help the cause of liberty for the proper price. But the proper price was never found, nor did the Natchez Committee deliver on its commitment, so Long had to divide his forces and live off the land. Undeterred, he and the Supreme Council declared Galveston a port of entry, authorized erection of a fort at Point Bolivar, and proclaimed Jean Laffite governor of Galveston Island—where he was of no more assistance than Freebooter Laffite. One trouble was that the Spanish did not look kindly on this incursion, and Governor Martínez sent Colonel Ignacio Pérez with more than 500 men to fight Long's settlement of more than 1,000 scattered men. Pérez captured isolated groups of filibusters and reached Nacogdoches on October 28. Within a month he had cleaned the Long settlers out of east Texas.

Long himself escaped capture by fleeing to Natchitoches. There he joined forces with José Felix Trespalacios, who was organizing another group to join the Mexican liberals. In April 1820, Long was at Point Bolivar, working again with Trespalacios, Ben Milam, and the resurfacing José Bernardo Gutiérrez de Lara to revitalize the Supreme Council. Long and Trespalacios soon disagreed, and Long pulled away from his Mexican colleague to lead an uncertain existence at Fort Las Casas on Point Bolivar until September 19, 1821, when he sailed with fifty-two men to capture La Bahía. On October 4 La Bahía fell, but here came Pérez again and four days later Long surrendered.

In some ways Jane Long's career is even more remarkable. Certainly it lasted much longer. Not only was she the first known Anglo-American woman to enter Texas, but she bore the first child of such parentage within the Texas border. Moreover she was determined, intrepid, courageous, and canny. As the wife of General Long of the Long Expedition, she and her sister had made a flag of white silk, striped and fringed in red, with a white star in the center of a red ground in the upper distaff corner.

When Long established his republic at Camp Freeman and took up life in the old stone blockhouse there, he had raised that Lone Star flag, an event of sufficient importance to be recorded in the *London Courier* of October 18, 1819. He had been gone from home only a few days on the expedition when his second daughter had been born. Although it seems to have been a difficult time physically for Jane, she took her two-weeks-old and her two-and-one-half-year-old daughters, Rebecca and Ann, and her Negro servant, Kiamatia or Kian, and without telling her family left the refined portion of Natchez-on-the-bluff, went down to the river, and booked passage to Alexandria, Louisiana. Alone with two wee ones and a servant, and evidently without funds, she nonetheless was setting out for a land unknown to her, probably without her husband's permission. She was a girl with purpose.

The trip required twenty days for a distance that can be driven legally in an hour today. By the time Jane Long arrived, she was ill. For another month she remained too ill to travel. When her doctor decided that her illness was induced by anxiety over her husband, she took care of that diagnosis by depositing the two babies with her sister in Alexandria, collecting several men as escorts, and heading for Nacogdoches. Finally the First Lady of the newly proclaimed Republic of Texas arrived at Nacogdoches to find her White House consisted of one room in an eight-room blockhouse. Furthermore, her husband told her that he had to move on to Galveston to negotiate with Laffite.

While General Long was away, back came Colonel Ignacio Pérez with the force to put down the revolution. Jane fled, along with all those males at Nacogdoches who didn't choose to stand, fight, and die. James Long, who had crossed her path on his way back to Nacogdoches, caught up with her at a place called Critchfield's Landing on the Sabine. Jane and her husband were the last to cross at night on the tiny ferry. Those remaining behind were killed in the night.

When finally she reached Alexandria, Jane learned that her baby, Rebecca, had died just a few days after she had first gone to meet her husband and that the sheriff was holding their possessions for debts. Dr. Long returned to his men at Point Bolivar while she waited in Alexandria. Long had lost everything and was even shot at by the agent he had left in charge of his trading post in Natchitoches. But he was a natural believer, while Jane was just as optimistic, and though friends in Alexandria and Natchez were having to bail them out, Long was making new plans to take Texas.

Any plans of James Long involved Jane. So the two of them with a friend of Laffite named Warren D. C. Hall set off at the end of February 1820 for Bolivar. And after a return trip to Alexandria and New Orleans, Jane resumed life at Bolivar at the close of 1820, bringing along her daughter Ann and her teenaged servant, Kian. Since by this time the wives of two doctors had arrived, Jane was no longer the only white woman in the area. General Trespalacios and Ben Milam soon took off for Vera Cruz, while Long left his pregnant wife for Copano Bay. With both leaders absent, the remaining soldiers lost their discipline and began to move out in two's and three's. None left without taking supplies. Soon the doctors departed, since a severe food shortage was in sight. But Jane refused to go. When the very last soldier had left, taking the remaining flour, he left behind only ammunition, muskets, a few fish hooks, and one line.

Alone on Bolivar except for Ann and Kian, plus a dog named Galveston, the twenty-four-year-old woman shot birds, fished, looked across the bay at the campfires of the Karankawa, and wondered whether they were as eager to barbecue her as she was simply to eat. When once the Indians gathered on the beach, Jane imagined that an invasion was at hand and that her little party would add to the list of more than 200 Americans whom the Karankawa reputedly had cannibalized. In defiance she hoisted her red-flannel petticoat to the top of the flagpole and fired the cannon from her memory of seeing the soldiers do it. The smoke and the noise sent the Indians scrambling from the beach, and she never had any difficulty in that direction.

The winter that followed was so severe that Galveston Bay is supposed to have frozen over for a quarter of a mile from shore, a claim that almost defies credibility. On one freezing cold night, with Kian desperately ill, Jane Long gave birth to her third daughter. The date was December 21, 1821, almost three hundred years after Cabeza de Vaca and Estevanico. By morning Jane was up and out in the cold wind looking for food, picking up frozen fish offshore, and with six-year-old Ann placing them in the brine of an empty pickle barrel.

On the day after a lonely Christmas Captain Rafael Gonzales showed up with six men from Monterrey and, glory be, a letter from James Long, which said that he was alive and well and in prison. When two days later the Gonzales party departed, Jane settled down for a winter of discontent and solitude. Once they did not eat for three days. Finally Jane hailed a sloop passing along the horizon. It turned to shore and landed a party of fifteen men, the first of Stephen F. Austin's colonists.

Thus arrived the first official colony of Anglo-Americans in Texas. No fanfare, no hoopla, but a happy greeting party nonetheless—a lonely, high-spirited, skinny, twenty-four-year-old girl-wife, a six-year-old child, a black slave girl, a babe in arms (name of Mary James), and a dog of unknown origin and future.

In fifteen years this group of colonists would grow and prosper, would revolt, would declare independence, and would make their declaration stick. And though Jane Long may be overrated as a heroine, and certainly she showed signs of capriciousness and wilfulness, she also had endurance. When the first white men came to Texas to stay, she was there to meet them. Beside her stood a Negro girl in her mid-teens. One has been called "The Mother of Texas." The other could as easily be designated as "The Mother of Black Texas."

6

Mexican Texas: Epilogue to the American Revolution

*T*HE story of the Anglo-American settlement of Texas, the subsequent revolt against Mexico, the period of independence, and the eventual war against Mexico by the United States has been chronicled principally by Anglos, whether patriotic Texans or critical New Englanders. While this account may not correct either view, along the way it might suggest certain considerations that have been given scant treatment heretofore.

For one thing, the Anglos did not move into Texas predetermined to excise the Texas territory from Mother Mexico. They moved in for that most fundamental of motives, greed, as signified by the presence of nearly free land. Texas was born in an atmosphere of what Sam Houston would later brand "the animating pursuits of speculation," [1] a gigantic land grab, and early cupidity had lasting impact on the Texas character: many of the scandals in Texas have been involved with land. Texans seem sometimes to be land-obsessed, like many westerners.

When you brought land hunger into conjunction with a Mexican government to whom Texas land primarily represented just

---

1. Sam Houston, Nacogdoches, Texas, to John A. Wharton, 14 April 1835, in *The Writings of Sam Houston, 1813–1836,* edited by Amelia W. Williams and Eugene C. Barker (Austin: University of Texas Press, 1938), 1:293.

so much dirt and grass and not much else, you created a situation into which ambitious men are going to move.

Such a man was Moses Austin. Born in Connecticut of a family which dates back to 1638 in North America, he had been a general merchandiser in Philadelphia, from which firm he had launched a branch house at Richmond, Virginia. Later he had moved to Wythe County, Virginia, where he had become involved in mining and smelting lead, an interest that stayed with him through life. In 1798, he moved to the lead sources in southeastern Missouri, where the Spanish granted him a league of land. Austin, now pushing forty, established the town of Potosi, built furnaces and a shot tower, opened another general store, and became a civic-minded first citizen of Missouri for two decades. When the War of 1812 with its consequent depression reduced incomes, Austin pledged most of his available capital for stock in the Bank of St. Louis in the belief that the bank could issue notes and increase local currency as a boost for business. But when the depression deepened in the Panic of 1819, the Bank of St. Louis failed, and Moses Austin's business empire lay in ruins.

Although he was nearly sixty, Austin wasn't a man to quit trying. Through connections in New Orleans, he had learned about the advantages of Texas and its ripeness for settlement. Austin realized that the Spanish would like to fill up Texas as a buffer against Louisiana and the remainder of the United States. And so he took himself to San Antonio de Bexar, where in December 1820 he proposed to Colonel Antonio María Martínez that he be granted permission to bring 300 settlers into Texas. Instead, Governor Martínez ordered him out of Spanish territory.

Austin was following the governor's advice and leaving town when he came across the Baron de Bastrop, a checkered character who claimed many nationalities and who was serving Spain in its last days in North America. After Austin told Bastrop his frustrations, the Baron intervened with the governor, and Martínez agreed to forward Austin's petition to General Joaquín de Arredondo, chief civil and military commandant of Texas, at Monterrey.

On January 17, 1821, Arredondo approved a grant permitting Austin to settle 300 families within an area of 200,000 acres. No provision was made for administration, geographical boundaries were unspecified, size and price of individual allotments were not defined, and Austin's role was not made clear. But most of the 200,000 acres was his if he could persuade 300 families to join him. He would call the shots, he would decide who came, and he would decide what they paid and what they did once they arrived. He had fashioned a speculator's coup for himself.

All that Austin received for his efforts was the elation of anticipation from March 1821, when he first received news of his grant, until he died the following June 10. Instead, his twenty-seven-year-old son, Stephen Fuller Austin, quiet, college-trained, lead miner and smelter, store operator, and member of Missouri's young territorial legislature, was the inheritor of this large spread.

When his father died, he was living in New Orleans in the home of a friend, studying law, and had recently taken the oath of office as circuit judge of the first judicial district of Arkansas (though probably he never held court). At first lukewarm about his father's big scheme, nonetheless he had helped in it. When Stephen learned of his father's death, he was in Natchitoches waiting to join Moses on a return trip to San Antonio. Instead, Stephen left promptly for San Antonio by himself, arriving there in August 1821. Governor Martínez passed along the mantle of colonization to Moses's son, who worked out certain administrative procedures with the governor. The two agreed that the acreage should be located on the coastal plain between the San Antonio and Brazos rivers, that Mexico would grant 640 acres to each head of a family, 320 acres for his wife, 320 acres for each child, and 80 acres for each slave. Essentially the land would be free, though Austin would collect 12½ cents an acre for his services. Austin also learned that the Spanish would provide no administration and that he himself must guarantee the good conduct of his colonists.

Back to New Orleans. Austin published the terms of settlement, invited colonists, and waited for the rush. As far as the

United States was concerned, the time was propitious: depression had been plaguing the nation since the close of the War of 1812, and people were eager for new starts, even in a new land. But further up the bureaucratic ladder in Mexico, officials refused to accept the grant approved by Governor Martínez and prepared to regulate colonization by a general immigration law.

This time young Austin went to the source—to Mexico City, where he pressured the *junta instituyente,* or rump Congress, to complete a new law authorizing him to bring in settlers. This law, which Emperor Agustín de Iturbide signed on January 3, 1823, offered heads of family a league and a *labor* of land (4,605 acres) and provided for various colonization agents, or empresarios, to promote immigration. Instead of the 200,000 acres which Moses Austin had envisioned, each empresario would receive 67,000 acres for each 200 families introduced. Once again, immigrants would not purchase the land from the government but would pay only a fee of 12½ cents an acre to the empresario for his trouble.

When Iturbide abdicated three months later, Austin reworked his contacts with the Mexican congress to receive a contract for 300 families on approximately the same terms. Then in August 1824 the new congress passed still another immigration law, vesting public land administration in the several states, which threw the project into the hands of the legislature of the state of Coahuila y Texas. In March 1825 the legislature passed another law confirming the original act approved by Iturbide. About the only difference was that the settler had to pay the state $30 within six years, not exactly an onerous fee.

Austin wasn't through. He persuaded the state to grant him three more contracts for a total of 900 additional families, and he worked out another contract in partnership with his secretary, Samuel May Williams, to settle 800 families in western Texas. The fact that the area he chose for the latter settlement overlapped the land set aside for another empresario named Sterling C. Robertson brought attacks against Austin's integrity which have continued to the present.

In 1825 Mexico had granted Robertson's Nashville Company a permit to settle 800 families along the Brazos River northwest of Austin's colony. Robertson was indefatigable, helping many of the resettlers to close out their affairs before leaving the United States. In dire cases he even underwrote the new settlers' moving expenses and equipment. Although altogether Sterling Clack Robertson settled more than 600 families prior to the Texas Revolution, he has been neglected by history. Instead, the glory and the memory have gone to Stephen F. Austin. Robertson's descendants are understandably resentful and feel that Austin cheated them out of their inheritance. They make a good case for their claim.

On the other hand, Austin's place in the history of Texas cannot be denied. Concocter of a gigantic land swindle or not, he knew how to run a proper colony and showed wisdom away beyond his years. Although· he had complete civil and military authority over his colonists until 1828, he invited his colonists to elect their own militia officers and *alcaldes* (justices of the peace). He drew up procedural forms and a simple civil and criminal code for his courts. As lieutenant colonel of militia he planned campaigns against the Indians. When with increasing population judicial pressures began to mount, he formed an appellate court of the seven *alcaldes*. And when in November 1827 the constitution of Coahuila y Texas took effect, Austin organized an *ayuntamiento,* a public body which would relieve him of the responsibilities of governing. With his background and his record of almost total devotion to the tasks of colonization, he easily was the strongest man in Texas.

Austin had to do everything. For instance, the Mexicans kept their record of titles issued on loose sheets, easily mislaid. Austin obtained permission to record titles in a bound volume with copies and originals both attested by a land commissioner. Austin prepared these forms. He hired and directed surveyors, checked field notes, gave out grants, prepared titles, chased Indians, corresponded with the states and with Mexican officials, and raised money. In his spare time he was a natural target for all visitors who might want to settle in Texas, and he ran a sort of open house without any hostess of his own to make small talk while he dealt with other matters.

Many of his settlers acted like Americans, refused to pay the

12½ cents an acre for services, and seemed aggrieved by the fact that Austin would bring up the issue. Finally they appealed to the political chief at San Antonio, who ruled that Austin could not collect.

Not incidentally, Austin's land commissioner was the Baron de Bastrop, who worked out an arrangement whereby he received $127 a league for signing titles and split his fee with Austin. But even this source of income merely kept abreast of Austin's expenses. In fact, he had to pay *all* public expenses, because no one else would pay them. When he died in 1836, he was still living on prospects because he had never received enough income to more than meet his running expenses. Before he could realize any wealth, he would have had to sell his leftover land.

In all policy questions Austin acted as go-between with the Mexican officials. He persuaded the federal government and the state legislature to suspend tariff payments for the Anglo colonists for seven years. He should have been wise enough to know that a permissive policy, even though temporary, spoils the child, but he did not. When the Mexicans started collecting, as they had every right to, the Texans cried as if they had been robbed.

On the slavery issue Austin was ambivalent. Free labor was non-existent, and most of his colonists were coming from the slaveholding South. Austin therefore persuaded the *junta instituyente* to legalize slavery, but the constitution of Coahuila y Texas prohibited further introduction of slaves by immigration. In effect, this meant that you had permission to do and not to do at the same time. Austin worked around this ambivalence by persuading the legislature that the constitution actually legalized labor contracts with nominally emancipated slaves. At the same time he talked readily and vividly about the evils of slavery, but when the colonists objected, he declared that Texas must be a slave state. Where Austin stood privately is inascertainable.

Politically and economically, Austin represented that curiously contradictory amalgam of populist and conservative that often characterizes Texans. Since many of his people had fled debts and judgments to come to Texas, he worked through the local *ayuntamiento,* the political chief at San Antonio, the state legislature, and the Mexican congress to obtain relief for them. Thanks to Austin, the legislature of Coahuila y Texas passed a law closing the courts for twelve years to plaintiffs seeking collection of such debts. The law also foreshadowed a homestead exemption law in that defendants could not be required to pay "if it affect[ed] their attention to their families, to their husbandry, or art they professed." Austin considered pushing for a law abolishing collateral security for loans and basing the credit sytem on "moral character" only.

On the other side, in current parlance no doubt exists that Austin belonged to the Establishment. Regularly he reminded his colonists of the generosity of the Mexican government and of their debt of loyalty to it. But his fellow Texans were not disposed to be patient with the "chronic revolutionizing" of Mexico, which usually had three governments—one on the march to power, one temporarily in power, and one on the way out. Although Mexicans had strong feelings for democratic government, the people who rose to the top were themselves strong men with equally strong personal drives. Thus devotion to democratic principle ofttimes became subordinate.

After men like Austin and Robertson had settled families in Texas, and after the families had been given heretofore undreamed-of amounts of land at nominal cost, the country slowly began to fill. The land was lush, well-watered, with giant spreading oaks and grass to a man's waist or shoulder. Wild game abounded, while a non-hunting man could live off the huge caches of honey found in the overhangs of the limestone banks along the creeks and rivers.

The cattle were fat on virgin prairie grass. There was enough seasonal change to keep down the dulling monotone of eternal sunshine. Even that close to the coast, sharp, sudden freezes can set in, and the weather can hurt enough to remind one of pleasurable days past and hoped-for pleasures ahead.

And behind it all worked without ceasing the slight figure of the busy bachelor, Stephen F. Austin, a legend in his own time but totally without the flamboyance that usually accompanies legends. Austin constantly counseled patience with the Mexicans for their clumsy administration of irritating laws (and any law irritated in these Elysian Fields) and as regularly reminded the Mexicans of the patience of his own people. In this continual rallying of two diverse forces, Austin moved forward the timetable of Texas.

In a later century the Texans and the Mexicans might have resolved their differences peaceably over the next several decades. But the problems of brand-new Mexico were well-nigh insuperable. Although the Mexicans possessed the same feelings for self-government and democratic institutions as the North Americans, Madrid had called colonial shots with considerably more authority than had London. Mexico was less prepared to rule herself. She was trying to absorb a mixture of peoples, each fiercely independent, while the United States was comparatively homogeneous. In Mexico people lived hundreds of miles from any seat of effective government, and roads were poor if indeed they existed at all. Mexico lacked navigable rivers for easy transportation of people and goods, or for broadcasting laws and moving officials. Although the Mexicans were good to the Texans, they did not administer the colonists efficiently any more than they administered themselves efficiently. Under such circumstances friction was bound to develop. It did.

7

Revolution

ALMOST from the arrival of the first invited Anglo-Americans into that portion of Mexico known as Texas, sporadic, isolated troubles ensued. Not that the immigrants necessarily came looking for trouble. But they had journeyed to Texas from their local enclaves, and everywhere they found foreigners—Mexicans especially, with a strange religion, a strange language, and a strange government; but also Alabamans, New Yorkers, and other queer folk. Many of the new settlers became good citizens of Mexico, grateful for the generous new start provided by a casual host. Others brought the same impatient and intolerant spirit that made them leave home in the first place. If they encountered anything—*any thing*—different, it was immediately branded as wrong. The times and the place called for mingling, and these newfangled Texans weren't ready to mingle.

All that was needed for real trouble was for the sporadic discontent to mobilize into one vast discord. The first really serious threat came along the Louisiana border, where a wealthy empresario, Haden Edwards, ordered preceding settlers with Spanish grants to get off his grant. The consequent struggle induced Edwards to take a trip back to the United States for assistance. While he was gone, his brother Benjamin launched the Fredonian Rebellion in an effort to divide Texas between the Indians and the Republic of Fredonia. When an alliance with the Chero-

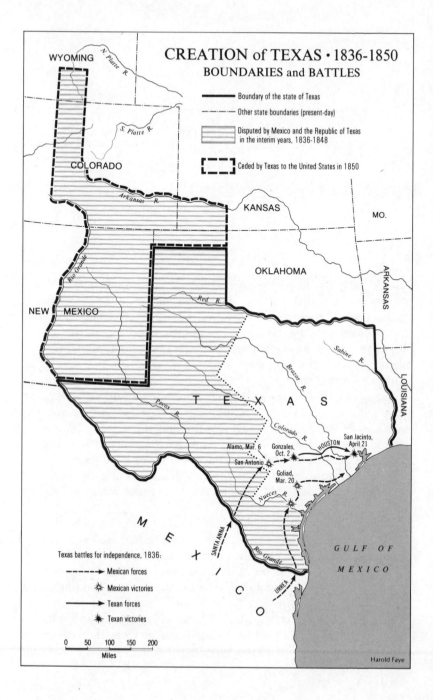

CREATION of TEXAS · 1836-1850
BOUNDARIES and BATTLES

Boundary of the state of Texas

Other state boundaries (present-day)

Disputed by Mexico and the Republic of Texas
in the interim years, 1836-1848

Ceded by Texas to the United States in 1850

WYOMING

N. Platte R.

S. Platte R.

COLORADO

Arkansas R.

KANSAS

MO.

OKLAHOMA

ARKANSAS

NEW MEXICO

Red R.

Sabine R.

LOUISIANA

Pecos R.

T E X A S

Brazos R.

Colorado R.

San Jacinto,
April 21

Alamo, Mar. 6   Gonzales,
Oct. 2

HOUSTON

San Antonio

Goliad,
Mar. 20

Nueces R.

M
E
X
I
C
O

SANTA ANNA

Rio Grande

GULF OF
MEXICO

URREA

Texas battles for independence, 1836:

Mexican forces

Mexican victories

Texan forces

Texan victories

0   50   100   150   200
Miles

Harold Faye

kee did not develop, and Stephen Austin not only refused to permit his colonists to aid the Edwardses but led militia to assist the Mexican troops, the Mexican militia pushed the Fredonians across the Sabine. Edwards failed to find recruits in Louisiana and returned to Kentucky.

The Fredonian Rebellion was an isolated incident and a bust. But it challenged Mexican authority. Henceforward every time someone found a Mexican ruling inconvenient, he would take up arms. Yet with their acknowledged faults the Mexicans still weren't that bad, were indeed random to the point of being careless. For instance, under the rules of colonization the new settler had to declare himself a Roman Catholic, which for 4,605 acres of land was not a bad bargain to many immigrants. And the nice thing about being a non-Catholic Catholic in Texas was that the Mexican priesthood was understaffed and haphazard. Priests came around about once every three or four years, sanctified the unions of fact, baptized and legitimatized the issues of such unions, and then disappeared for another several years. They were hardly a factor in anyone's religious life. When hotspur Texans protested the absence of religious freedom, technically they stood on sound ground. They *did* have to declare themselves Catholics. But pragmatically theirs was a paper issue.

Each boat load and each overland caravan brought in more Texans. The slightly more than 7,000 that lived in Texas when Austin arrived had grown to 20,000 by 1831 and to about 52,000 by the time the Revolution was completed in 1836. Not a spectacular flow, but steady enough to enhance dreams about population pressures, inflation of land values, and enlargement of market for fledgling merchants. From the beginning Texas was reasonably cosmopolitan; analysis of the 1836 population shows that about 10 percent were black, 7 percent Mexican, and 28 percent Indian. The remaining 55 to 60 percent were Anglo-Americans. Over the century-plus since, those figures have held fairly steady except for the Indians, who have unfortunately dwindled into the category of "Others."

The fact that the United States was making persistent noises about buying Texas exacerbated the situation. Perhaps the most significant point was that the most irritable Anglos within this eastern extension of Mexico were almost invariably the most lately arrived. The older settlers either were content with Mexico's general inattention or had been brainwashed by Austin's peaceful preachments. But the newer arrivals were impatient with their predecessors. They brought a certain missionary arrogance, having no understanding of why certain practices and institutions prevailed and why many problems should be nibbled at instead of swallowed whole.

The Mexicans of the 1830s were not unaware of the contentiousness, however unjustified, of their Anglo neighbors. Consequently they moved to cut off immigration by the Law of April 6, 1830, which annulled empresario contracts and prohibited settlement of immigrants in territory adjacent to their native country. Not much insight is required to gather what immigrants might not live in what territory adjacent to what native country. As usual, Austin worked successfully to exempt his own colony, as well as that of another empresario named Green DeWitt. Austin had found a loophole for continued immigration. But the law remained to offend others; and Austin, now a member of the state legislature meeting at Saltillo, worked to get the law repealed.

He also abandoned his long-time low-profile policy to join the cause of the sometime liberal, sometime dictator Santa Anna, who was trying to unseat President Anastacio Bustamante, a medical doctor turned cavalryman turned autocratic politician. When Santa Anna won, Texans felt that they should be rewarded for supporting him.

In October 1832 the Texans held a convention to inform the national government of their need for repeal of the prohibition against immigration from the United States, for extension of tariff exemption, and for separation from Coahuila and authority to establish a state government in Texas. Austin doubted whether the meeting was judicious, particularly since no Mexican delegates had been sent from San Antonio. The petitions never reached the federal government.

A second convention in 1833 repeated the previous petitions and framed a constitution for a Texas state government. Although Austin opposed the petitions, the convention elected him as the most influential man in Texas to take the petitions to Mexico City and to argue for them. Accordingly he left San Felipe, his headquarters, in April 1833, arrived in Mexico City in July, and in December persuaded the government to repeal the Law of April 6, 1830.

Starting home in December with the feeling that he had done well, despite the fact that nothing would convince President Santa Anna to approve state government for Texas, Austin was arrested at Saltillo in January 1834 under suspicion of trying to incite insurrection in Texas. Returned to Mexico City, he faced no charges. No court would accept jurisdiction of his case. But the Mexicans kept him in prison until December 1834, when he was released within the limits of the federal district. A general amnesty in July 1835 set him free to start the trip home to Texas. Whether he could have done anything to soothe Texas's fears is arguable, but his absence for twenty-eight months undoubtedly aggravated a deteriorating situation.

Back in Texas, he learned that still another convention was being called for the upcoming October. At a testimonial dinner for him in Brazoria on September 8, he not only came out for the convention but added the words that sent a chill and thrill through the Anglos in Texas: "War is our only resource." [1] And before the next convention could be held, revolution had broken out. An ebb and flow of confusion followed. Most of the time Texas was in a shambles with competitive governments of its own, and with regulars and volunteers in the field under separate leadership, bearing insufferable jealousies.

The fight began against the tyranny of the conservatives under President Santa Anna, and the battle flag of the Texans at the siege of the Alamo was the red, white, and green of Mexico with the numerals "1824" superimposed across the white. Texans were fighting for the liberal Constitution of 1824, not for freedom. But like all revolutions, the one in Texas progressed beyond its original aim. The men in the Alamo thought

1. *The Texas Republican* (Nacogdoches), 19 September 1835.

they died for the liberality of the Constitution of 1824, but four days before the Alamo fell a Declaration of Independence had been proclaimed more than a hundred miles to the east.

Moments in the fight are worth noting, for they have become part of the myth of Texas. The Lexington of the Texas revolution occurred on the west side of the Guadalupe River four miles above Gonzales on October 2, 1835. The settlement had been given a cannon four years earlier to defend itself against Indians. When General Domingo de Ugartechea, otherwise respected by the Anglos, sent for the cannon, the Anglos refused to surrender. *Alcalde* Andrew Ponton broadcast word of his defiance, and when Ugartechea sent Lieut. Francisco Castañeda to take the cannon, the number of defenders at Gonzales had grown from 18 to 160. Meanwhile the cannon had been buried and then exhumed, mounted on ox-cart wheels, and filled with chains and scrap iron. When the Mexicans appeared, they found a battle flag of a white banner with a rough drawing of the cannon and the words "Come and Take It." The battle that followed wasn't much, with one Mexican and no Texan killed. But the Mexicans retreated, the Texans cheered, and war was under way.

Ugartechea next moved on to San Antonio to join with his leader, General Martín Perfecto de Cós, a brother-in-law of Santa Anna. In Texas when the battle of Gonzales had occurred, Cós first disbanded the legislature of Coahuila y Texas in session at Monclova, landed 500 men at Matagorda Bay, and moved on to San Antonio to expel all Anglo settlers who had arrived since 1830 as well as to arrest all Texans odious to Santa Anna.

Into this situation stepped another former Kentuckian, older than most. Ben Milam, in his upper forties, had first come to Texas in 1818 as an Indian trader. He had been along on the expedition by General Trespalacios and Dr. James Long. As soon as Mexico adopted a constitution, he had joined its army, obtained Mexican citizenship, and attempted to become an empresario. At the time of the Texas revolution Milam had been in Monclova on land business—what else?—and was returning to San Antonio when captured by a Cós detachment. Milam escaped, found his way to the Texas volunteers, and moved on to where Stephen F. Austin was now commanding troops at Gonzales.

Austin placed Milam in charge of a company of scouts with the charge to determine the best route for assaulting San Antonio. The troops waited outside San Antonio, where they shortly determined to retire without attacking. According to folklore, Milam then made a stirring speech whose principal phrase was "Who will go with old Ben Milam into San Antonio!" Three hundred men would.

A split force hit San Antonio before daylight on December 5, 1835, leaving the main army outside the town. For three days the battle raged, as Cós had thirty pieces of artillery. On December 7, Milam was killed. On the next day the Texans began a house-to-house assault that drove the Mexicans backward, and on December 10 Cós signed a capitulation giving the Texans all public property, money, arms, and ammunition in San Antonio. He also agreed to withdraw south of the Rio Grande and not to fight the Texans again. Many Texans thought this victory marked the end of the war. Once safely removed from the Texans, however, Cós turned his army right around into Texas.

And the Texans hadn't reckoned with Santa Anna, a man of enormous ability and greater pride. Military experts have long praised Santa Anna as a master of logistics, a man who could take troops into the forbidding country in the north of Mexico and the south of Texas in the middle of winter and somehow live off a land with nothing to give. Determined not to be outdone by the aberrant Texans, Santa Anna came on with the single purpose of exterminating the *gringos* with their peculiar ideas of resistance—stopping long enough in Laredo to rest his forces and indulge his penchant for romance and fandango. Laredo greeted him as warmly as Philadelphia Quakers had the British while Washington was freezing at Valley Forge.

In February 1836, when the weather in Texas just might be moderating, Santa Anna set out for San Antonio. Just outside San Antonio stood the abandoned mission of San Antonio de Valero, known popularly as the Alamo (either for the town of Alamo del Parras in Coahuila or for a nearby grove of cottonwoods—or *alamos*). Mexican forces had occupied the Alamo from independence to the removal of the forces under General Cós the previous December.

On February 23, 1836, Colonels William Barret Travis and James Bowie entered the Alamo with a force of approximately 145 men. On that same day Santa Anna arrived at San Antonio. The next day the siege began.

Like all heroic fights it mixed a compound of courage and stupidity. Why a force of 187 men, which the Alamo subsequently came to number, would give everything to stop a force of 5,000 men who were bound to win defies logic. Why Santa Anna, with all his generalship, would tie up 5,000 men for two weeks when all he had to do was march around the Alamo, leaving a small holding force behind, and catch the Texans deeper into the interior also is difficult to discern. Call Santa Anna bloodthirsty, vengeful, and sanguine to the point of killing everything in his path; but the man was a good general, and not even sanguinity deters good generals. Later thirty-two men from Gonzales would sneak their way into the Alamo to join their companions in certain death. Why didn't they stay outside and die where it was practical? But these are the types of emotional stands that people make which bring them unconscious immortality.

Inside the fort-church, the purpose was single but procedure and command were at odds. Two men born to lead tried to share a command, but neither was disposed to subordinate himself to the other and each had his unswerving adherents. William B. Travis was a fiery South Carolinian. From the time he had hit Texas at Anahuac, he had been a leader of the so-called war party. In June 1835 he raised a company of volunteers to capture the Mexican garrison which had reoccupied Anahuac. In December 1835 the Texas government made him lieutenant colonel of cavalry, and in the following February he took his twenty-five men to reinforce James Bowie at San Antonio. Bowie, another man of heroic mold (but more than a little tarnished), and Travis disliked each other on sight, and the defense of the Alamo suffered from a divided command.

Bowie belonged to the half-man, half-alligator genre characterized by such worthies as Mike Fink and Davy Crockett. In Louisiana he had farmed, logged, and ridden alligators. He had also speculated in land with bogus titles and had smuggled slaves, frequently in collaboration with the pirate Jean Laffite. While recovering from a duel, he had fashioned a specially designed knife widely copied in Texas, the South, and the Southwest. Ideally the Bowie knife was built on the proportions of a short butcher knife, but with more curve on the blade near the point and a heavier handle, often of horn, and with handle, blade, and guard so well balanced that the knife could be thrown a maximum distance with deadly effect. The legend grew that the Bowie knife was "as handy as a shirt pocket"; certainly it was economical and practical for skinning, cutting up meat, eating, fighting duels, stabbing enemies, hammering, picking teeth, and all the other frontier needs. It was the weapon of the Southwest until the six-shooter supplanted it after Texas had joined the United States. It could be thrown faster than a rifle could be reloaded.

Bowie had come to Texas in 1828 and, in current terms, had gone native. He had been baptized into the Catholic Church in Bexar, had searched for a lost, probably nonexistent, gold mine that has come down into history as the Lost Bowie Mine, and on April 22, 1831, had married Ursula María de Veramendi, daughter of the Mexican governor of Coahuila y Texas. The death of his wife and children from cholera at the governor's summer home in 1833 is supposed to have turned Bowie to liquor. Although the Mexicans looked on Bowie as one of them and accepted him wholly, when the revolution broke out he joined the Texas forces. After the battle of San Antonio he commanded the volunteer force there, and he was in command when Travis arrived with his regulars. But God or germs intervened inside the Alamo, for from the very first day of the siege Bowie was confined to his cot with typhoid-pneumonia, and Travis took sole charge.

One more of the motley company, each of whose identity is known, should be mentioned. He was David Crockett, Tennessee frontiersman and congressman and already a legend. When the trouble in Texas began, Crockett and a few of his "Tennessee Boys" had joined Travis at the Alamo to fight against Santa Anna. He was probably the biggest man in the Alamo, more than six feet tall with broad shoulders and an athlete's waist and hips, and he was only a few months short of fifty years old in a company of mostly young men. But he acted as their cheerleader and spent the hours between volleys and assaults telling tall stories and being undoubtedly the best-liked person within the Alamo walls. Theodore Roosevelt once characterized him as "distinctly, intensely, American stock." Certainly he represents the citizenry of the Southwest in its most attractive form—friendly, a good talker, sober, considerate, and courageous. Although he lived in Texas for only two months, arriving just in time to die, the state claims him as one of its authentic heroes.

Ironically, the Alamo is not supposed even to have been there for the siege to occur. Sam Houston had ordered Bowie to demolish and abandon it, but Bowie had refused to do so. And so the Alamo remained for John Wayne and history. The struggle between Travis and Bowie for supreme command brought forth reactions which clarify the difference between Austin and Houston. Austin, unfitted for military command even though it was thrust upon him at times, opposed Bowie as a freebooter who fought only for what he could get out of a situation. But Houston valued him for his leadership and courage.

For thirteen days the siege continued, as the Texans held on gallantly. Santa Anna, on his arrival, had ordered a red flag—NO QUARTER!—raised over the tower of San Fernando Church. Travis answered the flag with a shot from an eighteen pounder, but before the round could be fired Bowie had sent a messenger under a flag of truce to seek terms of surrender. Santa Anna returned the messenger with the information that the red flag meant what it had always meant—unconditional surrender. Travis, his temper frayed, demanded an oath of "never surrender" from his men. He got it.

On the second day Travis sent out an appeal that has reappeared in anthologies of defiant statements. Some critics have called it the most heroic letter in American history:

To the People of Texas and all Americans in the world—Fellow
Citizens and Compatriots: I am besieged . . . I have sustained a
continual Bombardment and cannonade for 24 hours and have not
lost a man. The enemy has demanded a surrender at discretion,
otherwise, the garrison are to be put to the sword if the fort is taken.
I have answered the demand with a cannon shot, and our flag still
waves proudly from the walls. *I shall never surrender or retreat.*
Then, I call upon you in the name of Liberty, of patriotism, and
every thing dear to the American character, to come to our aid with
all dispatch. The enemy is receiving reinforcements daily and will
no doubt increase to three or four thousand in four or five days. If
this call is neglected, I am determined to sustain myself as long as
possible and die like a soldier who never forgets what is due his
own honor and that of his country. VICTORY OR DEATH.

William Barret Travis
Lt. Col. Comdt.

P.S.

The Lord is on our side. When the enemy appeared in sight we
had not three bushels of corn. We have since found in deserted
houses 80 to 90 bushels and got into the walls 20 or 30 head of
Beeves.

Travis [2]

Mostly the siege consisted of watching, working, and
waiting—placing guns, constructing platforms, throwing up
earthworks, sneaking out foraging parties, setting fire to nearby
houses which might give shelter to Mexican soldiers, and sending messengers eastward with frantic appeals for aid. Once in a
while the tedium was relieved by a Mexican charge or cannonade. Music would drift in to the Alamo from the Mexican
camp. Otherwise the Mexicans were doing about the same
things as the Texans. Occasionally Texas sentries would spot a
figure they thought was Santa Anna, passing on horseback
within musket range. They were never able to hit him. Two
Texas twelve-pounders did hit Santa Anna's headquarters, but
the general was not there.

2. William Barret Travis to the Citizens of Texas, Army Papers, Texas State Library,
Austin.

Travis spent much of his time sending out foraging parties and appeals. Travis wrote to a friend urging that a declaration of independence be proclaimed so that the world—and Texas—might better understand the defense of the Alamo. His position was indeed a very lonely one.

After March 3 no one either entered or left the Alamo. This is the period when Travis is supposed to have drawn his immortal line across the dirt floor of the Alamo and invited all who would stay and die with him to step over. According to patriotic folklore, Bowie asked, "Boys, will some of you kindly lift my cot across?" Whether Bowie made the move, the request is in keeping with his reputation. The symbolism of the line is as important as the veracity of the story. The Alamo is a place where ordinary men were ennobled as they died gallantly for a cause, unclear though they were as to what the cause was all about.

Early on the 4th the Mexicans began firing. All day the bombardment continued, but no attack was pressed. The next day was quiet, with only token fighting. Proabably all in the fort knew that the day represented a last lull. For eleven days they had hardly slept, eating at their posts—mainly beef and cornbread—and waiting. Coffee was only a memory. Many Texans fell asleep leaning against the walls, weapons in their hands.

But the 5th was as active for Santa Anna's forces as it was tranquil for the Texans. The infantry was being divided into four columns, each provided with picks, spikes, and scaling ladders. To the rear General Ramirez y Sesma was placing his cavalry to see that neither Texans escaped nor Mexicans deserted. When the call came, the artillery would remain quiet, for the infantry would be working right against the Alamo walls.

The attack began at 4 o'clock in the morning. It brought no surprise. The still of the chill March Sunday morning was interrupted by the blast of a bugle, and the Mexicans started shouting. From west, north, and east they poured out of the darkness to be met with Texan grape and canister. The Mexicans fell back.

But they were as brave as the Texans. Exhorted by their officers, they pressed forward again into the hail of bullets. In the background the Mexican bands were playing *"El Deguello,"* the "fire and death" call dating back to the Inquisition. Its music signified total destruction—death to enemies. Shortly three Mexican columns massed under the north wall. To the Texans inside it must have seemed as if the whole of Mexico were trying to mount the wall. It might as well have been, for the odds were thirty to one. Two waves fell back, but each suspension of attack left fewer Texans defending.

At daybreak the third assault began. Over the parapet came the Mexicans. Among the first was General Juan Amador, who seized the nearest Texas guns and turned them against the interior, shooting indiscriminately in almost every direction. He couldn't miss. Undoubtedly many Mexicans were shot by Mexican bullets, for the assault got out of all control. Madly, bravely, the Texans fought, but unfortunately for them, madly, bravely, the Mexicans fought also. The Texans had no place to retreat, even to fire blind, and the Mexicans just kept on coming on.

For three-quarters of an hour this barbarity continued, often hand-to-hand. Among the Mexicans Colonel Francisco Duque fell, and the belief is that he was trampled to death by his own men, though no one knew. It was that kind of brutal, close-in orgiastic fighting.

By 8 o'clock on that Sunday morning, old women and little children were walking to mass. Every last Texas soldier was dead, trying to hold off a force exceeding 5,000. For twelve days they had succeeded. On the thirteenth day they had joined a pantheon of heroes. Crockett was dead, mutilated, his Tennessee companions lying alongside him. Bowie was dead on his cot, and detractors and worshipers would argue for generations whether he died like a cringing coward or whether from his sickbed he and his fearful knife took a dozen Mexicans into eternity with him. Travis, who had pledged "Victory or Death," died beside a cannon, rifle in hand. He had set the stage for ultimate Texas unification and victory.

All day after the fight the exhausted survivors worked at gathering wood and dry branches and building a giant pyre: layers of bodies between layers of wood. Just before dusk Santa Anna ordered the torch to the pyre; in short time, the acrid air denoted that the Texans in the Alamo existed no more.

For the next six weeks Texans put aside their jealousies and little enmities, cried out "Remember the Alamo!" and caught Santa Anna dallying with Jenny the mulatto during siesta time alongside a bayou bend east of Houston called San Jacinto. The Napoleon of the West was captured, the Mexican Army surrendered, and Texas was free from the Mexican government.

To southwesterners the Alamo ranks alongside Lexington and Concord, Saratoga, and Cowpens. The shots there may not have been heard around the world, but they were certainly heard from Mexico City across Texas to Washington, and that covers enough distance to assure that the men who fell there would be remembered.

The effect on the Mexican psyche of losing Texas is impossible to determine. In the States great cheering ensued, except in New England, which had always resented westward extension and looked on the separation of Texas from Mexico as further evidence of a plot to enlarge the slave domain. Texas was one-third the geographical size of the then United States, larger than France, twice the size of Germany, larger than Spain. Had the United States been handed more than a quarter of a million square miles of territory, or had a third empire been created on the North American continent?

If Texas could throw off Mexican sovereignty, and if her prospects were as rich as they seemed, might not Texas grow in population and wealth to the point that it could absorb the remaining northern states of Mexico and eventually stretch all the way to the Pacific, creating a Pacific empire to match the growing Atlantic empire of the United States? These thoughts undoubtedly crossed many minds. Sighting down the long gun barrel of history, in the centuries ahead what target might Texas hit out there?

8

Of Myths and a Republic

$\mathcal{U}$NDOUBTEDLY one source of the traditional Texas image—or caricature—of roughness and political instability was the attitude of John Quincy Adams. In his latter-day congressional period, he carried on an effective campaign of opposition to its admission to the Union. Adams saw the admission of Texas as part of the southern plot to extend slave territory, and he had a strong bias against admission of any western territory anywhere. President James K. Polk's war against Mexico merely confirmed New Englanders' suspicion that Adams was correct.

Whatever the reasons for the myth and the almost universal dislike (and Lord knows Texas produces plenty of loud-mouthed politicians and spoiled rich who fuel the myth), the Texas myth is the cross that Texans bear. They naturally leave the state in a defensive posture, knowing that at the best they are likely to be treated as intellectual colonials and at worst as bizarre creatures. Walter Prescott Webb, a native Texan recognized as one of the most influential historians of the twentieth century, once observed that "Texans should learn silence." And J. Frank Dobie, another native, said, "Texans are the only 'race of people' known to anthropologists who do not depend on breeding for propagation.'' [1] Unfortunately Texans multiply over drinks, and by imagination.

Dobie himself brings home the point. A short, square-built man with a face carved from the old rock, he was steeped in classical literature, wrote with tender feeling about men and animals, and could build a sentence and a paragraph with as much craft as anyone in the nonfiction field. He published a score of books, none of which have gone out of print a decade after his death. His interest was man and his relationship with his environment, and he studied mustangs and coyotes for clues to universal behavior. And yet when he died, no less careful a newspaper than the *New York Times* started its lead as follows: "J. Frank Dobie, nationally known Texas humorist. . . ." [2] No one who knew Dobie would have called him a humorist to his face, but the *New York Times,* not a frivolous newspaper, could not see him as a Texan without also seeing him as a humorist—someone to be taken not quite seriously.

Without further belaboring the Texas myth, I should add that I believe its real genesis lies in the Texas Revolution, in which a group of upstart Anglos defeated a sometimes brilliant general leading an army of a nation whose roots are a century older than those of the United States and which in 1835–1836 was at least the equivalent of the United States in size and in strength. The fact that Texas persisted as an independent republic for ten years and itself showed some intimations of empire-building cemented the myth. The War against Mexico, fought to a great extent *over* Texas, merely sealed the mythical package. The facts that the Walker model of the Colt revolver was introduced in this war, that the Texas Rangers performed splendidly albeit without much discipline and with an utter lack of respect for regular army leadership, and that Texas provided a staging area for the invasion of Mexico tied the ribbons on the mythical package. Naturally Texans—native or newly arrived—have overglori-

1. Quoted in George Fuermann, *Reluctant Empire* (Garden City, N.Y.: Doubleday & Co., 1957), p. 277.

2. *New York Times,* 19 September 1964.

fied their period of independence and have created their own myth of a free and wild heritage.

Myth or not, some facts remain. On hearing that Texas had won its independence at San Jacinto, most Texans in the United States as well as most Anglos in Texas undoubtedly felt that Texas would immediately be annexed into the Union. But they didn't reckon with anti-Texas prejudice in the States on the one hand and with the confidence of Sam Houston in Texas on the other. At the same time Andrew Jackson did not feel that good politics permitted him to annex Texas, and his successor, Martin Van Buren, preferred to leave events as Jackson would have ordained them.

By this time Texans had a taste of independence. They began to see themselves as Spain and Mexico had intended them to be—effective buffers between the two major nations of North America. If they could whip Mexico in Texas, why could they also not whip Mexico in New Mexico, California, Coahuila, Chihuahua, Sonora, and who knew where else? They began to dream of an empire stretching to the Pacific. Likewise, they began to suspect they had their own Manifest Destiny, with the result that they were not going to supplicate before the altar of the United States. Prejudice and pride proved difficult to reconcile, and Sam Houston, the most remarkable Texan personality of the nineteenth century, was the type of man who could exploit such a situation for high stakes.

If in late spring of 1836 any Texans were arrogant, they simply did not understand the predicament into which they had projected themselves. True, they deserved to enjoy some elation over having defeated Santa Anna and having in effect run the Mexican army out of Texas. But they had no assurance that they could hold Texas against reinvasion by a determined Mexican army. They had no political parties, no viable government, no taxing authority, and no money. All they had accomplished was to defeat the Mexicans at San Jacinto.

Ten days after the Alamo had fallen, an *ad interim* government had been established under the presidency of forty-eight-year-old David G. Burnet. He had lived in Texas continuously since 1826 as a sometime empresario, had been a judge and a member of the conventions of 1833 and 1836. Conservative, sensitive, full of bombast and born to be unpopular, Burnet would have encountered insuperable problems under the best of circumstances. As president during eight months of chaotic transition, he lost his support and became extremely disenchanted. Once other Texans even tried to arrest him, but he refused to resign or to accept the resignation of his cabinet, thereby probably preventing a military takeover.

On the other hand, Lorenzo de Zavala, his vice-president, from a village in Yucatan, was an ardent liberal. During the Mexican revolution the Spanish imprisoned him at the castle of San Juan de Ulloa, where he studied medicine and English. Representing Yucatan in the Spanish Cortes in Madrid when he learned that Mexico had declared independence, he returned home to be a member of the Mexican legislature. He became governor of the state of Mexico in 1827 but fled because of persecution by the army. After another overturn he became national secretary of the treasury as well as governor of the state of Mexico, and then in 1829 he received an empresario contract to introduce 500 families into Texas. In 1832 he returned as governor of the state of Mexico, then became a member of the Mexican Chamber of Deputies in 1833 and minister to France under Santa Anna.

Like the Texans, Zavala in Paris decided that Santa Anna had no intention of observing the Constitution of 1824 and resolved to resist as a Texan. He built a home on Buffalo Bayou outside future Houston, moved in his family, and was at Washington-on-the-Brazos to sign the Texas Declaration of Independence. He remained as vice-president from March 17 until the following October 17. Less than a month later he was dead.

Zavala's presence further emphasizes that in great part the Texas revolution was a fight of liberals against tyranny, rather than Anglos against Mexicans. Although Zavala could foresee a long and assured role in the Mexican upper political hierarchy, nonetheless away off in the security of Paris he felt that Santa Anna was sabotaging the spirit of freedom and left for Texas to help restore that freedom. In a sense he is chicano *numero uno* in Texas.

In Texas Sam Houston was no undiluted hero, and citizens of the new Republic tended to factionalize according to the degree of favor or disfavor certain groups felt toward Old Sam. Pro- and anti-Andrew Jackson sentiment also infected many Texans, and Houston was still considered by many as the protégé of the president. In fact, Jackson supposedly was grooming Houston for the presidency when the latter walked out on his bride and on the Tennessee governor's office to disappear among the Indians along the western border of Arkansas, take an Indian wife, and drink a barrel or so of whiskey a day to forget whatever it was that had caused his walk-out in the first place.

But then Houston had sobered up, except for occasional aberrations, and had shown up in Texas, where he brought a fine reputation as a governor of a state and a frontier fighter. Without any previous recommendations he would have been an impressive man in any company; here he rose to commander-in-chief of the Texas forces. But as he had retreated steadily before Santa Anna, many soldiers and civilians alike had decided he was cowardly. When his Fabian tactics brought total victory in an 18-minute battle at San Jacinto, many others hailed Houston as a genius. His detractors regarded him as lucky.

Running for president against Houston were Henry Smith, notable primarily for having married three sisters in succession, and Stephen F. Austin, a reluctant candidate urged on by the anti-Houston element. But Austin was like many another prime candidate on the North American scene—when his opportunity arose, he had already passed his time. As seen, he had opposed independence at the outset of the trouble. He had also opposed placing Santa Anna before a firing squad. When the returns came in, Houston received approximately 80 percent of a total vote of nearly 6,000. His vice-president was Mirabeau B. Lamar, a man of letters whom we will meet again. In the same election on the first Monday in September 1836, the voters approved the new constitution, the only constitution accepted without acrimony in the history of Texas. Also placed before the voters was a referendum on annexation to the United States. Only ninety-one persons disapproved.

Under the constitution the President served three years, except for the first term, and could not succeed himself. Houston served from October 22, 1836 to December 10, 1838, Lamar until 1841, Houston again until 1844, and Anson Jones until the Texas flag was replaced by the United States flag on February 19, 1846.

The transition from colony to constitutional republic was accomplished quickly and with a minimum of disorganization. The progress of Texas in this experience proved a much smoother process than that of the earlier thirteen colonies into the United States. But in fairness to the United States, its problem was exacerbated by having to meld thirteen colonies into some sort of union, whereas Texas was a single entity to begin with.

Challenges were manifold. Texas wanted to be recognized by other nations of the world. It needed to become self-supporting. It had to be able to defend itself against the United States from the east and Mexico from the south (which has given Texans an historic sympathy for the plight of Germany, caught between Russia and France). The problem of peace with the Indians would remain for nearly another half-century. And the question of boundaries would help bring on the war against Mexico, as well as delay affiliation of the Republic with the United States. Also on hand were the expansionist elements from the United States, who had helped provoke the Texas war for independence and who asked regularly why San Jacinto should mark the end of territorial aggrandizement. They wanted to expand into other Mexican areas, to create a real empire that would compete with both the United States and Mexico on more or less even terms. And everyone wanted land.

Land was available and was given away prodigally. Since the Republic had no money, it paid its overdue soldiers in land scrip. Banks were outlawed, reflecting the Jacksonian bias against the speculative wildcat banks that helped bring on the Panic of 1837 back in the States. Since apparently people can no more live without banks than they can live without sin, some banking function was necessary—in fact, had been necessary since the whole revolution had begun. Just as the Continental Congress had its Robert Morris and the Union would produce its Jay Cooke, so the Texas Revolution and subsequent Republic witnessed the rise of the mercantile firm of McKinney and Williams to underwrite the Texas Revolution.

Thomas F. McKinney was a horse raiser and a man of action, while his partner, Samuel May Williams, from Rhode Island, had picked up experience and contacts in most of the Atlantic and Gulf ports, as well as in Latin America. As secretary and sometime partner to Stephen F. Austin, he also knew almost everyone among the older Anglo-Texan inhabitants. The firm operated in the little seaport town of Quintana and later in Galveston. When the upstart government of Texas could neither raise funds nor obtain credit, merchants in New Orleans and Mobile, as well as in such farther away places as Charleston, Baltimore, and Providence, advanced guns and powder, cloth for uniforms, and all the other sinews of war to the account of McKinney and Williams, which in turn forwarded these elements to whatever Texas government existed at the time. The result was that McKinney and Williams underwrote a good portion of the Revolution and their faith in turn led other merchants to help the struggling government. Without them, the Revolution possibly could not have been pulled off successfully, Texas would not have gained its independence at this time, and the Texas myth would be interesting but hardly overwhelming.

Penurious—or cheap—the Congress of the Republic of Texas and later the legislature of the State of Texas postponed paying the partnership for its efforts. After the original partners moved on to their graves, their heirs tried periodically to collect until the 1940s, when the Supreme Court of Texas ruled that the payment could be made to heirs only by passage of an amendment to the state constitution. At this point the heirs gave up, knowing full well that the Texas voting citizenry would never approve paying a debt more than a century old to people who hadn't even been born when the debt was incurred.

Patriotism was not a total loss to McKinney and Williams, however. They were given a banking privilege under a Republic of Texas constitution that permitted no banking. They could issue bills, but just couldn't call it a bank. Later, when Texas became a state, the state constitution also forbade banking, but again McKinney and Williams were permitted to continue their banking function. When Texas became a state in the Confederacy, its Confederate state constitution forbade banking, but McKinney and Williams continued their banking, even though Williams was dead and the partnership had really ceased to be active after 1853. Significantly, when bills issued by the Republic of Texas were being discounted 50 to 60 percent in the New Orleans mart and often in Texas, McKinney and Williams's bills were being discounted only 10 to 20 percent. In short, faith in the financial stability of these two men ranked much higher than faith in the Republic of Texas even though their treatment at the hands of successive Texas governments was shoddy, to say the least.

At the outset of independence Sam Houston, using his finely honed sensitivity and ignoring his personal preferences, chose a cabinet which he thought would work best for his country's interests. Among its members he named Austin as his secretary of state and Henry Smith as secretary of the treasury. Partially as a result of overwork and exposure in the service of Texas, Austin died about two months after taking office, only forty-one years old. He is often referred to as the Father of Texas, and the state is dotted with proud people who mistakenly say that they were descended from this bachelor.

So now Texas faced the joys of nationhood for a decade. Without regard to finances, its Congress established a standing army of 3,587 troops, in addition to a battalion of 280 mounted riflemen to protect the frontier. The Congress also authorized the President to accept 40,000 volunteers, an unrealistic figure that could only have been intended to be read in Mexico. Since Texas had no money, Houston's concern was reducing or eliminating an army payroll rather than enlarging it. Furthermore, the army was made up largely of latecomers who felt no more loyalty to Texas than they had to Mexico. These adventurers, invaluable though their services may have been, had refused to accept Lamar when the previous president, David G. Burnet, had named him their commander. Burnet had then made the worst possible choice for replacement, Felix Huston, a man of few qualifications who had left Natchez owing $40,000 while raising an army to assist Texas (after Texas had already won its freedom). Houston replaced Huston with Albert Sidney Johnston, a West Point graduate from Kentucky who became one of the more admirable Texan military leaders for the next quarter of a century. Huston challenged Johnston to a duel, wounded his replacement so critically that he could not take command, and remained on for a time.

But Sam Houston was wily, and while General Huston was busily trying to obtain the support of Congress for an invasion of Mexico, President Houston furloughed all but 600 of his troops. Soon the remainder were turned out, leaving Texas with only local militia and Rangers.

The worry that Mexico might invade remained uppermost in the minds of the Texians, as they then called themselves. Little basis existed for this anxiety, though Mexico never recognized the independence of Texas and still claimed the region. Nothing much happened during Houston's first term except that the president invited more acrimony by giving Santa Anna his freedom, providing that the deposed dictator go to Washington to persuade President Jackson to annex Texas. Although Houston knew that Santa Anna was not the right man for a forlorn mission, for Santa Anna no longer held either Mexico or Texas, he sent the Mexican general with an escort just to get him off his hands and out of Texas, where he was a nuisance. When Santa Anna arrived in Washington, Jackson sent him back to Vera Cruz aboard a United States frigate.

When Mirabeau Buonaparte Lamar succeeded Houston, he was much more straightforward in his foreign relations than his predecessor. He tried to effect an understanding with his former overlords, to the extent of sending Secretary of State Barnard E. Bee to Mexico in May 1839 to offer the Mexican government up to $5,000,000 to recognize Texas's independence and a Rio Grande boundary. Bee never proceeded beyond Vera Cruz. Where Texas would obtain the $5,000,000 is uncertain; but in view of later developments the sum, if paid, would have represented a bit of a coup for Mexico, who eventually lost Texas and received nothing in return. Lamar then sent another agent, James Treat, who did make it to Mexico City and hung around for ten months while the Mexicans encouraged him just enough to keep him from returning home.

The story of Texas-Mexican relations is too complicated to detail here. In the midst of Treat's mission a Republic of the Rio Grande was established formally in January 1840 as an antidote against the centralism of Mexico, backed by the states of Coahuila, Nuevo León, and Tamaulipas. Although Texas informally favored the new republic, it was so eager to obtain Mexican recognition of its own independence that it would not give official or forthright aid. When Antonio Canales of Camargo, one of the Rio Grande leaders, asked President Lamar for assistance, he was ignored. But because he thought that Texans were aiding the republic, President Bustamante of Mexico requested that the war against Texas be resumed. Lamar issued a proclamation admonishing all citizens of Texas "to abstain from all attempts to invade the territory of Mexico." When the Republic of the Rio Grande finally faltered in November 1840, Texas lost interest in the movement and undoubtedly congratulated itself on its forbearance.

On Treat's eventual return to Texas, Lamar recommended a declaration of war to force Mexico to recognize Texas. Congress refused. Lamar then sent one more mission, but the Mexicans refused to receive it. The president allied Texas with the Mexican state of Yucatan, in revolt against the central government, but the Yucatan revolution came to naught and did nothing for Texas. What next?

In his eagerness to fix the Rio Grande as a boundary Lamar attempted to push the Texas dream toward the Pacific. His first object was the string of settlements along the upper Rio Grande, of which the most notable is Santa Fe. This time a careful Congress vetoed his idea, but Lamar raised and equipped his own caravan. The party of 270 set out from Austin on June 21, 1841, and included among its three commissioners one Mexican, José Antonio Navarro, a signer of the Texas Declaration of Independence, a Mason, sometime legislator and congressman, and father of four future Confederate sons, who would lose almost four years of his life to the expedition. The purpose: take Santa Fe and establish the authority of Texas in New Mexico.

Whether the expedition was as visionary then as it seems now is debatable. Lamar had no Gallup Poll to tell him how the New Mexicans felt, but reports indicated that the hold of the Mexican government there was shaky. New Mexico, Lamar was eager to believe, was ripe for new leadership. For the economic determinists the Santa Fe expedition strikes another positive blow. Broke and not getting any better off financially with any alacrity, Texas was desperate for trade. In the United States a Santa Fe Trail had proved a two-way commercial highway from Missouri to New Mexico since 1821, when Mexico had abrogated the Spanish policy of exclusiveness in trade. Something akin to a road across the plains had been worked out, and mule- and ox-drawn wagons made the trip regularly, sometimes with military escort but not necessarily. The trail would continue to be important until the coming of the railroad in 1880, and its promise of enduring significance was not lost on the Texans. But how to divert this trade to Texas?

Although priorities get mixed, hope of empire seems to have outweighed even economics. On April 14, 1840, Lamar sent a letter to Santa Fe which was bold and undoubtedly ill-advised. He told the New Mexicans that their self-interest lay in joining the Republic of Texas, and that Texans would soon arrive to work out union. It seemed to him like such a good idea that the offer could hardly be refused. And so on June 19, 1841, the officially designated Santa Fe Pioneers set out. When commissioners, merchants, teamsters, and even journalists were added to the soldiers, the group totaled 321. Twenty-one ox-drawn wagons carried merchandise worth $200,000, plus the logistics for five companies of infantry and one of artillery.

When the first traders from Franklin, or Independence, Missouri, had reached Santa Fe, life for the visitors in the Mexican outposts had been one long fiesta. Texans thought that they too would be received as heroes, but instead Governor Manuel Armijo of New Mexico had called out his militia to resist what he looked on as an invasion. The Mexicans used a member of the Santa Fe expedition, Captain William G. Lewis, convincing him to persuade his fellow travelers in the advance party to lay down their arms. When the main force drew as close as Tucumcari on October 5, Lewis again persuaded the Texans that the Mexicans would treat them right if they would just put their fate in the hands of their hosts. Without firing a shot, the Mexicans took the entire expedition. Actually the Mexicans were getting secondhand goods, for the Texans had already been so done in by the desert plains that even capture seemed like succor.

Unfortunately the Mexicans looked on the Texans as something between prisoners of war and rebellious Mexican citizens. The visitors were subjected to a long, often brutal march to Mexico City, where they were imprisoned. When the United States got in the act, the Mexicans finally decided that discretion called for release of the prisoners. Those who made it home told harrowing tales.

Texas had no credit of good will with Mexico, and the Santa Fe expedition more than overdrew the account. In Mexico Santa Anna was once again in charge of the government, and early in 1842, he invaded the new republic. But the Mexicans ran out of steam quickly and retired to the far side of the Rio Grande. About all they accomplished was to fan anti-Mexican sentiment in Texas, to resurrect Texan vigilance against invasion from the south, and to scare the Texans witless.

Even Sam Houston panicked, declared a public emergency, and ordered the archives removed from Austin to Houston. Whether Houston was alarmed or opportunistic remains debatable. He had always preferred the town named for him, ostensibly because of its convenience to the sea but more likely because of his pride in name. The fact that in 1841 one Austin citizen was scalped at the town's nearby spa, Barton Springs; that a party of Comanches, led by a chief in war dress, marched near the French minister's house; and that in this raid a white boy was killed and a Negro boy captured, lends some credence to Houston's desire to remove the capital back toward the coast. Furthermore, like recent presidents he was deluded by having received three-fourths of the vote for president on his re-election bid. Just when he thought he had a mandate, Congress undercut him. With more than a thousand Mexican troops at San Antonio, Austinites fled, leaving only about two dozen families in the town.

Thus Houston gave the order for the archives to be removed, justifying his action on grounds that loss of the national archives would profoundly injure the country. Austinites were outraged. The move was opposed not only from a prestige standpoint but because property owners feared a sharp decline in real estate prices. And Austinites would sooner fight Sam Houston than Mexicans. At Bastrop, thirty miles to the east of Austin on the Houston road, a patrol was established to detain all wagons carrying government records. Houston had to back down.

The Mexicans gave him a second opportunity with an invasion in September, when General Adrian Woll again took San Antonio, this time for nine days. Houston asked Congress to permit the archives to be removed. If the Texans couldn't keep the Mexicans from taking San Antonio twice in one year, what hopes did they have in case a determined bid was made by Mexico to move another seventy miles farther to the Texas capital? Nevertheless Congress turned Houston down again.

Houston then ordered two military men to remove the archives secretly under pretense of saving them from an incipient Indian invasion. Accordingly twenty men and three wagons under the command of Colonel Thomas I. Smith loaded the wagons with papers from the Land Office. They headed north out of Austin and bedded down at Kinney's Fort. It was December 30, with a blue norther barreling in and rain falling as though poured from buckets, and nobody would get out on a night like this just to save an archive. But twenty men from Austin did, and no sentries had been posted. Colonel Smith treated his pursuers with discretion and agreed to return the archives on New Year's Eve, 1842. For one of the few times in his life, Sam Houston had lost permanently.

With the archive war over, the country could give more time to Mexican threats. But the invaders disappeared almost with settlement of the archives question. Texans had been all for chasing into Mexico that summer, but Houston had refused to be rushed into a war that he thought was unnecessary. By November 750 men led by General Alexander Somervell were ready to invade on their own. On December 8 they recaptured Laredo from the Mexicans; that seemed to satisfy the blood-thirst of many of them, who promptly returned home. Somervell took his men down the Rio Grande on a ten-day march and then turned them inland towards Gonzales. At this juncture a number of the men refused to go home and insisted on an invasion.

Under Colonel W. S. Fisher about 300 men began a march to Mier, a *pueblito* on the Mexican side of the Rio Grande. There the Texans ran into more resistance than they could handle and were forced to surrender. Marched deep into Mexico, they escaped once but were recaptured and drew black beans to determine which of their number should compose the one-tenth to be shot. Ironically, after months of confinement, the survivors were released by no less than Santa Anna.

Despite losing at Santa Fe, the Texans made a second try in that direction. In the spring of 1843 Colonel Jacob Snively gathered 180 men in North Texas for a raid on the Santa Fe Trail where it crossed the Panhandle area of Texas between Missouri and Santa Fe. But an escort of United States troops captured the Snively expedition, so that once again Texas pride was dented.

Although all of this coming and going proved abortive for both Texans and Mexicans, the expeditions had real value. They kept Texas advertised in the States, with the result that Texas never quite retreated from the public's mind.

With Houston and Jackson resisting efforts toward annexation on either side of the Sabine and Red rivers, the issue still would not die. The United States had recognized Texas almost at once, and Jackson's last official act before leaving office in March 1837 had been to name a chargé d'affaires to the Republic of Texas. Beginning in the following August and continuing into 1838, annexation remained an ever present issue in Washington. During the morning of every session of Congress from June 16 to July 7, 1838, John Quincy Adams made a speech opposing the annexation of Texas. When Congress adjourned without acting, the Texans, represented in Washington by Anson Jones, announced the "formal and absolute withdrawal" of the offer by Texas to be annexed.

For the nonce the issue died. Revived in 1842 and again in 1843, annexation could not be pushed through. Meanwhile Texas was hanging on as an independent nation and beginning to demonstrate some coziness with the British. Fear of British influence impacted on Washington, and on October 16, 1843, the United States open negotiations for annexation by treaty. The treaty progressed as far as being signed by two Texans and by John C. Calhoun, representing the United States. Within two months the Senate of the United States had rejected the treaty. A national election was imminent, and neither slaveholding nor free-soil senators wanted to lay their careers on the line on the Texas issue. The fate of Texas would be decided at the polls.

The leading Democratic candidate in the States was Martin van Buren, who had conducted an adequate administration following Andrew Jackson. When Van Buren refused to endorse the annexation of Texas, James K. Polk, another Jackson protégé who had succeeded Sam Houston as governor of Tennessee, received the nomination as an all-out supporter of Texas. Running against Polk was Henry Clay, the old Whig. In principle Clay approved the annexation of Texas, but for practical considerations he preferred to go slow.

In those days the election was held in November as now, but the president continued in office until the following March. Accordingly President John Tyler, reading the vote if not the polls, interpreted Polk's election as meaning that a majority wanted immediate annexation. A month after the election he placed the question before Congress. Probably wisely, the proannexation forces had decided that they could never summon the two thirds majority necessary to receive Texas by treaty. A joint resolution would require only a simple majority and could probably pass. They guessed correctly: on February 28, 1845, Congress passed a joint resolution providing for annexation.

Under terms of the joint resolution Texas could become a state if its people approved and if it left its boundary adjustments to the United States; if Texas would cede its public property, except for its public lands (which would be used in part to pay its debts), to the United States; and if Texas would prohibit slavery in any state created north of parallel 36°30'. Texas would also be permitted to divide itself into five states if it chose.

If Texans did not accept the offer before January 1, 1846, the whole process would begin again. Congress also authorized Tyler to withhold the proposal if he chose. Tyler didn't choose, and he named Andrew Jackson Donelson as his agent to submit the offer to Texas. When shortly Tyler left the Presidency and Polk replaced him, the only change in policy was Polk's urgency to complete annexation.

Once again Texas was on the throne. Both England and France were paying court, trying to persuade the Texans that their destiny lay in continued independence. Mexico too became tractable, preferring an independent Texas to having the United States crowding its border. The British chargé in Texas, Captain Charles Elliot, persuaded President Anson Jones to keep Texas uncommitted until he could obtain from Mexico a treaty guaranteeing Texas independence if Texas in turn would agree never to unite with the United States. But this was at the official level. Among Anglo Texas citizens the urge to return to the womb was growing, and Jones called a convention to meet on United States Independence Day, July 4. When Congress met, Jones had two propositions ready—the proposal of annexation and the treaty of peace with Mexico, which Elliot had somehow managed to put through Mexican official circles in an incredibly short time. Unanimously the Texas Congress accepted the offer of annexation to the United States, approved the president's proclamation calling for election of delegates to a constitutional convention for the State of Texas, and then went home. In two months the convention for annexation drew up a state constitution, a record short time which couldn't begin to be duplicated in Texas (or probably any other state) nowadays. In October the voters approved the terms of annexation and the state constitution. The constitution was accepted by Congress, and on December 29, 1845, President Polk signed the act that made Texas the twenty-eighth state in the United States of America. Texas had easily beaten the deadline of the United States Congress.

On February 19, 1846, Texans gathered in front of the state

capitol to watch the Texas flag taken down and the stars and stripes of the United States run up in its stead. President Jones announced his withdrawal as president in favor of J. Pinckney Henderson as governor and wound up his farewell speech with these words:

"The final act in this great drama is now performed. The Republic of Texas is no more." [3]

Nowadays most public places in Texas have two flagpoles, one for the flag of the United States and one for the Lone Star flag of Texas. Without consulting the law on the subject, most Texans intuitively believe that the Texas flag should not fly below the flag of the United States or any other banner, but alongside it as an equal.

In the more than a century since that historic day, both Texans and other North Americans have often debated whether anyone gained from associating Texas with the Union. Texas pride and Texas nationalism have been trying qualities to live alongside, while with some justification Texans have frequently felt that the United States held an animus toward them. At best the marriage has been uneasy, always threatening to come apart except that neither party had anywhere else to retreat. The advantages of staying together outweigh the advantages of separateness.

With the right to subdivide into five states, Texas has frequently considered whether it might wield more national power by having ten United States senators. But the temptation invariably founders on the practical belief that the five-state delegation might lose its unity. And besides, emotional issues exist—which state would inherit the Alamo, and which would have to accept the often hapless Houston Astros of the National Baseball League? East Texas, the "countriest" portion of the state, would have to claim Van Cliburn, the concert pianist, while Central Texas, with ever so much more sophisticated tastes, would enjoy Willie Nelson, the country-western Hall of Famer. In short, division would bring no end of problems.

Texas has produced its share of great men, both early and

---

3. Quoted in Herbert Gambrell, *Anson Jones: The Last President of Texas* (Garden City, N.Y.: Doubleday & Co., 1948), p. 419.

late, and none greater than Sam Houston. Still, probably no one
articulated the nationalism of Texas better than Mirabeau B.
Lamar, its first vice-president and second president, but more
than that: an eminently civilized man who wrote poetry, fa-
thered Texas education, and generally belonged to the type of
citizen who uplifts. He remains the supreme albeit sometimes
misguided philosopher of the state. In his inaugural he talked
about "the wealth, talent, and enterprise" of Texas and promised to promote the "true basis of all national strength and
glory."

"[Under] the most trying circumstances, from the dawn of
the revolution up to the present period [Texas] has maintained a
dignity, sobriety, and harmony which might stand as an example for older and longer established governments," he told
his listeners, adding that Texans possessed a larger share of the
world's blessings "than almost any other people on the Globe."
He averred that his eyes were "exclusively directed to the glory
of the nation," which harbored no evils that patriotism would
not remove. For the future he recommended that Texans look
"with a single eye to her glory and greatness and sacrifice all
narrow-minded selfishness upon the hallowed altar of patriotism." [4]

Lamar opposed annexation, saying that "however strong be
my attachment to the parent land, the land of my adoption must
claim my highest allegiance and affection." Annexation promised nothing positive for Texas but would only demonstrate
"that we had riven the chains of Mexican despotism only to fet-
ter our country with indissoluble bonds, and that a young Republic just rising into high distinction among the nations of the
earth had been swallowed up and lost, like a proud bark in a
devouring vortex." As only one of twenty-eight states, the sov-
ereign Republic of Texas would be "reduced to the level of an
unfelt fraction of a giant power," would become a tributary vas-
sal "pouring her abundant treasures into the lap of another people than her own," and as "the cornucopia of the world" would

---

4. Quoted in Dorman H. Winfrey, "Mirabeau B. Lamar and Texas Nationalism,"
Southwestern Historical Quarterly 59 (October 1955):184–205.

give the United States far greater wealth than it would be able to extract as a state.[5]

Lamar pointed out the frequent insults to the national pride of Texas. Official circles in the United States often looked on Texans as a "band of desperadoes" and heaped a "species of national indignities which a proud and spirited people may not bear, and which a patriot, jealous of his Country's as his own honor, should feel bound to resent." [6]

> And shall we blindly & madly precipitate ourselves into the deadly and destroying embraces of such a baleful people. . . . We have been told by them distinctly that they will not receive us as brethren—that our country is but the home of the wicked and the worthless, where vice is pestilential and virtue laughed to scorn; and like the spaniel that licks the hand that assails him, we continue knocking for admission at the door from which we are abruptly ordered with indignity and insult.[7]

These are just words, but they are words that, reiterated, drive home points. Constant repetition reinforced the natural pride which any underdog feels in winning against a favored opponent. Texans had plenty to celebrate in settling a frontier area, in achieving independence, and in making their independent nation work. They had heroes, particularly Sam Houston, who in his way could be as eloquent as Lamar but without Lamar's excess. But under Lamar Texas pride was elevated to a national characteristic, a way of life.

5. Winfrey, "Lamar and Texas Nationalism," p. 326.

6. Notes on the Annexation of Texas, 10 December 1838, in *The Papers of Mirabeau Buonaparte Lamar,* edited by Charles Adams Gulick, Jr., and others, 6 vols. (Austin: University of Texas Press, 1921–1928), 2:325.

7. Notes on the Annexation of Texas, p. 326.

9

Struggling Statehood

N mid-February 1845 Texas raised the United States flag, signifying its subordinate status as one of twenty-eight political entities within the United States. Fourteen months later, on April 25, 1846, a skirmish occurred between a contingent of Mexicans and an American scouting party in which several Americans were killed. American blood had been shed on Texas soil, and the new state was involved in that piece of violence known as the war against Mexico. Within two weeks two other battles had been fought in Texas: Palo Alto, in which 2,228 men under General Zachary Taylor defeated a Mexican force twice its size under General Mariano Arista in an artillery duel; and Resaca de la Palma, in which Mexican casualties ran 547 against 122 for the United States.

Zachary Taylor had brought his troops to Texas in July 1845, building a camp at the mouth of the Nueces, an uncontested state boundary that bordered a no-man's-land to the south. The Mexicans had about given up on reclaiming all of Texas but had indicated that a line along the Nueces would be fine for them. Texas and the United States held out for the Rio Grande, which meant that a hundred miles or more of brush country between the Nueces and the Rio Grande was disputed ground. In Texas, Taylor mustered several companies of Texas Rangers into the national service, though with some reluctance. They were a mishmash group insofar as military spit-and-polish was con-

90

cerned. But they could fight; oh, how they could fight. Their uniforms were not exactly a disgrace, for really they wore no uniform, just ragtag clothing to keep the insects from boring in and the chaparral from scratching or stinging. The one consistent piece of uniform among the Rangers was the Colt revolver, sometimes known as the Texas revolver, or a later model known as the Walker-Colt. The revolver became as much a part of the Ranger uniform as his sword, rifle, and horse and is inseparably linked with Texas Ranger lore.

As Taylor moved down to the Rio Grande and then pursued the Mexicans into their own land, the Rangers went along, never quite integrated into the forces of the United States and therefore always notable. A number of Rangers became prominent, including Jack Hays, by now a colonel, and Ben McCulloch, an uneducated Tennesseean who had left the first Texas state legislature to raise a Ranger company and spy for General Taylor.

When the Texans crossed the Rio Grande with Taylor into Mexico, the memory of all the imagined and real atrocities of the Mexicans evidently surged up in them. Revenge became their watchword, and no Mexican, regardless of age or sex, was safe. They gutted women, shot old men and children, and hanged civilians for no more offense than being there. On the other hand, they proved an incalculable help to Taylor's army during the capture of Monterrey, though again they ignored orders when told to hold the line at Monterrey's Bishop's Palace and overran the city's inner defenses instead. Taylor was outraged, as he had planned to shell the city with artillery before the main attack. When the Texans wouldn't leave the midtown they had captured, Taylor started the bombardment anyhow. Later, as scouts under McCulloch, the Texans dissuaded Taylor from running into a Mexican trap at Agua Nueva and persuaded him to entrench his troops near Buena Vista, where he won a victory that not only ended the war in northern Mexico but virtually drafted him for president.

Before Taylor could thank the Rangers, they had become celebratin' drunk, picked a fight with Taylor's regulars, and inspired a riot that required several hundred military police and a troop of cavalry to control. Although Taylor frequently paid tribute to the fighting abilities of the Texas Rangers, he could never forgive them for their lack of discipline. Still later, *"los diablos Tejanos"* under Colonel Hays joined General Winfield Scott as he moved through the Valley of Mexico. In Mexico City they misbehaved with such regularity that General Scott called in the Ranger captains to tell them that he would not "be disgraced, nor shall the army of my country be, by such outrages." One captain demurred that nothing was wrong with the Rangers except that they needed a good fight.[1]

In the meanwhile they would go on killing civilians. Whereupon Scott assigned them to chasing down a particularly troublesome band of *guerrilleros*. Thanks to a tip from a drunken señorita in a Tulancingo *cantina,* the Rangers caught up with the force of 450 at Zacualtipan one sunrise in mid-February 1848 and fought them with revolvers and Bowie knives until mid-afternoon, when the Mexicans with their padre-leader headed down the valley in full flight. The Texans sang and danced all night in celebration, taking care not to trip over the dead bodies at their feet. It was their last fight of the Mexican War, their last chance to kill Mexicans wantonly but legally. At the end of April they were mustered out at Vera Cruz and a few days later put aboard transports to Texas.

Undeterred by being a factor in a war, other Texans got on with the business of state-making. The Texans framed a constitution—the so-called Constitution of 1845—which worked so well that after several intervening constitutions, the people of Texas recopied it almost *in toto* as the Constitution of 1876, the fundamental law of Texas.

The group who framed the constitution were undeniably able and wide-gauged. Thomas Jefferson Rusk, president of the constitutional convention, had worked on the Constitution of 1836 and with Sam Houston was one of Texas's first United States Senators. J. Pinkney Henderson, the state's first governor, had served in Houston's cabinet and as minister to England and

---

1. See Stephen B. Oates, "Los Diablos Tejanos!" *The American West* 2 (Summer 1965):41–50.

France. Isaac Van Zandt had been a member of the Texas congress and a minister to the United States. R. E. B. Baylor had represented Alabama in the United States Congress and wrote the charter for Baylor University. Abner S. Lipscomb studied law in the office of John C. Calhoun and had been chief justice in Alabama, while Hiram G. Runnels had been governor of Mississippi. One of the framers was José Antonio Navarro, a Mexican native of Texas, while Tennessee contributed eighteen members, Virginia eight, Georgia seven, Kentucky six, and North Carolina five.

Texas leaned heavily on a new Louisiana constitution, drew from the constitutions of some of the other states, and, as intimated, utilized its own constitution of the Republic of Texas. The governor was selected for a term of two years and could not serve more than four years in a six-year period. The legislature was to meet biennially. Ministers of the gospel were prohibited from being members of the legislature—a prohibition pushed by Baylor, himself a Baptist minister. Participating in a duel also barred one from public office. The constitution was blatantly anticorporation, requiring a two-thirds vote of both houses to create any kind of a private corporation and forbidding incorporation of any bank (with, as seen, the devious exception of McKinney and Williams). The legislature could not incur debts in excess of $100,000. Exemption from foreclosure of homesteads of less than 200 acres was permitted. As noted, Henderson was elected governor and Rusk and Houston elected to the Senate. Houston would be twice re-elected, and Rusk would be re-elected to serve until he died in 1857. Texas had entered statehood.

With the exception of its boundary settlement, the issues in Texas during the latter 1840s and through the 1850s were essentially the same as in the remainder of the United States. In 1854 Governor Elisha M. Pease pushed through a school law which set aside $2,000,000 as a permanent endowment for public education. The legislature also set aside $100,000 in United States bonds to endow a university but absorbed the proceeds into the State Revenue Fund. Chartering or not chartering railroads was a continual issue, which Pease tried to obviate by advocating a "state plan" whereby Texas could build, own, and operate a system of railroads. The Know-Nothing Party became quite a force and once came within 800 votes of electing a governor. Sam Houston, ever the manipulator, flirted with the Know-Nothings, evidently not so much out of principle as with an eye on the presidency of the United States. The flirtation may have cost him a nomination for that office in 1860. By the middle 1850s Texans were aligning as a rule with either the Democratic or the Whig party, and although the Know-Nothing Party held an open state convention in 1856, by then it was already over the hill.

As the threat of secession and civil war approached, the state divided more and more into Jackson Democrats or Unionists, led by Houston, and Calhoun Democrats. Houston was magnificent in this period as he assailed Texans for their failure to observe the laws of the United States and to co-operate with the desires of the majority. Sometimes the peculiar problems of Texas coalesced with those of the nation, but on the whole Texas by annexation had taken on as much in the way of new worries as it had laid aside.

One overlapping state and federal problem was the boundary of Texas. Since December 1836 Texas had officially claimed as its southern and western boundary the Rio Grande from mouth to source and thence a line running northward to the 42nd parallel, a claim that went beyond the space allotted to Texas by both Spain and Mexico when it was a part of those two countries. Texas's claim also sliced into the boundaries of Tamaulipas and Coahuila as drawn by Spanish decrees of 1805 and 1811, included territory claimed by Chihuahua, and took in a good part of New Mexico, including Santa Fe. Texas made its claim with some legitimacy, because three weeks after San Jacinto Santa Anna had signed the Treaty of Velasco, which mentioned the Rio Grande without being precise about its role in the boundary between the two nations.

Texas also had another legitimate claim, that of any conqueror who tries to get as much as he can from the entity he has just defeated. The ambition of Texas is illustrated by the fact that most of the claim beyond the Nueces River consisted of empty country. Although scattered settlements existed along the lower Rio Grande, they were definitely Mexican in population and in character and had little feeling for Texas and its Anglo majority.

On the other hand, if the United States did not assume the Texas claim to the north, all of Texas, one state or five, might be south of 36°30′ and therefore slave territory. Here was a point for the free-soilers and the anti-Texans to consider. President Polk likewise was on the Texas side in the border dispute. During the war against Mexico the Army of the West under Stephen W. Kearny did what the Texans couldn't by occupying New Mexico and establishing a civil government there. Texans protested, saying quite correctly that the federal government was treating New Mexico as conquered foreign soil when in reality the army had merely occupied Texas territory. Secretary of State James Buchanan temporized by throwing the issue to Congress. He also soothed the Texans by promising that New Mexico's civil government was only temporary and would not affect their claim to all territory east of the Rio Grande. Not wishing a war on two fronts, the Texans accepted the reassurance and turned back to assaulting Mexico.

The Treaty of Guadalupe Hidalgo, ending the war, settled the borderline between the United States and Mexico but not the upper boundary of Texas. The lower Rio Grande was made the international boundary, as Mexico relinquished all claim to territory north and east of that river and ceded New Mexico to the United States. Though some Texans thought this solved their problems, the more perceptive view was that the United States Army and not Texas was controlling that territory to the north-northwest.

Then came the slavery question again. David Wilmot had introduced his proviso frequently in Congress. Under it, slavery was prohibited in any territory acquired by the United States as a result of the war with Mexico. As the slave states fought the proviso, their success strengthened their determination to resist the spread of free-soil territory. The issue aroused Senator Sam Houston, who spoke and wrote regularly against the proviso, arguing that the Missouri Compromise of 1820 had served for nearly thirty years and should continue to serve. The debate gave Houston one of his opportunities to attack a pet distaste, the "moonstruck seer" John C. Calhoun, and to make a number of forthright statements against disunion such as he would be making for the next dozen years—statements which would polarize his support and opposition.

While Congress dawdled, Texas created Santa Fe County on March 15, 1848, with boundaries including most of that part of New Mexico which it had claimed. Shortly, Texas told the United States it was sending civil officers to take over and asked the army to sustain them. When the first man, Judge Spruce M. Baird, arrived to become the new county judge, the commanding officer at Santa Fe, Colonel John M. Washington, told Baird that he would maintain the government established by General Kearny until ordered to desist by President Polk. Actually Polk had already ordered Washington to assist the Texans rather than interfere. But Washington continued his resistance and nonassistance until Baird left the territory in the summer of 1849.

By that time the United States had a new president, Zachary Taylor, considerably less enchanted with Texas than was Polk on the basis of on-the-scene experience.

Meanwhile Texas created three more counties to the south of Santa Fe County between the Pecos and the Rio Grande and sent a commissioner, Robert S. Neighbors, to organize the counties. Neighbors, who had organized El Paso County without meeting resistance, found that New Mexico was another story. By now Taylor had let it be known that he favored statehood for both California and New Mexico, and the people in the latter region were more interested in their own statehood than they were in organizing counties for Texas. Governor Peter Hansborough Bell demanded that President Taylor explain his prejudiced conduct and called a special session of the Texas legislature to meet in mid-August 1850.

Before the legislature could meet, New Mexico had adopted a constitution for its proposed state that took in the disputed territory plus territory undoubtedly belonging to Texas. President Taylor was now dead, but his successor, Millard Fillmore, threatened to send troops against Texas. Although at first the

boundary dispute was a party fight, with the Democrats supporting Texas and the Whigs disputing the Texas claims, party
alignment collapsed as the slavery issue thrust itself into the
fight, just as it did to almost every other contest within the nation.

When finally moderation prevailed, Texas received the
boundary which still holds: beginning at the intersection of the
100th meridian and parallel 36°30′, going west along that parallel to the 103rd meridian, following it south to the 32nd parallel, turning west along that parallel to the Rio Grande, and then
following the river southeastward to its mouth. For agreeing to
take less than it claimed, Texas would receive $10,000,000.
The people of New Mexico would be authorized to organize
their own territory. The settlement was part of a larger package
known as the Compromise of 1850, whose passage most historians believe delayed the breach in the Union until 1861. At a
special election Texans accepted the proposal—less than they
had claimed but probably as much as they could ever hope to
get—by a two-to-one majority. The legislature in special session
then approved it, and Governor Bell signed the act of acceptance on November 25, 1850. Texas now had its fixed outlines,
presumably in perpetuity.

The question of the public debt remained. Nearly five more
years passed before it was worked out. A complicated obligation, its simplest explanation is that Texas paid 77 cents on the
dollar with the money coming from the federal government,
$5,000,000 of it in bonds and the remainder held in the United
States Treasury. Some justification may be made for Texas not
paying in full, for at the time the republic had assumed the
obligations no one advanced credit at par value. Of the
$5,000,000 in bonds turned over to Texas, about $3,750,000
remained after the nonrevenue obligation had been paid. Texas
set aside $2,000,000 to endow its public schools and then
turned around and lent most of that to railroads to aid construction.

With the money in hand, Texas remitted nine-tenths of its
taxes to the counties for a total of six years, and the counties
used the windfall to construct public buildings and the like.

Thus Texans early became used to outside funding of needed improvements and a low tax rate—and have never worked to establish a broad and equitable tax base. Having enjoyed the windfalls of taxes from petroleum and petrochemicals for more than sixty years, Texas is even now unable to face up to imposing new taxes to maintain itself with public services as revenues from taxes on petroleum are beginning to diminish. Unless Texas can get away from this lottery mentality and can go to work on a solid tax structure, the state will continue to rank where it does now: usually in the lowest 20 percent in education and social services.

In many ways Sam Houston dominated the decade and a half of Texas's first attempt at being a state in the Union. Whether he was denouncing the use of a regular army as inconsistent "with the genius of our institutions," as he did at the time of the Mexican War, or declining a commission as major general during the same period because he did not wish to be "encumbered with all the splendor and pomp" which accompanied General Winfield Scott; or whether, as in 1848, he denounced those senators who campaigned either for themselves or for presidential candidates during an election year, he was invariably newsworthy.

Gradually Houston was mapping out a personal philosophic position. He was angered over the Texas boundary settlement, claiming that while the United States had a right to settle a boundary with Mexico without consulting Texas, it possessed no right to settle unilaterally the boundary between Texas and the United States. He assailed President Taylor for what Houston looked on as intransigence and even coercion. Boiling mad as only he could be over the slurs against Texas by Taylor and by "the usurpations of the military authorities in Santa Fé," Houston asserted a states-rights interpretation of the Constitution. But he vehemently denied any threat of secession by Texas.

> Think you, sir, that after the difficulties they have encountered to get into the Union, that you can whip them out of it? No, sir. New Mexico can not whip them out of it, even with the aid of United

States troops. No, sir!—no, sir! We shed our blood to get into it, and we have now no arms to turn against it. But we have not looked for aggression upon us from the Union.[2]

Within a week Taylor was dead from typhoid fever, and Houston was writing the new president, Millard Fillmore, in conciliatory phrases.

Houston stood in the midst of most of the large issues of the day. He defended the Indians and castigated the United States' treatment of the red men, which won him few friends in that era. When the Nebraska bill came before the Senate in January 1854, and the South influenced President Franklin Pierce to take a stand denying the right of Congress to legislate slavery out of the territories, Houston made public his intention to vote against the bill—an action which alienated both Democrats and Southerners. Houston answered critics in the Senate and elsewhere by saying that while he was from the South, he did not regard himself as a sectional person.

As the nation moved into the year 1855, Houston spoke at Tremont Temple in Boston on Washington's Birthday, with William Lloyd Garrison himself delivering a rebuttal. Houston closed his speech as follows:

> Our country is too glorious, too magnificent, too sublime in its future prospects, to permit domestic jars or political opinions to produce a wreck of this mighty vessel of State. Let us hold onto it, and guide it; let us give it in charge to men who will care for the whole people, who will love the country for the country's sake, and will endeavor to build up and sustain it, and reconcile conflicting interests for the sake of prosperity. This can be done, and let us not despair and break up the Union.[3]

All during the 1850s Houston was regularly making news by threatening to retire from public life. But he didn't retire—Texas itself retired him from the Senate, after which, to the consternation of a number of people, he ran for governor because

---

2. Llerena Friend, *Sam Houston, The Great Designer* (Austin: University of Texas Press, 1954), p. 207.

3. *Writings of Sam Houston,* 1:177.

(as he said) the people wanted excitement and he might as well give it to them as anyone. But "the people" sided with their legislature and turned him down in 1857 by a margin of 4,000 votes.

Although Houston suffered the humiliation of seeing the Texas legislature unanimously elect his successor two years before his own senatorial term expired, events conspired to keep Houston from having to vote against the will of his state and his section during the remainder of his term. He behaved so circumspectly and was awarded such national attention that many Texans began to second-guess themselves, with the result that in 1859, as he was leaving the Senate, he succeeded Hardin R. Runnels, the man who had defeated him two years before, as governor. But the time was not propitious for a man whose heart belonged to the Union to be a governor of a people whose minds and spirits were drifting rapidly toward the shoals of secession.

Texas had definitely begun a career of statehood, uneven though its path might be. The nagging question remained whether Texas lacked the constancy to endure as one of the stars in the flag of the United States—whether, like a capricious coquette, it would follow the next attractive drummer for a medicine show who promised quack cures for its real diseases.

Texas had the makings—but could the erratic, sometimes swashbuckling, sometimes pestilential, invariably audacious people who inhabited the state fashion anything of them? Or would they blow all following the rascals of disunion, that destructive leadership of the Georgians and the Carolinians against whom their senior citizens had warned them? As everyone knows, they blew their opportunity to be constructive and spent a century remolding their psyche and reshaping their promise.

10

A Tagalong Confederate

*W*HEN Texas united her destiny with that of the United States, . . . She entered not into the North nor into the South, . . . her connection was not sectional, but national." [1]

So spoke Sam Houston at his inaugural as governor of Texas at the close of 1859. His sentiments were bound to provoke a state legislature already outraged by the fact that he was going over its head to the people, delivering the address to a huge crowd on the grounds of the capitol.

What was Texas doing in the camp of the rabid secessionists? Ninety percent of Texas' white population had come from the Old South or had been born of southern parents. Their mores were southern, and their political opinions were southern. The west was a long way off in time, and Texas showed no inclination to fulfill its later role as the transition state between south and west.

Part of the trouble among the Union-oriented people in Texas was that they never got organized. Only the regular Democrats knew what they were doing; their opponents just sputtered in frustration. Furthermore, Houston had been elected as an independent on a platform endorsing the Constitution and pledging allegiance to the Union. Houston had campaigned mightily for his political resurrection. He had won by 9,000 votes. No

---

1. *Writings of Sam Houston*, 7:383.

one had doubted where he stood, for just before leaving the United States Senate he had said:

> I wish no prouder epitaph to mark the board or slab that may lie on my tomb than this: "He loved his country, he was a patriot; he was devoted to the Union." If it is for this that I have suffered martyrdom, it is sufficient that I stand at quits with those who have wielded the sacrificial knife.[2]

And when one critic had retorted that he preferred disunion to the violation of constitutional rights, Houston had answered:

> I hope that my honorable colleague does not suppose I would submit to any infraction of our rights. Our rights are rights common to the whole Union. I would not see wrong inflicted on the North, or on the South, but I am for the Union, without any "if" in the case; and my motto is, "it shall be preserved." [3]

Although in his late sixties, Houston nonetheless seemed to relish the contest, despite the fact that the Texas legislature had been disinclined even to furnish the new governor's mansion for its latest occupant. But Houston fought a lonely battle. When South Carolina invited Texas to send delegates to a Southern convention to protest against Union invasion of the rights of the South, Houston warned the Texas legislature that the Union was created to be perpetual. His opponents responded with charges that he had in effect outlived his time.

While the governor was counseling patience, Texas was wondering whether Old Sam was planning some sort of a coup. His reputation for being crafty had only been enhanced with the years, and while his enemies still accused him of cowardice against Santa Anna, they also realized that he had sprung a trap on the Mexican general at San Jacinto. Could there be a San Jacinto awaiting the secessionists? Rumors even spread that Sam would move himself—and the government?—to a haven in Mexico. While the election of Abraham Lincoln had touched off shock waves throughout the South, all that Houston offered in

2. Friend, *Sam Houston,* p. 349.
3. *Writings of Sam Houston,* 7:216.

the way of action was an unenthusiastic acknowledgment of his election.

While Houston deliberated, a group of citizens called for a secession convention to meet on January 28, 1861. A week before, Houston convened the legislature in an extraordinary session—only to see that body authorize the convention to act for Texas. Under a future governor, O. M. Roberts, the convention approved on the second day a resolution stating: "It is the deliberate sense of this convention that the State of Texas should separately secede from the Federal Union." The vote was 152 to 6. Shortly after, the convention adopted an ordinance of secession which was passed before packed galleries, with only eight dissenting votes. When J. W. Throckmorton, another future governor, voted against secession to the accompaniment of hisses from the gallery, he called out: "Mr. President, when the rabble hiss well may patriots tremble."

Texas drew up a declaration of causes not unlike those proclaimed by other seceding states. Boiled down, they argued that the Union was bent on coercion, and coercion was the one force with which the people of the state could not live.[4]

South Carolina, Mississippi, Florida, Alabama, Georgia, and Louisiana had already left the Union, had begun to form a government at Montgomery, Alabama, and were sending delegations to Austin to attempt to enlist Texas in the movement. On February 16, after the convention had adjourned, Ben McCulloch seized the United States arsenal and barracks at San Antonio.

When the referendum on secession was held on February 23, the vote was 46,129 to 14,697 in favor of the ordinance. Whether Texas's sentiment favored secession by three to one is debatable, for many Unionists stayed away from the polls and eighteen counties actually voted against secession. Secession, according to the rules, was to take place on March 2, 1861, exactly twenty-five years after Texas had first declared its indepen-

4. *Journal of the Secession Convention of Texas, 1861,* edited by Ernest W. Winkler (Austin: Austin Printing Co., 1912), *passim.* The Texas journal is probably the most complete one for the South, containing all sorts of biographical information about the delegates.

dence at Washington-on-the-Brazos. Ironically it was also Sam Houston's sixty-eighth birthday. On March 4 Houston issued a proclamation that Texas had seceded. That same day Lincoln was inaugurated in Washington.

Events were moving almost frenetically. Texas applied for membership in the Confederate States of America, but before the application could be made the Confederate congress had already admitted Texas. The convention sent a delegate, George W. Chilton, to order the governor to appear at high noon on Saturday, March 16, to take the oath to support the Confederate States. When Chilton arrived at the governor's mansion at 8 o'clock the evening before, Houston asked him to wait until noon the next day.

After dinner Friday, the Houston family and servants gathered in the dining room. The governor read from the family Bible. They all knelt in prayer. Then Houston went upstairs to his bedroom, leaving word that he should not be disturbed. In his stocking feet and without his coat or vest, he walked all night. When he came down in the morning, he had chosen to sacrifice his office, rather than his conscience.

At noon on Saturday, the convention was meeting upstairs in the Capitol while Sam Houston was sitting in his chair in the basement. He was summoned three times to take the oath of allegiance, but he sat silent. Thirty years of serving Texas had ended, and the man who had once been hailed as savior was now repudiated, nailed to the cross of the Confederacy.

Away off in Washington, President Lincoln was not unaware of Houston's unswerving loyalty to the Union. Accordingly, he offered troops to the beleaguered governor, while the rumor spread that the president would make Houston his secretary of war. Back and forth between Austin and Washington went an intermediary offering to concentrate Federal troops in Texas to sustain Houston as governor, even after he had been deposed. But Houston declined, instead requesting that all troops be removed from the state as soon as possible. After the firing on Fort Sumter, the remaining Federal troops were held as prisoners of war.

The forced abdication of the Old Hero represents a high point of drama for Texas during the Civil War. Most of the war was fought east of the Red and Sabine rivers. Not that Texas sat out the war in comfort. As a border state, it felt exposed to attack from Kansas through Indian Territory on the north, from New Mexico on the west, and from the Gulf on the south. It also worried about the degree of encouragement the Indians might gather from the confusion.

At first, companies of minutemen faced the Indian threat. In 1862 they were replaced by a frontier regiment, while another regiment was assigned to guard the Rio Grande frontier from Fort Brown near the Gulf Coast to Fort Bliss outside El Paso. But only two major engagements with the Indians took place. When in October 1864 the Comanche and Kiowa raided Young County, about 100 miles northwest of present-day Fort Worth, frontier people "forted up" inside the stockades, reducing the likelihood of isolated attacks. During the following January, several hundred state and Confederate troops attacked the Kickapoo, whose intentions were peaceable, and paid for the unwarranted attack with heavy losses. The most notable fighting took place in the relatively empty West, where John R. Baylor, an ex-Indian agent, led troops into Arizona, organizing that territory with himself as governor. For a while Confederate troops occupied the area south of the 34th parallel as far west as Tucson.

Meanwhile General H. H. Sibley raised a Confederate force to drive Federal troops out of New Mexico. On February 21, 1862, he defeated the Union at Valverde, took Albuquerque without a fight, and headed for Santa Fe. On March 28, he was defeated in a hand-to-hand battle at Glorieta Pass and retreated through the mountains back to Texas, having lost 500 men. The Union held New Mexico.

Three months after firing on Sumter, the Union extended its naval blockade into Texas. Fifteen months later Union forces forced the Confederates out of Galveston, the state's principal port. Fresh in Confederate command of the district of Texas was John Bankhead Magruder, who had been made a lieutenant colonel for his excellent leadership at the battle of Chapultepec and had shown "superior generalship" in harrowing General

George B. McClellan's advance on Richmond in the spring of 1862. General Magruder decided to retake Galveston with a ragtag landing fleet armored with cotton bales and manned by 300 veterans of Sibley's abortive New Mexican campaign. At the same time he concentrated a land force at Virginia Point opposite the island of Galveston. On New Year's Day 1863 the two forces converged on the island and recaptured the town, along with four ships and 300 Federal prisoners.

Another memorable fight took place at Sabine Pass, a sort of border lake between Texas and Louisiana where the Sabine and the Neches rivers empty their waters for the enjoyment of the Gulf of Mexico. In September 1862 a Federal patrol had forced out the Confederates. In the following January the Confederates recaptured the pass and gave Texas one of its few legitimate Civil War heroes. Richard W. Dowling, out of Galway County, Ireland, and still in his twenties, had participated in the recapture of Galveston three weeks earlier and had been placed in command of Company F, Texas Heavy Artillery, with orders to spike the guns at Fort Sabine. Instead of obeying, Dowling had taken rails from the Eastern Texas Railroad to strengthen the fort and left the guns intact.

Undoubtedly Dowling gave Texas its most spectacular Civil War victory. The Federal leadership had launched an expedition of twenty ships with 5,000 troops for an apparent major invasion of Texas. Defending against this group was Fort Sabine, with a small earthworks, six cannon, and forty-two men known as the Davis Guards, most of them Irish out of Houston. Three of the Federal gunboats—the *Clifton,* the *Arizona,* and the *Sachem*—were to conduct a prelanding artillery assault, after which the troops would move ashore.

The engagement began on the afternoon of September 8, 1863, when the *Clifton* and *Sachem* in parallel formation moved up the channel of the pass. When the ships came within 1,200 yards of the fort, the Confederates opened fire on the *Sachem* and on the third or fourth round put the gunboat out of action. The Confederates then turned their guns on the *Clifton,* which lost the use of several of its guns, was grounded, and finally surrendered. Then the *Sachem* surrendered. Altogether the battle took only forty-five minutes.

Major General William B. Franklin, in command of the expedition, turned what was left of it back to New Orleans, and gained his place in American military history as the first American general to lose a fleet to land batteries alone. The losses weren't great—the Federals lost 19 killed, 9 wounded, 37 missing, and 315 taken prisoner. They also lost two steamers. Dowling was an overnight hero.

The small Sabine Pass operation had international repercussions. Doubts about the efficiency of the Federal navy were strengthened. The *New York Herald* credited Dowling's victory, together with the Federal loss at Chickamauga, with drastically lowering the credit of the United States.

General N. P. Banks, who with Admiral David G. Farragut had planned the invasion through the Sabine Pass, tried again at another point. In the winter of 1863 his combined naval and land force of 6,000 men moved against the lower Rio Grande, where the Confederates lacked even the strength of the forty-two men at Fort Sabine. One by one the Federals picked off the coast towns—the island of Brazos de Santiago, Brownsville, Corpus Christi, Aransas Pass, Indianola, and points between, until Galveston and Sabine Pass remained the only ports open to Texas and the Confederates.

In the spring of 1864 Banks mounted his last campaign against Texas. With 25,000 veterans and a flotilla of gunboats, the armada moved up the Red River from Alexandria, Louisiana, planning to unite with 15,000 men under General Frederick Steele moving southward from Little Rock. The pincers movement was supposed to clear out all of northern Louisiana, southern Arkansas, and eastern Texas, the latter area including Confederate ordnance shops at Marshall and Henderson as well as the garden for feeding Texas. Under Magruder Texas turned out almost every male who could stand alone, except for those deserters who were raising the devil on the Texas frontier. First General Sterling Price stopped Steele at Camden, Arkansas, using 8,000 cavalrymen. On April 8 with 11,000 effective troops, General Richard Taylor stopped Banks's army at Mansfield, Louisiana, fifty miles below Shreveport and close to the Texas border. Banks fell back, eventually to the Mississippi.

The last battle of the war was fought (and won) under John S.

Ford, an old Ranger hand, at Palmito Ranch near Brownsville a month after Appomattox. The defeated Union soldiers brought news of Lee's surrender. The news was distressing, for Governor Pendleton Murrah and General E. Kirby Smith preferred to continue the war in the west. But the Texans had seen enough of the war, and besides it was almost too late to get in spring planting. General Kirby Smith formally surrendered at Galveston on June 2.

The fact that Texas was not a prime battle area for the Civil War should not obscure the fact that tens of thousands of Texas soldiers participated in that bloodiest of all American war adventures. Although at first Texans were told that troops from their state would not be needed, by the end of September 1861 ten regiments had been organized and were soon on their way to Virginia. Early in 1862 Governor Francis R. Lubbock answered a Confederate call for fifteen more regiments of infantry. Before conscription was enacted on April 16, 1862, Texas already had about 20,000 men in military service. At first the conscription laws applied to men from eighteen to thirty-five years of age; in the following September the upper limit was raised to forty-five, and finally it stretched from seventeen to fifty. Exemptions were liberal, covering officeholders, the professions, agriculture, and industry. In addition, Texans were exempted for frontier defense. Substitutes could be hired. Texas also beefed up its own militia.

How many Texans saw service is impossible to determine. The census of 1860 revealed 92,145 white males in Texas from the ages of eighteen to forty-five, and probably at least two-thirds, or more than 60,000, put on some kind of uniform. Of those, approximately one-third saw service east of the Mississippi, in either the Army of the Mississippi or the Army of Northern Virginia. Several individuals and units gained a measure of legitimate fame.

Benjamin Franklin Terry, a Fort Bend County sugar planter, went to Virginia to participate in the first Battle of Manassas and then returned to Houston to organize a regiment of cavalry known as Terry's Texas Rangers. The Rangers left Houston in September 1861 and fought with considerable valor in such engagements as the Five Days' Battle, Shiloh, Murfreesboro, Chickamauga, and Knoxville. They were still around to surrender to William Tecumseh Sherman in Greensboro, North Carolina, at the end of April 1865. Terry himself was killed while leading a charge against Union troops in the Rangers' first days of combat near Woodsonville, Kentucky, on December 17, 1861.

Another notable group was Ross's Brigade, a mixed Confederate army unit dominated by Texans. Organized at Grenada, Mississippi, in November 1862, the brigade took in the 3rd, 6th, 9th, and 27th Texas Cavalry, all of them with some war experience as dismounted cavalry. After their horses arrived, the troops were placed under the command of General Earl Van Dorn, later were commanded by other Civil War Confederate generals, and then on December 16, 1863, were placed under the command of Lawrence Sullivan Ross, an Iowan whose father had been a United States agent of the Brazos Indian Reservation near Waco for three years just prior to the Civil War.

Ross should be remembered for having entered the Confederate army as a private, which hardly anyone of substance did. He rose through the ranks with amazing rapidity and was a brigadier general before the fall of Vicksburg. Altogether he took part in 135 engagements and was rewarded with the governorship of Texas in 1886, becoming the first governor to occupy the present Capitol Building, and then the presidency of the Agricultural and Mechanical College of Texas. Sul Ross State University is named for him. As for Ross's Brigade, it fought almost continuously during the fifteen months of Ross's command, participating in major battles at Lawrenceburg, Harpeth River, and Murfreesboro.

Hood's Texas Brigade developed when John Bell Hood was made a brigadier general and given command of the Texas Brigade. It was attached to Lee's Army of Northern Virginia and James Longstreet's Second Corps and fought nearly continuously in such memorable battles as Gaines's Mill, Second Manassas, and Antietam (Sharpsburg) in 1862; at Gettysburg and Chickamauga in 1863; and in the Battle of the Wilderness in 1864. The brigade started out with 3,500 men and rose to a peak of nearly 4,500, but by Appomattox war had reduced the number to only 557. Hood, "the fighting general," lost his right leg at Chickamauga and lost his reputation around Nashville in the winter of 1864–1865. Texas also lost Ben McCulloch, the old Texas Ranger, at Pea Ridge and Albert Sidney Johnston at Shiloh. Terry's Texas Rangers left about two-thirds of its men in graves scattered over a half-dozen states.

On the civilian front Texas suffered because it was associated with an upstart, wrong-headed government in a losing cause. The state contributed John H. Reagan, a Tennessean who in Texas became a district judge and congressman, as postmaster general. In the last few weeks of the Civil War he would also hold the hopeless position of secretary of the treasury for the Confederacy. Reagan lost his chance to be a hero to embittered Texans following the war, for as a former cabinet officer he was imprisoned for several months at Fort Warren in Boston Harbor. But on August 11, 1865, he issued a letter advising the people of Texas to acknowledge the loss of the war, accept the extinction of slavery, and give the Negro full civil rights, including the right to vote with the proper educational and property qualifications. What he evidently wanted was to avoid the evils of an imposed military government and unqualified black suffrage, but die-hard Texans misread him and turned on him for a time as a turncoat. In later years he served as a Congressman and Senator.

The wartime Texas government established a military board to dispose of the bonds of the United States then held by the state. Texas suspended all laws for the collection of debts and in a special session called for February 2, 1863, doubled taxes— something it would not dare try today. The state appropriated $600,000 for the use of needy families of soldiers and $200,000 for a hospital fund for wounded Texans in the Confederate armies. It tried to allay dissatisfaction with the Confederacy, even to abolishing substitution in the army.

But basically concentration of military activities east of the Mississippi left Texas pretty much to its own devices, which meant that its citizens felt pleased to be on their own and at the same time felt neglected. Because the feeling was shared by

Arkansas, Louisiana, and Missouri, Governor Lubbock called a meeting of the governors of those states to meet with him at Marshall, Texas, on July 18, 1862. Only Governor Claiborne F. Jackson of the Confederate government of Missouri showed up, though the other governors expressed interest. Nothing much happened, for the Confederate government was in no shape to do much. It did send General E. Kirby Smith as a commander of a trans-Mississippi department.

When General Smith called a conference for the following August 1863, after the stalemate at Gettysburg and the fall of Vicksburg, every western state sent representatives. The conference agreed that the western Confederate States should seek amicable footing with the French under Maximilian and Carlotta in Mexico and expressed its confidence in Smith. A dispute arose as to whether cotton for exchange with Mexico for supplies should be impressed, as favored by the Confederate government, or whether cotton should be purchased, as favored by Texas. An act of February 6, 1864, empowered the Confederate Congress to prohibit exportation of cotton except under regulations made by the president, which meant the Texas plan was dismissed.

Although about three-fourths of the Texas government's budget was expended on the war, receipts nearly doubled expenses, so that the state did not hurt particularly. Unfortunately considerable portions of the receipts turned out to be worthless money, and the state dipped into its school and university funds to keep going. After the war was over, a party looted the state treasury, but all it found that was negotiable was $5,000 in specie. If state taxes were not a particular burden, Confederate taxes were, and the government at Montgomery and Richmond collected $37,486,854.34 from Texas in the four years from 1861 through 1864.

In some ways, the people hurt worst by the war were the neutralists, particularly the Germans in their settlements in Central Texas. The Germans had been around almost as long as the Anglos, having begun to immigrate in the latter days of Mexico's sovereignty in Texas. Some counties became so packed with Germans that German-language newspapers continued to be published in these towns into the middle 1950s and German was frequently the first language of the people. Trouble was, the Germans had come to Texas to embrace freedom, and freedom was what they expected. Accordingly, as far back as May 14–15, 1854, at the annual *Staats-Saengerfest* in San Antonio, delegates from the German political club had adopted resolutions declaring that slavery was evil and that Texas should obtain help from the federal government to abolish the institution. Anglo-Americans were horrified. The Germans had also come to the United States when they entered Texas, but the Confederacy was not the United States. Therefore, at the beginning of the Civil War sixty-five Union sympathizers, all Germans, left Kerr County for Mexico. Kerr and its contiguous counties were placed on martial law, and a party took out after the disaffected Germans. Over half were killed before they could reach Mexico.

Not all Germans opposed the war, and some served with considerable valor. On the other hand, neither did all Anglo-Americans approve the war, especially if they were going to be conscripted. North Texas particularly, with an immigrant population from the free and border states, showed opposition and by the end of the first year of the war had formed a secret organization called the Peace Party, so secret that we still don't know much about it. Its members did try to resist the draft and to spy for the Union Army, though they lacked much to spy on. When a drunken Peace Party man attempted to enlist as a Confederate loyalist, the conspiracy was exposed and a Gainesville mob lynched 25 of the conspirators by hanging and gave 150 more a purportedly fair trial before hanging 40 of them. Others in other North Texas towns were hanged as soon as they were identified or suspected. Still others were forced into the Confederate Army, where the valor of their service is unrecorded. In addition, in some counties the deserters were so numerous that they intimidated loyal Confederates.

Times were relatively hard, though nothing to compare with Vicksburg or Atlanta or Virginia. Crops were good, though farm labor was frequently short. Salt became scarce. Medicines and hospital supplies proved insufficient. The military authorities sponsored the growing of poppies for opium, but without much success. The ladies worked as assiduously in the Civil War as in other wars before and after, rolling bandages, rounding up clothing, establishing relief committees, and in general looking after wives and children of soldiers long gone. By 1863 the citizens of Houston were contributing $3,000 a week for this latter purpose. The people learned to use substitutes—ashes from corncobs for soda, parched sweet potatoes, rye, and okra for coffee, and shucks and straw for hats and fans. Governor Lubbock was inaugurated in a homespun suit, and the "homespun dress that Southern ladies wear" was frequently hailed in song. "Making do" became almost a fad.

Like the remainder of the South, Texas lacked industrialization. An arsenal for cannon and a cap and cartridge factory were established in Austin. In East Texas some iron goods were manufactured, and Texas increased its output of wagons, ambulances, harness, and saddles. The state penitentiary in Huntsville provided the largest amount of manufactured cloth. The state had a paper shortage, which might be a blessing at the governmental level but forced a number of newspapers to suspend. But Texas had the advantage of being next door to Mexico, which served as a funnel for many materials.

The trade route with Mexico was not an easy sluiceway. Between the border and the settled portions of Texas lay 300 to 400 miles of largely empty territory except for the intrusions of Indians, but the combination of necessity and profit justified the trip. Since cotton was bringing from 30 cents to a dollar a pound in the North, which paid hard money when Confederate bill were worth 5 cents on the dollar, a considerable amount of the white gold found its way eventually into Union hands. This trade could be considered treasonable, except for the fact that the Pennsylvanians and the New Englanders had carried on such trade during the American Revolution and Carolina factories were turning out uniforms for Union troops during the Civil War. Speculation abounded, and war profiteers flourished.

Once Texas broke his heart by seceding, Sam Houston was caught up in the emotional surge that accompanies any man whose home is invaded. As he wrote a month after the firing on

Fort Sumter, "The time has come when a man's section is his country. I stand by mine. All my hopes, my fortunes, are centered in the South. When I see the land for whose defence my blood has been spilt, and the people whose fortunes have been mine through a quarter of a century of toil, threatened with invasion, I can but cast my lot with theirs and await the issue." [5] Ambition had gone out of his system, and about all he could contribute was a role of elder statesman and critic. In his last public appearance in July 1863 he visited with Federal prisoners in the penitentiary in his hometown of Huntsville, talking about the war and the Union. On July 26 he died from pneumonia. He did not live to know that the Union would survive the multiple fractures of the present blow, but in part he had gone down in trying to prevent that Union from falling apart.

As the renewed Union tried to salve its wounds and knit its broken bones back into place, Texas faced the challenges of a new age with results that would keep its name in the forefront of the nation.

5. Friend, *Sam Houston,* p. 349.

TEXAS

A photographer's essay by A. Y. Owen

Photographs in Sequence

Windmill at sunset near Lubbock.
West Texas driver on Highway 298 near Sudan.
Houston skyline.
The *Southern Eagle* loading grain at the port of Beaumont.
Kilgore College Rangerettes under a derrick, Kilgore.
Oil pumps, Permian Basis oil field, near Sundown, Texas.
Trees bent by coastal winds, Rockport.
Cattle on the Trans-Pecos range in Southwest Texas.
Whooping cranes in the Aransas Wildlife Refuge north of Corpus Christi.
Bishop's Palace, Galveston.
Texas-Eastman petrochemical plant, Longview.
West Texas farmer inspects irrigated land, near Sudan.
Modern-day and early Texas Rangers at headquarters in Waco.
El Paso at night, looking southwest toward Mexico.

11

More Resurrection than Reconstruction

*O*N June 19, 1865, Major General Gordon Granger of the United States Army, fresh from service with General William S. Rosecrans's army, arrived in Galveston to make the federal presence felt in Texas. Almost immediately on landing, he proclaimed that all Negro slaves were free and voided all legislation passed during the Civil War. One result is that in Texas blacks do not celebrate the anniversary of Lincoln's Emancipation Proclamation but observe June 19 as their emancipation day.

The experience of Texas over the next several years was not unlike that of the other ten Confederate States. Confusion reigned at first, but then from July 1865 to April 1870 Washington, D.C., dictated the policies of the state government. After that, the state endured another four years during which its government rode out of phase with most of its experienced citizens. About the pleasantest thing you could say of Texas in those nine years of Reconstruction is that its direction was flexible and its politics were fluid. The state adopted a new constitution in 1866, then spent $200,000 completing another constitution, and in 1875 put through its third constitution in nine years. Obviously the leaders of the state either did not know what they were doing or were chronically dissatisfied.

In that first Constitution of 1866 Texas refused to approve the Thirteenth Amendment to the Constitution of the United States, although the document as a whole treated blacks more generously than the fundamental law of any other state of the recent Confederacy. Negroes were made secure in person and property and were generally given the same rights before a court as a white person. The constitution not only repudiated the war debt but cancelled all state debts incurred during the war, whether they had to do with the war or not. In the election which followed, James W. Throckmorton, president of the Constitutional Convention, who owned the best of both worlds by being a former Unionist who had become a brigadier for the Confederacy and who supported the Reconstruction policy of President Andrew Johnson, was elected governor by a four-to-one majority. On August 20, 1866, President Johnson proclaimed the end of the insurrection in Texas.

Most Texans thought the end of the war on the battlefield meant the end of political strife as well. They expected to return to the pre-1861 fold, having expiated their sins by losing on the battlefield and giving the black his freedom. But the Radicals in Congress under the leadership of the incorrigible Thaddeus Stevens and straight-backed Charles Sumner were determined that Johnson would not let the South off the hook too easily. When Texas sent up two senators, neither of whom could take the "iron-clad oath" of "never voluntarily" having "borne arms against the United States . . . or yielded a voluntary support to any pretended government . . . hostile or inimical thereto," the United States Congress refused to seat either the senators or the three representatives who later joined them. Furthermore, Texas turned down not only the Thirteenth Amendment but also the Fourteenth and passed a labor law which spoke against enticing away of laborers, a subterfuge for keeping the black in some sort of peonage. The Texas laws for freedmen remained offensive to those who believed in full freedom, for they forbade laborers leaving home without permission or having visitors during working hours.

Another point that rankled was Texas's understanding that civil authority had been restored to supremacy over military authority. While constitutionally correct, Texans had not reckoned with the vindictiveness of the Radical Republicans. To head off any kind of confrontation Governor Throckmorton tried to restore law and order, remove garrisons away from centers of population to the frontier, and eliminate interference by the military and the Freedmen's Bureau in civil affairs. He succeeded rather well in all except the last objective. Both the Freedmen's Bureau and military officials regularly violated civil rights, jailed civilians for speaking out in opposition, and arrested contrary editors. Almost no soldiers were permitted to be tried by civil authorities for violating state laws. When Negro troops burned the town of Brenham, no one was ever brought to trial. Aggravating the situation was a double handful of lawless people who disliked blacks and Unionists but were willing to join those two groups in harassing the Southern white for the sheer joy of making mischief.

When on March 2, 1867, the Radical Republicans passed the First Reconstruction Act over President Johnson's veto, they legislated the governments of the Southern States out of existence and divided the South into five military districts. Texas was placed in the Fifth District along with Louisiana, under the charge of General Philip H. Sheridan. Charles Griffin, one of the commissioners previously chosen to receive the surrender of the Army of Northern Virginia, was named commander of the military district in Texas with headquarters at Galveston. Although Throckmorton had been a Unionist, the fact that he was now a governor who resisted military thrust led other Unionists to undermine his influence. On July 30 General Sheridan removed him.

As Throckmorton's successor Sheridan appointed former Governor Elisha M. Pease, a Unionist and a moderate. But the new military governor of Texas, Joseph Jones Reynolds, made the deceased loud-talking Griffin look good. Reynolds cleaned the state of all rebel officials, and he interpreted the word "rebel" liberally; he stacked Texas voter registration boards with Radicals, convened the 1870 Reconstruction legislature, and finally ran for the United States Senate, where Texas showed its low opinion by defeating him.

When voter registration had been completed, nearly 60,000 white voters and 50,000 blacks had been enrolled, while the number of men disfranchised ran between 7,500 and 10,000. The military made every effort either to place blacks in the majority or to control the Negro vote. By this time the Ku Klux Klan had invaded Texas from Tennessee, determined to scare the Negro out of voting, even to the point of bloodshed. The situation was not exactly stable. When the next election was held in mid-February 1868, the Democrats stayed home, hoping to defeat the Reconstruction program. The Republicans carried the election and wrote the Constitution of 1869—better than anyone had anticipated, but misused by the Radicals.

In the midst of all this politicking Texas became involved in a landmark suit whose decision is usually cited in any constitutional history of the United States. On February 15, 1867, during the administration of Governor Hamilton, Texas sought an injunction to restrain George W. White, John Chiles, and others from using Texas Indemnity Bonds paid to them by Texas after secession for supplies for the Confederate States of America, and to obtain restoration of fifty-one of the bonds.

Although the case was argued on all its points, from the outset both sets of attorneys and the court recognized that the main issue was the status of Texas. Involved was the legality of all Reconstruction government in the South. The chief attorney for Texas, George W. Paschal, a former Union editor who disliked Black Republicans, argued that since the Union was indestructible, Texas therefore had never left it and the status of Texas had remained unchanged. The defense argued that Texas, having seceded from the Union and having waged war against the United States, had lost its status as a state in the Union. Therefore Texas had no right to sue in the United States Supreme Court.

The court limited its decision to the specific issues involved rather than considering the validity of all acts of the secessionist state governments. In a five-to-three decision read on April 15, 1869, by Chief Justice Salmon P. Chase, the court held the Union to be indestructible and thus not dissoluble by any act of a state, the government, or the people.

The decision in Texas *v*. White therefore repudiates the doctrine of state sovereignty and clearly supports a federal as against a consolidated system of government. As the decision summarizes: "But the perpetuity and indissolubility of the Union, by no means, implies the loss of distinct and individual existence or of the right to self-government by the states."

On a smaller point, White and Chiles had to return the bonds since they were unlawful holders, having received them in a situation which sought to destroy the Union and benefit the Confederacy. When Paschal later sued for his legal fee of nearly $65,000 because Governor E. J. Davis had refused his claim, Paschal won the case and was allowed to retain all the bonds as his fee.

At the end of November 1869 Texas voted for a new governor. General Reynolds apparently counted the returns, for he never made them public. He simply announced that Edmund J. Davis, a Radical, had defeated A. J. Hamilton, a moderate former governor, by 39,901 to 39,092. Hamilton never really believed the tally. The Radicals also elected three congressmen. In a show of democracy they permitted the Democrats to claim the fourth congressman, J. C. Connor, who was both an army officer and a carpetbagger.

The Radical Republicans also won control of both houses of the Texas legislature. With Reynolds in firm control the legislature ratified the Fourteenth and Fifteenth amendments and elected James W. Flanagan, a former Whig who in the Texas legislature had introduced a bill for the first insane asylum in Texas, and Morgan Hamilton, an ardent Republican, to the United States Senate. On March 30, 1870, President Grant signed the act admitting Texas senators and representatives, and on the following April 16 General Reynolds formally ended military rule by remitting all authority to the civil officers.

Some now claimed that Reconstruction was over, but actually it lasted four more years. The direction was established when the new legislature, the Twelfth, postponed regular elections (which should have been held in the fall of 1870 for congressmen and in 1871 for state officers) until November 1872, thereby giving themselves at least an extra year in office. When eleven Democrats and three conservative Republicans opposed certain authoritarian moves of the Radical majority in the legislature, the latter arrested a part of the minority and expelled one member. In May 1871 the legislature removed its speaker, Ira H. Evans, for having opposed pushing back the election date. The legislature gave the governor power to declare any county under martial law plus a state police force of about 200 men. It also enlarged the appointive power of the governor until Davis could name an estimated 8,538 employees or officers.

In a way the Davis period witnessed a businessman's administration, but with little sympathy for holding the line in taxes and debt. At first the legislature gave the International Railroad Company, which was to build slaunchwise across Texas from Laredo to Jefferson, 8-percent bonds to the amount of $10,000 for each mile of railroad constructed. When the State Supreme Court declared the law unconstitutional, the state settled with the company for twenty sections of land for each mile constructed and for tax exemption on the company's property for twenty-five years. The state also gave the Southern Pacific and the Southern Transcontinental Railway companies provisional grants in bonds aggregating $6,000,000. Charges of bribery broke out all over the place, none of it proved. By the Constitution of 1869 the legislature could not grant land to railroads, but the legislature put this prohibition out for amendment in 1873—after which it gave away tens of millions of acres for railroad construction until the public domain had been exhausted.

But the worst abuses lay in Governor Davis's use of the police force and imposition of martial law. Undoubtedly the police force contained men who were either criminals or had criminal intent, as evidenced by their occasionally arresting men on little or no provocation, killing them in cold blood, starting riots and moving in to create reigns of terror, and misusing black policemen to stir up racial hatred. When a black state policeman killed a white man in East Central Texas, Davis moved troops into the area, suspended ordinary rights, and taxed the citizens of the two counties involved three cents on each hundred dollars of property valuation.

On the other hand, the Radicals gave Texas several overdue pieces of legislation. They tried to provide a public roads system, which remained a disgrace until the 1920s. They enacted a homestead law. They beefed up the frontier defense. They looked ahead to a true free public school system, making attendance compulsory and levying adequate taxes. Adequate then, at any rate.

Whether Davis and the legislature could have held power in the state if they had been more moderate is debatable, given the mood of the time. Quite aside from increased taxes, many Texans felt that this administration was an imposed one. That the Davis administration also maintained certain Radical newspapers through official patronage in the form of public printing did not set well with the general citizenry either.

But then came the delayed election of autumn 1872; and despite the fact that the polls were crowded with Davis henchmen and militia and that canvassers tried to reject enough votes to win, the moderates prevailed. When the Thirteenth Legislature assembled in Austin in mid-January 1873, it withdrew official patronage from newspapers, thereby closing down a number of Radical journals; it repealed the Police Act; it removed substantially the power of the governor to declare martial law; and it took away most of his appointive power. It also provided for a general election of state officers for early December 1873.

That election may well have been the most fraudulent in Texas history. Radicals threatened blacks who might vote Democratic. Democrats ordered blacks away from the polls. Underage boys voted. The issue became one of who would out-intimidate whom. The election proved to be the last stand for Davis, who lost to Richard Coke by a two-to-one margin and took his fellow Radicals down with him. The Radicals turned to the courts, holding that the election was unconstitutional since the Thirteenth Legislature kept the polls open for only one day instead of for four, as they had done. The State Supreme Court backed them, but the public did not.

Davis refused to give up his office and appealed to President U. S. Grant to send troops to Austin to sustain him. Coke and his new legislature organized the administration on the second floor of the Capitol, while Davis and the rejected legislature maintained their positions on the first floor, guarded by Negro troops. For several days Texas enjoyed dual government and anticipated an armed clash. Friends of Davis brought up his black troops at night, equipped with torches, and they paraded around and around the Capitol Building, chanting as they marched. The scene had all the eeriness of an Indian war camp by torchlight. Austin citizens stood armed and grim, waiting for the inevitable fight.

But the fight was not inevitable. President Grant, who earlier had advised Davis that it would be wise to accept the voters' wishes, sent a second message through his attorney general stating that he would not intervene. Davis yielded.

Davis has been given a rather hard time by historians. Personally he seems to have been a rather decent person, undeniably able and the most influential Texas Republican during Reconstruction. His belief that all Democrats and conservatives were rebels did not make him any friends in Texas. But after all, the Confederates had tried to hang him while he was recruiting for his regiment of Unionists near Matamoros during the Civil War. The fact that he had been elected originally by little more than 800 votes in a total of nearly 80,000 and that he ran as strong a government as if he had a popular mandate caused many Texans to chafe more than usual under his leadership. But the further fact that he remained in Austin until his death in 1883, prospered as a lawyer, and was given strong support by Texans for a place in President Chester A. Arthur's cabinet indicates that he must have been a man of considerable ability.

Those private Texans who suffered through the collapse of the Confederacy and the chaos of Reconstruction found themselves generally just barely holding on. In the remainder of the United States a downward trend in profits and prices had set in following 1866, and the year 1873 witnessed a panic which deepened into a severe six-year depression. Besides, the whole social system had to be reconstituted, taking into account a new body of free Negro labor which was as free not to work as slaves had been "free" to work. At times thousands of acres lay idle. Land values fell off to one-fifth of 1860 prices, and a decade after the war cotton dropped steadily from its high Civil War price down to 13 cents a pound. Since cotton production also fell off, the real loss in cotton income was calamitous.

Like the remainder of the South, Texas turned to the sharecrop system under which landowners supplied tenants with housing, equipment, and seed and took a share of the resulting crop, sometimes as high as two-thirds. Cotton moved northward and westward; Texas continued to grow in population, which regularly opened new markets and helped to drive some prices and incomes upward; and the North discovered Texas cattle. In the ten years following the war railroad mileage quadrupled, but most of Texas remained unconnected by rail.

In politics Texas also joined the Solid South, even though that solidity has been regularly overestimated. But the reaction against Davis and the Radical Republicans was so intense that "Republican" became a nasty word. Texas did not become exactly a one-party state, for the Democrats consistently split on political issues and any Texas Democrat with strong opinions invariably carried a prefix indicating his variety of Democrat.

Hurt worst of all was the black, who lost his early political gains in the reaction against Republicans. Perhaps he would have lost them anyway, but the fact that he was associated with an authoritarian administration which overused martial law and overburdened citizens with new taxes certainly damaged his cause. White Texans associated black suffrage with Radical Republicanism and started taking measures that were sometimes subtle, sometimes disconcertingly direct to disenfranchise the black. In the long run the black lost more than the white in Reconstruction, though the white lost also because of his failure to utilize the elective and collective power of the black in putting Texas back on its feet.

At the conclusion of Reconstruction Texans wrote another constitution designed to eliminate the Radical Constitution of 1869. First they tried to change that document by legislative joint committee, but the House of Representatives refused this method as being too centralized in approach. The people had to be reassured, and so the issue was put to the voters, who approved a convention of three elected delegates from each of the state's thirty senatorial districts. The convention met on September 6, 1875, for eleven weeks. Seventy-five of its members were Democrats, six were Negroes, and fifteen were Republicans. While this wasn't exactly proportional representation, it may have been better than expected. One of the members had helped write the Constitution of 1845 which had brought Texas into the Union, eight had been members of the Secession Convention of 1861, and one had helped write the Constitution of 1868–1869. Nearly half of the delegates—forty—belonged to the farmers' group called the Grange, three were former Union soldiers, and more than a score had been officers in the Confederate Army.

Perhaps it was the hard times or perhaps it was the presence of the Grange members, but the delegates at the convention set an all-time record, even in Texas, for cheapness. They refused to employ a stenographer, nor would they permit the proceedings to be published, so the convention that produced the constitution under which Texas has operated for a century furnished no official record for posterity. The delegates showed their penury in other ways: they provided for short terms of office; low, almost miniscule salaries; and limited power for officials. In almost every way possible they indicated that public administrators were a nuisance who needed to be turned out almost as quickly as they assumed office. The system provided for little continuity or time for planning, and Texas has suffered from it for a century. The constitution also can be faulted (as can others of the same era) for being too detailed, so that it hamstrung the state in its efforts to progress. So much was stated so explicitly, invariably as seen through an 1875 lens, that Texans have become inured to voting for from three to seven amendments to their constitution at almost every general election. Altogether 346 amendments to the Constitution of 1876 have been submitted, an average of seven per biennium, of which 220 have passed. Almost ten times as many as the federal Constitution in almost half the time! The Constitution of 1876 was no lofty statement of principles and organic law, but a piece of detailed legislation born of reaction.

Sadly, when the Texas legislature met as a committee of the whole in 1974 to draw up a replacement for the Constitution of 1876, its members repeated all the old mistakes and added a few new ones. Basically they showed no more concept than their predecessors of the fact that the greatness of the federal Constitution lies in its broad statements of principle and its elasticity, and became embroiled in arguments over inclusion or non-inclusion of right-to-work laws, proportion of highway funds to urban mass transportation, and the like. Every group with a special interest—some good, some bad—received its day, and the legislature attempted to include most of their requests. A constitution resulted that no one really wanted, not even the legislature which had drawn it, and after several months and several million dollars the legislature at first refused to accept its own document or to send it out to the voters for approval or rejection. The 1975 session of the legislature decided to let Texans vote separately on eight of the more controversial sections. In November the voters spoke overwhelmingly: by margins that usually ran three-to-one, all eight propositions were voted down. Whether Texans were voting to retain the present constitution, to reject these particular proposals, or to spank the legislature for having written a constitution themselves instead of turning it over to a citizens' committee remains an unresolved question. Only one fact is certain: in the Bicentennial year of 1976 metropolitan Texas lumbers along with a constitution that was written for a horse-and-buggy age.

The 1875 drafters were trying to shuck off an immediate past and prepare a future more to their liking. Politically the majority established a system which suited them. What they really came to like—economic growth—owed little to the constitution but everything to God and grass. They did not know that underneath all that hardscrabble farming lay seas of oil placed there by the Good Lord and geologic capture through no fault of their own. Nor could they quite foresee how the hunger for beef in more affluent areas would give them an international image for no other reason than that they had grass and cows and learned what to do with both.

12

The Circumstance of an
Unfenced World

*T*HE Trail—and Trail deserves to be capitalized—pointed to the North Star. Like rivulets feeding into a stream which joins other streams to make a river, the Trail increased its flow until it strung out hundreds of thousands of cattle over hill and prairie to the horizon's infinity, carrying them to market somewhere to the north. In one year 700,000 walked the Chisholm Trail, the most storied of several from Texas to Kansas—an almost continuous file of hoofs and horns.

Of extraordinary endurance, they were an ungainly-looking group, for they had no consistent color but were stippled, dappled, dirt-colored, ugly—unless you owned them or had some reason to be sentimental. Everyone remembers their horns, though most of those which hang in offices and gamerooms have been heated and melted and stretched and shaped. Nature, less poetic, gave some Texas cattle horns that were thick and short-curved like buffalo horns, or again one horn shooting up and its mate turned down, while some were true collectors' items spreading ninety inches or better from one gracefully curved tip to another.

They were a part of the American epic, celebrated and cheapened and made a *cliché* through excess, as is the American wont. But once the epic was real, and it saved a state from the

126

economic readjustment that ten other states faced following the collapse of the Confederacy. Texas was lucky when the range-cattle industry came to rescue it from the financial doldrums of Reconstruction. The nation was lucky also, for the range-cattle era placed an indelible stamp on the American character that transcends Texas, the West, and the frontier. In a way, that era represents the story of the United States in a capsule.

It started with Cortés, the Spanish conquistador. Back in Andalucía Spanish sheep and cattle ranged. Cortés unloaded horses in Vera Cruz to scare the daylights out of the confronting *indios,* and Gregorio de Villalobos came along shortly after with that Spanish-Moorish bovine, and then both animals ranged upward and inward into Mexico. Coronado took them on journeys of thousands of miles into the high plains of the Southwest, and those two redoubtable padres, Eusebio Kino and Junípero Serra, led other cattle and horses into Arizona and California.

When the Spanish built a chain of missions across Texas, cattle and horses moved with the Spanish cross. Loosely tended, the livestock multiplied. Although at first Indians were terrified by horses and then in the gentlemanly tradition of the Spanish *caballero* were forbidden to ride because they were servile people, they soon learned to handle the horse because the Spanish needed hired hands on horseback to cover the vast breadths of the ranges. In the New World the Spanish developed a *hacienda* system, adapted a system of cattle tending to the ranges of Mexico's plateau, and built a considerable hide trade within Mother Mexico and in California. Meanwhile the cattle which came to Texas were almost as feral as the handfuls of people who lived there.

Before Mexico ever separated from Spain, *haciendas* had been established on either side of the Rio Grande. The Mexicans continued the system, and the Anglo-Texans inherited it. At the time of the American Revolution Mission Espíritu Santo near La Bahía was herding 15,000 head of cattle; Mission Rosario, 10,000 head. That country of low chaparral between the Nueces and Rio Grande became, as we have seen, disputed territory between Mexico and the Republic of Texas, ripe for raids. And the raids occurred. The Texans stole the Mexicans' cattle and were labeled patriots by their fellow Texans, branded as *banditos* by the Mexicans. The Mexicans ran off Texans' cattle and were branded as bandits by the Texans, and labeled as patriots by their fellow *Mexicanos*.

Over the eons the Spanish cattle themselves adapted to the New World, growing taller and lankier while their horns spread into the storied longhorns. They were built for travel, because they had strolled their way a thousand miles from Vera Cruz; and they grew long horns because they had to learn to fight off predators in the brush. In the days of the Republic of Texas and thereafter they cross-bred somewhat with cattle brought in from the Old South, which helped their beef content without destroying their mobility. Like two-legged Texans, they operated best when left essentially alone, and they needed looking after only at twice-a-year roundups—one for branding and one for slaughter.

With God providing the grass and the brush and the Spanish providing the cattle and mustangs to tend them, the situation was ripe for the perceptive Anglo to move into the ranching business. Consequently into the no-man's-land between the Nueces and the Rio Grande came one of the more remarkable though little-known adventurers in a state pockmarked with freebooters. Henry Lawrence Kinney came to Texas at the start of the Republic and moved right into the center of trouble at Brownsville. By 1841 he was ranching on a large scale near Corpus Christi, a town he helped to found, and was trying to buy out all the small ranchers in the area. Whether ''buy out'' or ''euchre'' is the more nearly precise verb is debatable. But he proved that an Anglo could ranch the country, although he himself was not a money-maker. His talent lay in promotion with other people's money, and contributed that oft-repeated social role of a speculator—he opened an area to trade and settlement.

While Kinney was building up a retinue of followers in the brush country, a sixteen-year-old named Richard King was developing a career as a steamboat pilot on Alabama rivers and taking part in Florida's Seminole War. In Florida young King met Mifflin Kenedy, veteran clerk and substitute captain on river steamers from the Ohio and Mississippi to Florida. The Mexican War brought both men to Texas, where they helped transport troops and supplies for Zachary Taylor's army. After the war Kenedy ran a pack train to Monterrey and kept a herd of sheep in Hidalgo County. Meanwhile King, still only twenty-seven, bought Santa Gertrudis, a Spanish land grant of 75,000 acres. In early December 1860, on the eve of the Civil War, he sold half of the tract to Kenedy; and for the next eight years the pair engaged in large-scale ranching, steadily increasing their ranch holdings from profits made in supplying European buyers with Confederate cotton.

Out of this partnership grew the famous King Ranch, at one time the largest ranch in the United States and still a name with which to conjure. When the partnership dissolved in 1868, it took thirteen months to round up and divide the stock in cattle, sheep, goats, and mules, which ranged from the Nueces to the Rio Grande. Kenedy kept the Laureles division of the ranch, which he enclosed in 1869 on three sides with thirty-six miles of smooth wire fence—one of the first Texas ranches under fence. Eventually he expanded the ranch to 242,000 acres, all fenced, and sold it in 1882 to a Scottish syndicate which renamed it the Texas Land and Cattle Company. As for King, the King Ranch is still the King Ranch, with its headquarters in Kingsville, though it is now run principally by the in-law side, the Klebergs.

Whatever money Kinney, King, and Kenedy made in cattle came principally from hides and tallow. Cattle as beef were almost a drug on the market. During the Civil War the women and old men left behind had too many other things to do to tend cattle, and the hide and tallow industry proved difficult to maintain. So Texas cattle disported themselves biologically, found the grass good, and multiplied.

Before the war Texas cattle had been trailed to points on the Mississippi from New Orleans to St. Louis, but the drives had not been particularly profitable. Nonetheless the range cattle industry spread onto the upper Texas prairie. Cattle were herded through the sites of Dallas, Fort Worth, and Denton for decades before those towns existed. Indians and Civil War halted the western movement of the cattle industry, but after the war the ranchers began to move up onto the higher plains. By 1876 they had moved beyond the 100th meridian into the eastern Panhandle. They also moved onto the plains to the north and into New Mexico and Colorado.

The beef situation boiled down to a simple problem of practical economics. Every year Texas was salting down and pickling some of its finest beef and feeding millions of pounds to the hogs or to the Gulf of Mexico, cooking it first to render the tallow. Millions of cattle, estimated as high as 5,000,000, ranged over Texas. Up north were new-rich appetites with new-rich money. The resource existed. The market existed. And a thousand impossible miles separated the resource from its market. In Texas people were outnumbered by cattle by up to ten to one. In New York appetites were denied beef at almost any price. This is the kind of profit problem that calls out the American genius.

Texas was rescued by a twenty-six-year-old from Illinois, Joseph G. McCoy. McCoy persuaded the Kansas Pacific Railroad, building west, to erect a full-grown cattle town at a whistle-stop known as Abilene and then went south in 1867 to persuade Texas cattlemen heading north, generally toward Sedalia, Missouri, to take the more westerly route to that unheard-of town. His must have been a masterful salesman's performance, for no one from Texas knew McCoy and no one on the trail had an opportunity to check on his credentials. But they arrived to find that Abilene was indeed what McCoy had promised—a reasonably complete town with everything from loading pens and corrals to gambling dens and soiled doves. Abilene became the first of a string of cattle depots which dotted the West and gave rise to millions of words and millions of feet of film, the whole cowboy myth celebrated from Moscow to Manila.

In their profit-seeking, cattlemen learned a number of things. By traveling west of the population line, they avoided quarantine laws against Texas cattle, brought on by the fact that the latter dropped a tick to which they were immune but which devastated local herds by carrying a sort of bovine typhoid quickly branded as "Texas fever" (although Texans naturally called it "Spanish fever"). Further, the cattle fattened on the trail north. Cattlemen also found that northern grass was considerably richer, though the growing season was shorter, and so they stocked the northern ranges with Texas cattle. The market for stock cattle soon equated with the market for beef. When Northerners found that cattle could survive rugged winters, the cattle industry spread like the large end of a cornucopia onto the plains of Nebraska, the Dakotas, Montana, Wyoming, and even into Alberta and Saskatchewan. Texans found what any entrepreneur likes to discover—that the price of Texas cattle increased from $5 a head in Texas to $30 a head and upwards in the North ($85 in New York was the likely highest known price), and that a considerable profit margin lay in between. And every year nature restocked the range, so that your capital resource never seemed to dry up. As one stockman observed, raising and selling cattle resembled running a house of prostitution—no matter how often you sold your product, the inventory was always there to sell again.

Some of the profits were fantastic, and stories of the beef bonanza reached all the way to western Europe. Narrators undoubtedly exaggerated their accounts of profits, and though the listeners probably suspected it, nevertheless greedy Germans and careful Scotsmen rushed to sink their money into the western plains. The influx of European capital again provided a kind of lend-lease to the United States, freeing American capital for other sorts of development. Meanwhile Texas and the other plains states raised their own entrepreneurs, who followed no set stereotype except one of men who knew what to do with opportunity.

Thus Major George W. Littlefield came stumping home on his crutches from the Civil War, mustered out months before its end because of his wound. In Texas he found that his mother had taken care of the home place, but that Army worms and June flooding proved as formidable enemies as Yankee guns. He was also paying 2 percent interest a month. As his debts grew heavier, his creditors demanded pay in gold instead of paper. Come the spring of 1871, and like other Texans with cattle and horses, he pointed them north, 600 head of his own and 500 more bought on credit. At Abilene he found a "sporty looking" man who bought his herd at from $40 to $50 a head.

Back in Texas, Littlefield paid off his debts, freed himself from his interest chains, and thenceforward hired men to do the trailing for him. When he died years later he owned the LFD and LIT ranches in the Texas Panhandle and in New Mexico; was founder-president of the American National Bank of Austin, which he had organized in 1890; had been a member of the board of regents of the University of Texas for nine years; had owned Austin's historic Driskill Hotel; was widely known as a philanthropist; and had a town named for him in the Texas Panhandle.

Even multiplying such individual accounts as one-generation wealth on the range does not equal the significance of the discovery that the Great American Void, the reputed Sahara of the United States, was habitable and, glory be, profitable. While no accurate account of the number of cattle driven over the trails exists, the 1880 census estimates that the drive to Abilene, 1867–1871, totalled 1,460,000; to Wichita and nearby depots, 1872–1875, 1,072,000; to Dodge City—"the Bibulous Babylon of the Plains"—and Ellsworth, 1876–1879, 1,046,732; to Dodge City and Caldwell, 1880, 382,000. Estimates for the whole period to 1890 run as high as 10,000,000 head. Eventually Texans became acquainted with the land from Texas to Montana, dropping off men along the trail as they also dropped off cattle.

Several factors appeared to close down the open range. Naturally any profitable venture attracts investors and speculators. Too many ranchers and would-be ranchers got in the act, violated natural laws governing good range, and overstocked. They destroyed the grass, or so reduced the range that when the first drouth came along, the range virtually disappeared and the cattle dried up and died. Then too, the longhorn was a traveling animal who incidentally carried beef on his bones. Consumers with taste demanded better beef while breeders with taste began an effort to improve the quality through upbreeding, gradually phasing out the longhorn until he became an endangered species.

Furthermore, the virgin land of the prairies, never broken by plow, attracted farmers. Having gone broke in Kentucky or in East Texas, they decided that new soil could help them recoup their finances, and so they moved out onto the grasslands with their farming tools. With their somewhat tidy minds they filed for titles, slicing athwart the open range like a vein of stubborn gristle through the center of a fine roast. The Industrial Revolution contributed its bit through the invention of barbed wire, which the nesters used to fence *out* range cattle and which the ranchers eventually used to fence *in* their own charges. Cattle profits attracted huge syndicates which could both buy land and fence ranges and hastened the closing. The advance of railroads into Texas relieved the necessity of trailing to Kansas, while the transfer of the windmill onto the plains to tap a hitherto unknown but quite adequate ground-water supply finished the process. In short, orderliness and system replaced romance.

Closing the range led to another violent period in which cattlemen cut fences to get at water, which invariably the farmers had enclosed. Texas courts seldom convicted a man for fence-cutting, because so frequently the violator was faced either with cutting or with ruination. Fencing also reduced the success of rustling, a way of life by which a number of later respectable cattlemen started their herds. Finally, the first great efforts at fencing were financed by eastern and European capitalists, so that fence-cutting could be sold to local juries as a last-ditch stand of embattled Texans against the greed of outsiders. Gradually morality seeped into the scene, the Texas legislature in 1884 made fence-cutting a felony, and a threat of actual civil war in Texas was averted. Altogether, estimates of damage by fence-cutting run as high as $20,000,000. And as of today it remains against the law in Texas to carry a pair of wirecutters, even in your automobile.

Even though the open range shut down, Texas has retained its open range image. Too much acreage is needed for a steer to survive for ranching to be intensive, so the Texas rancher snorts at Californians for referring to their ten-acre prune farms as ranches. To a Texan a ranch has to have vastness, and its soils must not be exposed to the plow except to produce truck to be used around the house. Exceptions are made to this rule. To speak of your wheat ranch is legitimate. But raising cotton over thousands of acres, as many West Texans do, does not permit the owner to speak of owning a "cotton ranch." Cotton has an association with 40 acres and a mule and stoop labor, and in no way, no way, can a cotton farmer ever evolve into a cotton rancher.

With enclosed ranching the Texas cattle industry lost some of its more spectacular characteristics. No longer did men have to lie with or sing to the herd at night, cattle grazed rather than ranged, and eventually herding by helicopter and pick-up was introduced. Still in 1954 there were at least nineteen Texas ranches with 150,000 acres or more. The largest was the King Ranch, which retained almost three-quarters of a million acres in Texas plus lesser ranches in pre-Castro Cuba, Montana, and Australia. Several other ranches had more than 400,000 acres. The longhorn was confined to wild life refuges, to breeders of exotics on tourist ranches, and to a relative handful of sentimentalists. Instead, the white-faced Hereford served practically as a symbol of Texas, along with Durham, Angus, and Brahman. And the cowboy became a deromanticized employee.

If any romance surrounded sheep and their culture, Texas would have carved another chapter in this branch of the livestock industry. Like cattle, sheep had come in during the early Spanish era, starting in South Texas and gradually moving up into the state. A myth grew that sheep and cattle could not inhabit the same range because sheep cropped the grass too short. While calm observation has refuted this belief in part, the fact remains that where grass is short and scarce, sheep and goats can just about ruin an area.

Sometimes sheepmen and cattlemen fought each other for ranges, with results not always pretty. Courts almost always decided for the cattlemen, possibly because they wielded more power rather than on the legal merits of the case. By 1880 the Texas range included more than six million sheep, after which the industry declined somewhat until 1930. By World War II the sheep count, which had declined to less than two million early in the twentieth century, had increased to nearly eleven million, after which it dropped off again.

Angora goats were introduced from Turkey to the hill country of Texas in 1849. More than four million goats with a value of $20,000,000 to $30,000,000 now range the Texas countryside, and three-fourths of all Angora goats in the United States live on fewer than 8,000 ranches in a few counties from San Angelo to Uvalde. San Angelo, in fact, is the nation's largest market for sheep and wool, as well as for goats and mohair. About 100 wool and mohair warehouses lie in the San Angelo vicinity, both to serve the industry and to provide lamb feedlots.

The value of Texas sheep has run as high as $155,000,000, and Texas as the leading state in the nation contains about one-fifth of all the country's sheep. But few Texans know this statistic, and none mention it. The goat situation is even more unmentionable, for Texas produces 97 percent of all U.S. mohair. Texas has its share of wool and mohair millionaires, but they never make the movie scripts.

The cowboy has his chroniclers and poets. Without doubt he has been heroized until he would have been almost unrecognizable to his contemporaries, and yet in today's complex world he appeals to the poetry in today's urban soul as he appealed to the professional poet in previous ages. Sometimes those poets caught him, perpetuated him, and tied him particularly to Texas, so that the Texas myth is wrapped around his saddle and chaps.

Here then is the Holy Trinity of Texas. What the cod and fisherman and God meant to New England, the mustang, long-horn, and cowboy meant to Texas. They symbolized a freedom which probably never really existed, but which people like to think existed. Most Texans would no more know what to do with that freedom than would any other American, but they perhaps delude themselves in believing that they understand the hunger for freedom as no one else.

13

Exit Frontier, Enter Hogg

IF it had not been for the unanticipated development of the range-cattle industry, Texas concerns during the latter nineteenth century would undoubtedly have paralleled those of the other southern states, with a few aberrations because of Texas's semiwestern status. Democrats reigned supreme; the only difference in statewide candidates lay in the degree to which they embraced Greenback and then later Populist tenets. The Greenbackers advocated an income tax, improved schools, less central government coupled with more state regulation of railroads and other bodies; they demanded that the federal government issue more paper money, or greenbacks, on the theory that if more money were in circulation, more would naturally filter down to the farmers, who were hurting. While they lasted, the Greenbackers made a lot of noise and elected George Washington Jones, a renegade Democrat, to Congress from 1879 to 1887. They also ran him for governor on the Greenback ticket in 1882, where he lost with 102,501 votes to John Ireland's 150,891. He tried again against Ireland in 1884 but lost by even more. The result indicated the beginning of the end for the Greenback Party in Texas, as various Democrats took over successive planks of its platform.

In a public sense the state continued to be poverty stricken, not unusual for a former Confederate state. Receipts in 1874 did not meet one-half of expenditures, but no matter how much the governor tried to retrench, demands of a growing state always offset economy. O. M. Roberts—the Old Alcalde, as he was called—curtailed expenses stringently, even to discontinuing payment of rewards for the arrest of criminals and by turning out convicts from the crowded prison system. The legislature caught the spirit by discontinuing Confederate pensions and substituting a grant of a section of land to each veteran, an amount later doubled. By the time Roberts retired as governor, he had reduced the public debt by more than a million dollars and had annoyed everyone who desired the continuation or initiation of a public service.

As much as retrenchment, good crops improved the Texas financial record. Cotton production more than doubled from 696,000 bales in 1876 to 1,514,000 bales a decade later. The growth of the livestock industry has already been noted. Meanwhile in a decade railroad mileage quadrupled from 2,000 miles in 1876 to almost 8,000 miles in 1886. Population increased from 818,579 people in 1880 to 2,235,527 twenty years later. For tax purposes property evaluation grew from $257,632,000 in 1876 to $630,525,123 a decade later. Various public services enlarged: the state built a new prison at Rusk, a second hospital for the insane at Terrell in 1885, a state orphans' home at Corsicana, a school for deaf and blind black youth at Austin, and a new capitol at Austin, completed in 1888.

The capitol remains an imposing red granite structure, the largest state capitol in the Union built with the least expenditure of money. To get the capitol built on a scale to fit Texas pride, the state advertised for bids, with payment in land. A Chicago syndicate won the bid, received 3,000,000 acres in ten counties along the New Mexico line plus another 50,000 acres for surveying the land, and went to England for its finances. The syndicate had nothing to do with the land except turn it into a ranch, the famous XIT, at one time the largest ranch under fence in the world. The owners strung 6,000 miles of single-strand fence wire around its 94 pastures and outer perimeter.

One reason that Texas had alleged it was resigning from Mexico was that the Mexicans had failed to provide a system of public education, including a public university. To rectify, the

Republic of Texas set aside fifty leagues (211,400 acres) of land to establish two universities. The state established a University of Texas in 1858, but the Civil War prevented its actual beginning. Then the Constitution of 1876 granted a million acres of land to the university and its branches but did not compel the legislature to open a school. When the Texas State Teachers Association, organized in 1878 as a result of a meeting called by Governor Roberts, pushed for the legislature to make good on a university, the governor got behind the educators and the legislature put the plan into operation, selecting Austin as the site for the main university and Galveston for its medical school. The university has been a thorn in the side of the legislature ever since, and vice versa: at its regular sessions in 1883 and 1885 the legislature refused to appropriate money for its maintenance out of the General Fund, and the fledgling school had to limp along on fees and income from its unproductive property.

In 1876 the legislature came up with another answer to Mexican neglect of public education by instituting a community school system which had no district boundaries, no means of acquiring and controlling property, and no assurance of continuity. When economy-minded Governor Roberts vetoed the school appropriation bill in 1879, the citizens of the state became annoyed enough that they began to push for a system whereby the schools would receive income independent of a sliding share in the General Revenue. In 1883 they pushed through a constitutional amendment which repeated a provision in the Constitution of 1876 granting the public schools a poll tax of $1, adding to that amount one-fourth of the state occupation taxes, providing that the legislature should levy a special school tax not to exceed 20 cents on a $100 valuation, and guaranteeing a school term of at least six months. The following year the legislature rewrote the school law to provide for an elective state superintendent; divide the state into school districts with the privilege of voting a local tax; widen the school age to 8 through 16; require teachers to hold certificates; and prescribe a system of registers and reports. Since the citizens would not vote local taxes, the schools starved. In rural areas the situation was so disgraceful that the public schools of Texas are still trying to catch up ninety years later.

Probably the public problem whose settlement pleased Texans the most was securing its several frontiers. The Texas Rangers had made their reputation long before the post-Civil War years. Indian depredations pretty well came to a halt, as particularly the Comanche and Kiowa made their last stands for freedom.

The best-known source of trouble was Juan Nepomuceno Cortina, known as Cheno, a natural bandit and natural leader who had worked both sides of the Rio Grande since the mid-1840s. He became a living folk hero in 1859 when he attacked Brownsville, took Fort Brown, and proclaimed his mission as that of a Texas citizen defending the rights and property of Mexicans. The Ranger force that made the mistake of attacking him and hanging his lieutenant was soundly beaten; Cheno's supporters began to talk of driving the Anglo-Americans back at least to the Nueces and perhaps beyond the Sabine.

The U.S. Army finally moved to take back Fort Brown, but it took nearly two weeks. In 1860 both the Rangers and the Army—under Colonel Robert E. Lee—fought him back across into Mexico. During the Civil War he crossed the border again, co-operating with both Confederate and Union forces without playing favorites. With the rise of Benito Juárez, Cortina declared himself governor of the state of Tamaulipas on January 12, 1864; later, he switched sides but wound up with the same title. But with all his inconstant political loyalties, he remained true to his one love: cattle stealing. Finally, with the U.S. Army under E. O. C. Ord, commanding general of the Military Department of Texas, facing the possibility of crossing the border into Mexico to end lawlessness on the Rio Grande frontier, the Mexican government arrested Cortina and saw to it that he behaved until his death in 1894. He was buried with full military honors.

Cortina is a legitimate chicano hero, a man who successfully thumbed his nose at Texas authority for a long generation. More recent Texan chicanos who have triumphed—Lee Trevino, Trini Lopez, Congressmen Henry Gonzales, and Eligio de la Garza, for example—have joined the Establishment. Cortina defied and physically ridiculed Anglo concern and authority.

Actually, internal rowdyism represented a considerably greater concern than did Mexicans. Texas remained a haven for people who had gotten into trouble elsewhere and for young toughs who had to quench the rising sap of youth along some Texas frontier. Many of them were not criminally minded but just needed to prove their manhood.

In his 1879 message to the Texas legislature Governor Roberts commented on the "unprecedented" amount of crime in the state. The editor of the *Jacksboro Frontier Echo* estimated that 100,000 horses had been stolen in the state during the three years preceding March 1878 and that not more than one in ten of the estimated 750 thieves regularly engaged was ever brought to justice. After the Northwest Texas Stock Association was organized at Graham in 1877 to suppress horse and cattle theft, its members became discouraged because leading citizens were committing a considerable part of the stealing. Naturally vigilante justice appeared, and undoubtedly a number of people were shot or hanged without proper attention to their civil rights or guilt. Stage robbery, in the words of one observer, "became almost an epidemic," while Sam Bass turned into a legend.

Into this situation stepped the Texas Rangers, the most effective state enforcement agency in the history of the United States. While their heroes already included such names as Jack Hays, Samuel Walker, Ben McCulloch, Rip Ford, Big Foot Wallace, and Sul Ross, in some ways the greatest of the Rangers appeared in the unlikely person of Captain Leander H. McNelly, a soft-spoken consumptive who moved in on Texas feuds, Indians, and Mexicans with equal felicity and ferocity. McNelly had been a Confederate soldier at seventeen, a captain of scouts—and hero—in Sibley's brigade at nineteen. This small thin lad with the timid voice grew into a small, thin, and timid-sounding man of courage, impatience with rights, racial arrogance, and commitment to six-gun law and order.

In the mid-1870s McNelly took a troop of Rangers into the so-called Taylor-Sutton feud in DeWitt County, where neither feuding group would permit the courts to operate. He recruited his companions himself, rejecting many for fear that they could not face the moral and emotional problem of shooting their own relatives. While McNelly stayed in the county, ensuring that both sides received justice, Ranger headquarters in Austin received a telegram from the anguished sheriff of Nueces County asking his help.

Off to Corpus Christi went McNelly and his troops, where he found a mixed situation. Ranches had been burned; retaliation was being met by retaliation, with the Mexicans receiving the worst of the exchange. Woe unto the *tejano* whose eyes were black and whose English was accented or nonexistent. Even McNelly, no racial liberal, was moved to protest.

Here McNelly changed historic Ranger tactics. He passed over the latest model repeaters—Henrys, Spencers, and Winchesters—and chose for his troops the Sharps, a heavy, single-shot rifle in .50 caliber, a favorite among hunters of buffalo, which seldom shot back. The Sharps had long-range accuracy but was almost impossible to handle in a running fight. The Ranger had to think before he shot.

When McNelly arrived near Brownsville in June 1875, he received word that fifteen Mexican nationals had crossed the border below the town. A week later he caught up with them at Palo Alto. The Mexicans took refuge on a small island in the river surrounded by salt marsh, confident that the Rangers could not penetrate. But McNelly sent his men from three sides, killing twelve raiders.

Serenity set in, not only for the Mexicans but for McNelly and his men, until October, when through his spies McNelly learned that the Mexicans had contracted to deliver 18,000 head of cattle to Monterrey within ninety days. At a going price of $18 a head, that meant a third of a million dollars' worth of cattle. No wonder men like Cortina were willing to risk. A bright moon came, ideal for moving herds, but nothing happened. But then a month later when the moon rose bright and clear again in November, here came Cortina's men, about sixteen or seventeen of them who successfully took out seventy-five head of stolen cattle. McNelly drove his men sixty miles in five hours trying to intercept, but they missed the raiders.

The captain decided that the time had come to make a bold illegal strike across the border straight at the bandits' heart. Whether for a cloak of legality or for assistance, McNelly tried to persuade federal troops to cross into Mexico with him, but they refused beyond promising to cover his return if he made it across. At one hour after midnight on November 19, 1875, Captain McNelly and thirty comrades invaded Mexico, straight into a force probably ten times as large as theirs, seeking the ranch of Las Cuevas, which doubled as a depot for stolen cattle. Fortunately they found Las Cuevas after daylight, because possibly 300 men were drawn up to intercept. McNelly retreated to the Mexican bank of the Rio Grande, using the riverbank as earthworks. When the Mexicans under Juan Flores, owner of Las Cuevas, showed up, they thought the Texans had escaped to the opposite side and moved into almost point-blank range before the Rangers opened fire. As the first volley took care of Flores, the leaderless Mexicans retreated to the brush.

On the United States side of the river sat the federal troops, watching like spectators at a football game. Some became so excited that they abandoned caution and correctness and crossed to Mexico to assist. The Mexicans, not knowing how many more would come, raised a truce flag and promised to return the stolen cattle if McNelly would withdraw with his Rangers. In the midst of all this activity, McNelly received a telegram from the secretary of war of the United States instructing him to get back on United States soil. By flash, McNelly sent a terse reply, telling the secretary of war to go to hell, he was staying in Mexico, where his quarry were.

Legal or not, the raid accomplished McNelly's purpose. Tales of his daring spread throughout Texas and northern Mexico, with the result that the Ranger reputation for swift meting out of justice was enhanced to the point of mythology. Texans believed in Ranger justice; Mexicans just plain hated the Rangers, which they still do. But McNelly's Las Cuevas War, as it came to be called, proved successful. Border troubles diminished noticeably and immediately.

In the end purists and tuberculosis brought McNelly down. He violated too many procedures for the politicians not to demand that he be fired. Seemingly oblivious of danger and pain, McNelly was brutal with transgressors. Yet some of the Mexicans in the Nueces Strip, which had been part of Mexico only a generation or two before, may have had as much right to the cattle as Anglo cattlemen.

It is possible that the Texas Rangers should have been abolished by 1881. But they weren't, and they threaded their way through other notable periods down to the present. Nowadays they are under fire in Texas for badgering chicanos and *huelgistas,* or strikers. They ride in cars, sometimes transferring to planes or boats, always with their saddle in the car's trunk. Traditions persist—they do not wear uniforms, and they are required always to have a horse available for immediate use, so that they may leave the roads and trails and go where the criminal may hide and the difficulty may lie. As the oldest state law enforcement agency in North America, they forged an imperishable chain in the national state of mind that has created the myth of Texas.

Some Rangers' excesses have to be considered in context, as when they were ordered out by Governor Ireland to help put down a strike of 9,000 members of the Knights of Labor against the Jay Gould railroad system in late spring of 1886. They performed as strikebreakers and labor baiters, but so did every other state militiaman throughout the United States and so did many federal troops. The trouble is, in 1976 Rangers still intervene on the side of management in labor-management disputes while in most democratic countries government forces endeavor to be neutral. Add the Rangers' labor-baiting to the fact that many of the laborers are chicano, and you can readily see why in many Texas circles feeling grows that the Texas Rangers should be retired to contemplate rather than enlarge their myth.

Not so exciting but equally important in settling Texas, and much more in tune with what was happening in the remainder of the nation, was the advent of business regulation and reform in Texas. Regulation naturally centered in the railroad industry, whose post-Civil War quadrupling of mileage has already been cited. Because of its size and vast distances, Texas was a natural for railroad building, and by 1890 had nearly 9,000 miles of railroad. Leading roads (which frequently underwent a series of name changes and ownerships) included the Southern Pacific;

the International and Great Northern, which connected with the Mexican National Railroad in the 1880s and became part of the Gould empire, eventually a part of the Missouri Pacific system; the Gulf, Colorado and Santa Fe, built from Galveston and missing Houston because of Galveston's annoyance at Houston's regular enforcement of a seasonal quarantine against the port city for periodic epidemics of yellow fever; and the one railroad most nearly Texan, the Texas and Pacific Railway, formed in March 1872 to proceed from the border of East Texas until it hit the Southern Pacific track ninety-two miles east of El Paso. In 1880 Jay Gould and Russell Sage took over the Texas and Pacific and put General Grenville M. Dodge, the Civil War logistics genius who had constructed the Union Pacific, in charge of construction. Dodge reached the eastbound Southern Pacific by the beginning of 1882. Meanwhile another railroad running from Fort Worth to Denver crossed the openness of the Panhandle, so that Texas could be entered and left from almost any direction. In 1893 the Fort Worth and Denver City became part of the Burlington system.

The legislature's liberality really showed through in granting public lands to railroads from 1854 until 1882, except for a four-year period when the Constitution of 1869 prohibited such bounty. Usually Texas gave sixteen sections for each mile of road constructed, and forty-one railroad companies received state land before the act was repealed in 1882. The greatest beneficiary was the Texas and Pacific, with 5,167,360 acres. Altogether Texas gave away 32,150,000 acres of the state's public domain, an area the size of the state of Alabama.

Arguments for and against contributions of public lands for railroad building existed in Texas as with the federal government. The generous grants caused some lines to be built that would have been just as well not built. Grants caused lands to be held off the market, thereby retarding development. Whereas lands held by roads like the Santa Fe, which had received bounty from the federal government, later turned out to be rich in timber or in uranium, the Texas lands enhanced little in value and produced little profit. Most sold at a few cents an acre as undercapitalized railroads tried to unload their land to avoid receivership. Yet certainly the railroads helped to promote the settlement of Texas, just as they acted as unofficial immigration agencies for the western portion of the United States.

Although the Grange and the Greenback Party criticized established administrations, no really organized opposition to corporate advancement of wealth appeared until the farmers began to protest during the 1880s. As the price of cotton dropped (from 31 cents a pound in 1865 to less than 5 cents a pound in 1898) and farmers saw their income drop from $88,000,000 to $68,000,000 between 1887 and 1890, they began to wonder at whose door lay the fault, for they had raised 25 percent more cotton in the lesser income years. Like their contemporaries in Kansas and Minnesota, they fought taxes and mortgage charges and seemed to pay through their noses beyond what was demanded of city dwellers. Whose fault? The faceless corporations, the railroads with which they had some intimacy because they shipped produce, or the equally obnoxious and intimate middlemen, who charged too much commission?

Out of this argument stepped a new movement, the Farmers' Alliance, along with its political outgrowth, the People's Party of America or Populists. The Farmers' Alliance was Texas-conceived, founded originally in Lampasas County as a stockman's organization to eliminate livestock thieves and loan sharks. By 1887 it had become a national organization with a strength of one to three million members. While Alliance members ostensibly eschewed partisan politics, nevertheless in a state meeting at Cleburne in 1886 the Alliance translated its demands into a political program, with a preamble that spoke of "the shameful abuses that the industrial classes are now suffering at the hands of arrogant capitalists and powerful corporations." Among other measures, the Alliance demanded that public school lands be sold only in small grants to actual settlers, that railroad property be assessed at full value, and that the federal government enact an interstate commerce law. Later the Alliance previewed the Sherman Antitrust Act of 1890 with a request that an antitrust law be enacted. To a degree the Knights of Labor co-operated with the Alliance, and the combination of farmer and laborer meant that the Texas Democratic Party had to notice and to an extent accede.

All the reform movement needed was a personifier, an articulator. He appeared in James Stephen Hogg, still in his middle thirties and a rarity as a Texas gubernatorial candidate—a native son. As a newspaper publisher in Longview and Quitman, he fought subsidies to railroads, corruption of the Grant administration, and lawlessness, three issues which provided nearly daily fodder. By 1876, when he was twenty-five, he received his only defeat for public office when he ran for a seat in the Texas legislature, his first uncertain step up the political ladder as county attorney, district attorney, and in 1886 attorney general. He was one Democrat for whom blacks would vote.

In each of his races Hogg proved a fearless exponent of reform, naturally reaching his zenith when he attained a statewide constituency. As attorney general he encouraged new legislation to protect the public domain set aside for school and institutional funds and instituted suits which returned more than a million and a half acres to the state. He forced railroads and land corporations to sell their holdings to settlers within certain time limits, and he made the life of "wildcat" insurance companies untenable.

Most of all Hogg educated or propagandized Texans, depending on the viewpoint, about their needs, focusing on the establishment of a railroad commission to regulate corporate railway interests. While he wasn't a single-issue candidate, he knew how to parlay one issue into championing the white hats against the black ones. In addition, for instance, he called for abolition of the national banking system and for that hottest of all issues nationally, free coinage of silver. Although his espousal of all of these issues won him national attention, the railroads remained his prime target.

Meanwhile Texas was caught up in another national movement, prohibition of alcoholic beverages. The issue surfaced about 1870 with the appearance of the United Friends of Temperance and Bands of Hope, the latter a juvenile society of similar purpose. The Woman's Christian Temperance Union entered

Texas in 1882, and besides its educational campaign for prohibition it obtained a reformatory for boys and a state orphans' home. Although Texas had enacted a local option law in 1876, enemies of liquor insisted on statewide prohibition. The Grange, the Greenback party, and the Alliance in turn joined the prohibition movement, though the churches and temperance organizations kept the issue alive.

Finally the legislature acceded to the pressure by submitting a prohibition amendment in 1887, the first blow in a running fight that would set neighbor against neighbor in Texas for the next thirty years. Every public person had to take a stand. Among the leaders were both United States Senators, John H. Reagan and Sam Bell Maxey, along with a rising young man named Joseph Weldon Bailey. Attorney General Hogg and Congressman Roger Q. Mills opposed Prohibition, and their view prevailed by nearly two to one in the election which followed. The Texas Brewers' Association fought successfully against submission of another amendment until 1911, when once again the prohibitionists lost, this time narrowly, 237,393 to 231,096. When Governor James E. Ferguson was impeached in 1917 on charges indicating that he had received illegal favors from the brewers, the prohibitionists took heart. Using the charge that liquor interests were buying a Texas governor and patriotically pointing out that beer and liquor reduced the war potential of the United States during World War I, they put through a law in the spring of 1918 forbidding the sale of liquor within ten miles of any place where troops were quartered and followed that up with a law closing all saloons, beginning in the summer of 1918. Then the federal government took over, and on January 16, 1920, the Eighteenth Amendment to the federal constitution made Prohibition a national policy. Texas ratified the Eighteenth Amendment and on May 24, 1919, in a sort of *ex post facto* action, adopted a Prohibition amendment to the state constitution by a three-to-two margin. It was as regularly violated in Texas as in Brooklyn and Brookline.

For the first time since the days of Sam Houston in the United States Senate, Texans began to make their presence felt nationally. For nearly twenty years Roger Q. Mills served in Congress, rising to chairmanship of the Committee on Ways and Means. He was a losing candidate for the speakership in the Fifty-Second Congress. In 1888 he wrote the Mills Bill, an attempt at tariff reform in a period when the United States Senate favored ever higher protection for American industry. The bill passed the House, bogged down in the Senate, and became a Democratic Party cause in the election of 1888 with reform going down to defeat along with Grover Cleveland in that somewhat lackluster year. Mills later became a United States Senator.

Even better known and more powerful was John H. Reagan. Restored to political respectability, and elected to Congress again in 1875, he had been re-elected almost automatically until named to the Senate in 1887. He had been chairman of the House Committee on Commerce for ten years, and in the Senate he obtained membership on the equivalent committee. Always an advocate of open government, he pushed for and helped write the Interstate Commerce Act of 1887, which marks not only the beginning of federal regulation of railroads but also the regulation of business in general. Both the United States and Texas were beginning to assert the power of the people over the growing concentration of power in business and industry.

The next decade in Texas could very well be called the Hogg decade. Earthy but not profane, this native son knew his people, how to criticize them, and how to move them. He permitted no one in Texas to remain indifferent. In a Victorian age he would strip off his coat in the hot Texas sun, loosen his suspenders, and take on "the interests" which in his view were discriminating against the common man, especially the farmer. Possessed of a wide vocabulary, he utilized it with precision; he could talk at the level of any audience without sounding uncomfortable or talking down. Hogg also had a feeling for the bold stroke that Theodore Roosevelt could have admired. When, for instance, the Southern Pacific Railroad dropped off 700 marchers in Coxey's army in the West Texas desert in 1894, Hogg delivered to that potent corporation an ultimatum to get those men across Texas so they could exercise their right of protest in Washington in such unmistakable tones that the railroad backed down. Not many governors since, if any, would have stuck their necks out in such a cause with so much courage and conviction. The railroads and insurance companies would have liked to trim him down, but the people got in the way.

The Texas Constitution of 1876 provided for railroad regulation, and from time to time various legislatures even showed a disposition to keep railroad practices within bounds. But until Hogg came along as attorney general, attempts at enforcement were weak. He compelled one railroad that had quit operating to resume service. He forced dissolution of the Texas Traffic Association, which operated a pool of nine railroads with headquarters outside the state. This pool controlled all Texas lines except one, set their rates, and prescribed levels of service, not always in the public interest. In general, he diminished out-of-state control of Texas railroads and brought their offices home.

As attorney general Hogg worked steadily to establish a railroad commission and made his desire a cornerstone of his campaign for governor. Since some responsible people doubted the constitutionality of such a commission, Hogg persuaded the legislature to submit an enabling amendment to the voters. Particularly he pointed out inequitable freight rates, which persisted into the 1950s, so that northern manufacturers could receive Texas and southern resources at cheaper rates than they could be laid down in neighboring towns within a state. The most frequent example given in Texas was that lumber from East Texas forests could be shipped to Nebraska more cheaply than to Dallas 150 miles distant.

When the voters adopted the amendment, the legislature acted by establishing a commission with power to fix rates and fares. Gradually its power was enlarged, including the right to control issuance of stocks and bonds for railroads. Originally the governor named the three commissioners, but since 1894 the commission has been elected. The importance of this commission in Texas is indicated by the fact that John H. Reagan resigned his certain seat in the United States Senate to accept the chairmanship at a lower salary, even though he was in his seventies. The commission proved immediately effective, reducing freight rates, thereby increasing milling and manufacturing within the state and in two years saving a million dollars on shipment of cotton. When the railroads contended that the commission's rates were confiscatory, courts sided with the state.

In the gubernatorial election of 1892 the Railroad Commission and Hogg's regulatory inspirations remained the issue. Opposing Hogg was George Clark of Waco, a railroad attorney, who earlier had branded the commission as "wrong in principle, undemocratic and un-Republican." Although many Republicans broke ranks to support Clark and the conservative Democrats, Hogg won re-election easily.

In general the Railroad Commission proved an effective regulator for railroads. When, later, Texas fields began to bloom with oil derricks, the commission enlarged its supervision over transportation to include not only pipeline administration but also the burgeoning petroleum industry in general. Many of its procedures proved effective and in the public interest, and Texas turned up in the surprising role of being the first state to legislate worthwhile conservation of petroleum resources. However, in the name of conservation the Railroad Commission has frequently used its authority to maintain high prices for petroleum products. And as conservatives in the state have become increasingly effective, voters have reflected that conservative leadership and have elected commissioners who see regulatory issues through the lens of major petroleum corporations. People-minded political leaders, of whom the numbers grow proportionately smaller each decade, criticize today's commission as being in the pocket of the petroleum industry. Unfortunately their charges have considerable validity.

Hogg was likewise a strong supporter of antitrust legislation. As attorney general he pushed through a Texas antitrust law in 1889, just four weeks after the first such state law had been passed in Kansas. Unlike the Sherman Antitrust Law passed at the federal level in 1890, so frequently turned against labor unions, the Texas law specifically exempted labor and farm organizations. The law had teeth and the state used them until gradually in the twentieth century the state's business interests defanged it.

As governor, Hogg pushed through an alien land law prohibiting foreigners from owning land in Texas. This act flew in the face of the giant combines, particularly from England and Scotland, which were developing ranching in West Texas. When the state supreme court declared it unconstitutional, a second law was passed in 1893 prohibiting establishment of corporations for the special purpose of dealing in land. Those corporations already in existence were given fifteen years to phase out. Other corporations already holding lands not necessary to their business were likewise given fifteen years to dispose of their excess holdings. But no one paid much attention to this law, and out-of-state and foreign corporations hold considerable bodies of Texas land today which lie idle against the day they might prove useful or precious to some purchaser.

When in 1892 Grover Cleveland returned to the presidency after an absence of one term, not all Texas Democrats cheered. Although Cleveland represented an island of reform in a sea of big-business Republicans, he was no progressive. As a result Texas drew closer to the Populist cause. The state was crisscrossed by stump speakers, including James H. (Cyclone) Davis, a Chatauqua regular who doubled as president of the Texas Press Association. Many of these stump speakers were Protestant evangelical preachers, who mixed religious conviction with desire for political change. After all, nowhere do the Scriptures sanctify railroads.

To head off the rising tide of populism the Democrats borrowed a leaf from the Republican black book and through corrupt tactics began controlling the growing Mexican vote in South Texas. The Populists retaliated by going after the Negro vote, using influential men both white and black ('' 'fluence men'') to obtain it. Although vote-buying through petty bribe is wrong in itself, a greater wrong occurred because the Democrats in response refused to permit Negroes to vote in their primaries for generations. In 1896 the Populists thought they might pull off a winner in their candidate for governor, a forty-seven-year-old former Arkansan named Jerome C. Kearby, a Democrat who had wandered to the Greenback Party, the Union Labor Party, and the Anti-Monopoly Party before turning Populist. With Republican assistance Kearby polled 238,692 votes against 298,692 for Charles A. Culberson ("chippy-chasing Charley," his enemies called him). The fact that the national Democrats under William Jennings Bryan had stolen the platform of the national Populists undoubtedly blunted Kearby's quest for votes. Except in the gubernatorial race, the Populists had reached their zenith two years before, when they held 22 of 128 seats in the lower house of the state legislature and elected two state senators as well as a small host of county and precinct officers.

But good times were coming. Both the major parties were beginning to pick up pieces of Populist dissent, particularly the Democrats who under Bryan's leadership gave more effective representation to Populist needs than could the Populists themselves. Besides, Culberson, a former Alabamian who had shown Hogg sympathies as the latter's attorney general, turned in a reasonably reform administration himself and the average Texas voter could feel that the state remained in good hands. In Culberson's administration Attorney General M. M. Crane brought suit under the antitrust law against Waters-Pierce Oil Company. Since Standard Oil Company held a large share of Waters-Pierce, Culberson was taking on the giant of them all; the case became nationally famous and one of the most important in Texas judicial history. When Texas won the suit, Waters-Pierce was ordered to close out its affairs in Texas and leave. The company president, Henry Clay Pierce, appealed to Congressman Joseph Weldon Bailey. Following Bailey's advice, Pierce reorganized his company presumably to mesh with Texas laws and in 1900 renewed business activities in the state. Waters-Pierce might have gotten away with the re-entrance if the State of Missouri had not also brought suit against the corporation, revealing that Standard Oil still held 3,000 shares of stock at the time of its readmission to Texas.

In 1906, following an investigation, then Attorney General Robert V. Davidson filed suit to cancel the right of Waters-Pierce to conduct business in Texas. Davidson asked $5,000,000 in penalties. Inferentially the suit became a contest between the State of Texas and Bailey, now a United States senator whose star was rising rapidly. The forty-three-year-old

Bailey was accused of accepting a retaining fee of $100,000 as company counsel as well as having unethical relationships with Standard Oil and with the John H. Kirby lumber interests. Although Bailey had the qualifications to become a national force and was later exonerated by a state legislative joint committee, the accusation terminated his effectiveness. After continuing as senator long enough to make his point of innocence, Bailey resigned on January 8, 1913. Once he came back to run for governor but was defeated. The charges against Bailey were as sensational and as profoundly felt in Texas as the later charges against Shoeless Joe Jackson, the hitting wonder of the Chicago White Sox at the time of the so-called "Black Sox" scandal in 1919. That same apocryphal story about the kid running alongside Shoeless Joe, awash in tears, crying, "Say it ain't so, Joe," was told for years on Bailey. Certainly his political demise broke a lot of hearts, probably including his own. He even debated Davidson publicly about the propriety of a public official's accepting fees for counseling a corporation in a case in which the public had an interest, but enough people remained unconvinced to prevent his wholesale reinstatement in the heart of the voters.

When the verdict came in, the court ruled Waters-Pierce guilty of violating the Texas antitrust laws insofar as it was owned in part by Standard Oil Company, contrary to a re-entry affidavit made by its officers in 1900. In other words, the corporation's officers had lied to the state. Because of the lie Texas cancelled Waters-Pierce's permit to do business and fined the company $1,623,000. Naturally Waters-Pierce appealed, only to have the judgment sustained in the supreme court of Texas and in the Supreme Court of the United States. On April 24, 1909, interest plus fines brought a payment of $1,808,483.30. A few months later the properties of the company were sold at auction by its receiver. The fine, the largest ever assessed in Texas, was one of the largest in United States history to that time. Only when Judge Kenesaw Mountain Landis assessed Standard Oil a $29,000,000 fine several years later did Texans quit bragging about their own severity.

Behind the Texas sentiment that made the Waters-Pierce suit

practicable stood James Stephen Hogg, almost as powerful out
of office as in. In 1903 at the Hancock Opera House in Austin
he concluded one speech with an appeal to Texas pride that had
endured: "Let us have Texas, the Empire State, governed by
the people; not Texas, the truck-patch, ruled by corporate lob-
byists." In 1905 he summarized his political views in a paragraph that sounds remarkably current seventy years later.

> I should like to see: Rotation in office permanently established;
> nepotism forbidden; equality of taxation a fact; organized lobbying
> at Austin suppressed; the free-pass system honestly, effectively
> abolished; oil pipe lines placed under the commission's control;
> insolvent corporations put out of business; all bonds and stocks of
> every class of transportation limited by law; corporate control of
> Texas made impossible; and public records disclose every official
> act and be open to all, to the end that everyone in Texas shall know
> that, in Texas, public office is the center of public conscience, and
> that no graft, no crime, no public wrong, shall ever stain or corrupt
> our State.[1]

Ironically Hogg stands at the apex of the Texas executive system. Probably every governor since has been introduced by
some master of ceremonies as "the greatest governor of Texas
since Jim Hogg." Naturally each man has accepted the identification as consummate praise, though no intervening governor
has yet qualified to take Hogg's place. Yet each of them (with
the possible exception of New-Dealish James V. Allred) would
have felt a severe distaste for Hogg as a politician had he been
that governor's contemporary or if Hogg were alive now. A
later governor might have dismissed Hogg as a dangerous radical and in his private and even public moments have wondered
whether Hogg wasn't a tool of the Communists. Hogg was
indeed the last people's governor of Texas, perhaps the only
one.

The Hogg tradition has continued in Texas. In a moment of
less than usual perception the Board of Regents of the Univer-

---

1. *Addresses and State Papers of James Stephens Hogg,* edited by Robert C. Cotner
(Austin: University of Texas Press, 1951), p. 532.

sity of Texas once secretly named as that institution's president Pat M. Neff, a former governor, unequalled debater, and generally all-around fine man who did not understand the quest for intellectual excellence. Hearing of it, one of Hogg's sons beat such a drumfire of protest throughout the state that the appointment was withdrawn before it was ever announced, and most of the state never even knew the post had been offered. Hogg's only daughter, Miss Ima Hogg—known throughout the state simply as Miss Ima (no other identification required)—reigned into her mid-nineties as securely and with as much considered grace as though she were the queen of the state. When several years ago the Establishment of Texas decided to hold a fundraising for one of Miss Ima's favorite charities with a high-priced black-tie dinner in her honor, the affair was oversubscribed by Texas conservatives, who largely came out of affection and appreciation for the grand lady. Miss Ima, whose only concession to age was a cane, hobbled to the rostrum and startled nearly everyone there by beginning her speech with, "I am delighted to see that you're all here . . . and that you're all Democrats!"

James Stephen Hogg would have been as proud of her as she was of him.

Lest any reader get the idea that Texas was totally concerned with agrarian discontent and cows and politics and James Stephen Hogg during this latter nineteenth century, let us take note of one other, unnoticed development in Texas during this era. In the late 1870s and into the 1880s a little black boy, second son of an ex-slave laborer, was being taught musical discipline by a German teacher in the northeast Texas border town of Texarkana. The probabilities that away off in Texarkana, population (1880) 1833, a German music teacher would be teaching "one-two-three-four" fundamentals to a black boy who would become world famous are meager. But the boy went on to a Methodist black college called George Smith, played in medicine shows and vaudeville, published his first song in Temple, Texas, and wound up playing for the Maple Leaf Club in Sedalia, Missouri, where his tribute to his employer, "The Maple Leaf Rag," brought him temporary wealth and enduring fame.

He went ahead to write many another song and an opera and then disappeared from public view, as forgotten as when he was playing on the streets of Texarkana.

Then in the 1970s the world rediscovered Scott Joplin and learned that he was the king of ragtime, a music combining the scale, key, and harmony of the white culture with the polyrhythmic drive which the blacks brought from Africa. In other words, Joplin played and composed in "ragged time," the juxtaposition of a syncopated treble against a steady bass. In 1911 Irving Berlin would commercialize ragtime with his own "Alexander's Ragtime Band," marking the descent of raggy music and the rise of a newer American music form known as "jass," often corrupted into a stylized popular music that has been more commercial than original.

In all of this seemingly static period in the history of Texas then, a black tad is skipping around in a red-dust town that is hardly more than a border village, undoubtedly humming incipient tunes that enter his head from nowhere. This sort of unseen development is what lends hope to Texas and elsewhere that in less inspired moments, something unseen and unsuspected may be going on. Joplin would write a rag-tango called "Solace" about 1909, and solace is what his memory gives us, even though in typical American fashion the American performing entertainer seems bent on overplaying Joplin until his music becomes hackneyed. The contribution of this anonymous lad outlives all other contemporary Texans and his eventual arena was—is—larger than even James Stephen Hogg's.

14

Sometimes Progressive,
Sometimes Timid

*T*HE first part of the twentieth century has been designated variously as the Progressive Era and the Good Years. Texas fit the trend, sometimes trying to move ahead with the needs of the time, at other times waiting out the world.

In politics it raised Colonel Edward M. House, a former Houstonian of independent means who as a kingmaker liked to sponsor progressive candidates. House made his national move after William Jennings Bryan visited Austin and talked to him about Woodrow Wilson, then governor of New Jersey. House went to New York and had Wilson come in from Trenton; politically it was a case of love at first sight for both men. When Wilson became President of the United States in the election of 1912 on a minority vote, House moved to Washington as a sort of benign Rasputin in Wilson's court.

The result was that Texas and the South moved to Washington to a degree not to be repeated until Lyndon B. Johnson became president a half-century later. Albert Sidney Burleson, a congressman for eight terms, served as postmaster general throughout Wilson's presidency. For secretary of agriculture, Wilson turned to Texas academia, naming David Franklin Houston, a former president of the Agricultural and Mechanical College of Texas and later of the University of Texas. At the

157

time of appointment Houston was chancellor of Washington University, which removed his immediate Texas taint. A good college administrator, Houston reorganized the Department of Agriculture and aided American agriculture by helping sponsor several significant laws. In the last year of the Wilson administration he served as secretary of the treasury, as well as chairman of the Federal Reserve Board and the Federal Farm Loan Board.

Thomas Watt Gregory of Austin, who had served as special counsel for Texas in prosecuting the Waters-Pierce case, had been a House-selected delegate to the Democratic national convention in 1912 and had helped devise the strategy which brought Wilson the nomination. Wilson first named Gregory as special assistant to the Department of Justice to bring suit against the New York, New Haven, and Hartford Railroad in an antitrust suit. In 1914 Wilson appointed Gregory attorney general; Gregory created the War Emergency Division of the Department of Justice, enlarged the Bureau of Investigation, and continued to prosecute antitrust violations. When Charles Evans Hughes retired as chief justice in 1916, Wilson offered the post to Gregory, who declined.

Texas had enjoyed the Spanish-American War as much as the remainder of the nation, possibly even more. Theodore Roosevelt resigned as assistant secretary of the navy to come to San Antonio to put together his famed Rough Riders. San Antonio went wild socially as lads from eastern finishing schools, some with their valets, came to San Antonio when the word went out that Roosevelt was looking for men who could ride. Every mother with a frying-size daughter held a party and spent the family bank account in the hope of landing a prize. Another group of men who also could ride, $30-a-month, unlettered cowpokes from the unfinishing schools of the Texas Panhandle and New Mexico Territory, likewise were recruited by Roosevelt, but not by the mothers of San Antonio's beauties.

Kissing the Texas boys goodbye as they left for Cuba became the big entertainment, particularly since most of them returned before the girls had time to form new liaisons. The fact that the war was ineptly run and that these men, chosen because they could ride hell-for-leather, could not take their horses to Cuba was a bitter disappointment, but to a nation short on heroes, these lads who charged up San Juan Hill on foot proved reasonably legitimate.

Through its participation in the Spanish-American War, Texas really rejoined the Union. The principal reason, an emotional one, for the change was that General Joe Wheeler, who as a twenty-six-year-old brigadier had fought with distinction at Shiloh and elsewhere, carved a new reputation for himself as a general of cavalry in the Spanish war.

If the United States was good enough for Fighting Joe Wheeler, it was good enough for Texas. Altogether Texas sent about 10,000 men into military service, claiming Colonel Leonard Wood and Theodore Roosevelt as two of its own heroes.

Later that summer, as the first weekend of September 1900 approached, the United States Weather Bureau warned that a tropical cyclone was moving westward in the Gulf of Mexico. On September 7 the surf became dark and menacing, too angry for late-season bathers. On the next morning the hurricane struck with full fury. By 4 o'clock that afternoon all of Galveston, a city of 38,000, was under one to five feet of water, and an hour later the Weather Bureau wind gauge registered a velocity of ninety-six miles an hour. In an era without radio, Galveston, "the hand of Texas extended in greeting," was completely isolated from the outside world, cut off as if it were set adrift.

In effect it was adrift. Three hours later the wind had reached 120 miles per hour, shifted from east to southeast, and was pushing a tidal wave fourteen feet high across a stilt-built city barely above sea level. The storm drifted across two-thirds of Texas, and in Weatherford 300 miles to the northwest the afternoon turned so dark that the chickens went to roost at 4 o'clock.

After midnight, when the winds slackened in Galveston, the people crawled out from under the debris to assay what had happened. Immediately they could tell that half the city had been destroyed. When daybreak came and they began to seek friends, they learned that possibly 6,000 persons had been killed, 2,600 structures devastated, and every building damaged at least by wind and salt water. Property loss was placed at $25,000,000. It was the greatest natural disaster in American history.

On a thickly settled, low, flat island, with the jumble of the hurricane plus snakes and crabs, no way existed to bury 6,000 people. Galvestonians loaded the corpses on barges, towed them out to sea and dumped them. In a short time most of the bodies had washed back upon the shore, bloated and smelly. The town fathers used idlers and blacks to round up the dead and to build a funeral pyre. Many of the workers, particularly blacks, did not want to touch the dead bodies. A Catholic monsignor, as pragmatic as his church, ordered out all the remaining spirituous liquors, especially rum, and soon had all his necessary workers happily drunk enough that they lost their fear of working with human carcasses. The result was a gigantic cremation such as no other American city has ever known.

Out of the disaster emerged Galveston's contribution to American political science. In charge of one of the prime cities of Texas, comparatively more important then than now, the city fathers resolved to re-form the city government—none too good to start with and paralyzed by the magnitude of their clean-up and resurrection problems.

Thus the business element in Galveston, in existence since 1882 as the Deep Water Committee, decided that the mayor-alderman political machine could not cope and would have to go. They were in the van of a progressive movement led by businessmen throughout the nation to clean up "the shame of the cities." In Galveston they organized the first lasting commission form of city government, enunciated in the new Galveston charter of 1901, under which its members became heads of the various city departments. The new government promptly built a seventeen-foot seawall to head off a repetition of the disaster. When Galveston was hit by a second strong hurricane in 1915, the ten-mile-long seawall held out the Gulf's waters and Galveston underwent nothing more than a stormy weekend.

The commission form of city government worked so well in Galveston that in 1905 Houston obtained legislative approval to revise its own government under a commission charter. Des

Moines, Iowa, switched in 1907, the first northern city to try the plan. Five more Texas cities immediately followed Houston, others joined over the years, and by 1950 approximately 200 cities in Texas alone followed the commission form. The general idea was adopted by cities throughout the United States until the plan began to reveal its own weaknesses. It stalled about 1920, when progressive city elements began to favor the city-manager plan, and even Galveston abandoned the commission plan as the 1960s began.

Financially the government of Texas tried to provide services through a general property tax, so that real estate paid a lion's share of the tax burden. Not until ownership and use of the automobile became widespread and the petroleum industry began to develop fully did Texas transfer the burden of taxation to natural resources and to production and exchange of goods. Between 1899 and 1919 the value of manufactures in Texas increased almost 700 percent, but this figure remained negligible because it started from such a small base. Twenty years ahead of the federal government Texas tried a system of insurance on bank deposits, making such a plan compulsory in 1909. At first the experiment worked well, but too many bank failures in the early 1920s caused the system to shake and Texas repealed it in 1927.

In 1917 Texas created the Texas Highway Commission, at first no better than any other state's but later pretty well removed from political influences and one of the better state highway agencies. Financed by a designated percentage of the state tax on gasoline, the highway department has consistently possessed sufficient money, so that Texas probably has as good a reticulation of highways as any state in the Union. The marvel remains the number of smooth, narrow, ribbon-roads that go from no town to no place.

The practice of Texas politics displayed about as much cynical fraud as that of the other southern states and the big-city machines of the North. Political parties ran their affairs about as they pleased, which meant that the Democrats excluded blacks. Corporations consistently bought power and planted candidates who would serve their interest. Frequently conventions were

held with scant notice, or held under conditions or at places that
made it nearly impossible for voters to attend. Voting procedures were such that the ballot was often in no way secret. In
1902 Texas pushed through a poll-tax law, which provided a
system of sorts for voter registration. And in 1907 primaries replaced conventions as a means of nominating candidates. By
1918 any candidate not receiving a majority of votes in a primary had to run against the second-place candidate in a runoff.

Texas found restoration of Negro voting rights a difficult
task. In 1923 the legislature enacted a "white primary law" to
exclude Negroes from Democratic primaries. The Supreme
Court of the United States threw out this act. Thereupon the
legislature conferred upon political parties the power to exclude
black voters. The Supreme Court said that this law was unconstitutional also. The Democratic Party, operating more or less as
a private club, excluded blacks from its primaries while recog-
nizing their right to vote in national elections. In a state primarily Democratic, denying a person's right to vote in a Democratic primary just about disfranchised him. When in 1944
Texans with relatively little grumbling opened their primaries to
Negro voters, the world failed to cave in. By and large blacks
began to vote without incident or white protest, although the
numbers remained comparatively insignificant until the middle
1960s.

Now and then racial antipathy has stoked the fires of tension
in Texas as elsewhere, causing ugly incidents in which the state
takes no pride. What was riot and what was diversion is sometimes unclear, especially in the earlier days, when people lived
farther apart and could relieve their frustrations by beating a
pony or chasing a mule-eared jackrabbit. But riots identifiable
as riots began to occur altogether too frequently following the
Civil War. Between July and December 1870, for instance,
Governor Davis's state police made 124 arrests for rioting. Racial discord caused riots in 1871 and again in 1872, but each
time the state police put down the trouble without much loss and
with no punishment. In 1877 the Salt War, centered in El Paso,
brought out a mob of five hundred, mostly Mexican nationals,
to protest private claims on territory that they considered public

domain. Five men were killed, and property damage estimates ran as high as $31,000.

When a black trooper was killed in 1881, about fifty Negro troops at Fort Concho broke open an arms rack and invaded San Angelo, wounding one man and wrecking some property. There was not a whole lot to destroy. Twenty years later a mob rioted at Brenham for two days over employment of a black brakeman by a railway. In 1906 in Brownsville a race riot involving Negro soldiers occurred, with proportions large enough that a couple of books have been written on it in the past decade, while at the time President Theodore Roosevelt issued one of his more threatening pronunciamentos.

Probably the worst racial riot took place at Houston following several days of insults by its less enlightened citizenry and policemen directed at Negro troops stationed there in August 1917. By the time order had been restored, the soldiers had seized arms and ammunition from Camp Logan and had gone into town seeking specific white policemen as targets. Undoubtedly two of the police officers deserved severe disciplining, but as usual others were caught in the crossfire and confusion. Box score: seventeen dead, most of them white; a small host of wounded; serious threats of white retaliation; martial law for four days.

Two other riots deserve mention. The most tasteless one occurred at Sherman in 1930, when a black man allegedly assaulted a white woman. The mob formed, but before the Texas Rangers could arrive to disperse it, the group had burned the courthouse where the Negro was held, and had lynched and mutilated the prisoner.

The other riot occurred less than a decade ago—in May 1967—when some police thought that every black, every student, and every antiwar demonstrator must be a dope-crazed Communist tool. At Texas Southern University in Houston, after some sporadic shooting, police invaded a university dormitory, guns in sight. The frightened students allegedly shot back, though the evidence is vague and fragmentary. One policeman was killed, and two black students and two policemen were wounded. Undoubtedly racial tension was a factor. Compared with earlier and later riots, vigilante justice, and lynching, the Texas riots weren't even good warm-ups. But they remain nonetheless as ugly blotches on the Texas record.

With less resistance Texas felt its way toward a program of public welfare for the unfortunate. It established a state hospital for epileptics in Abilene in 1904, a hospital for tuberculars, a training school for delinquent girls, hospitals for the mentally ill in Wichita Falls and at Rusk, and another for retarded children at Austin. The state banned child labor where machinery was used, outlawed compulsory trading at company stores, established a Bureau of Labor Statistics, set up factory safety laws, regulated the hours of women workers, and limited state workers to an eight-hour day. Under Governor Oscar B. Colquitt, who had risen from a tenant farmer, Texas pushed through a workmen's-compensation act before World War I.

The legislature passed a suspended-sentence law, which permitted a convicted person to avoid prison by future exemplary conduct, and an indeterminate-sentence law, which provided that the length of imprisonment should be determined by the convicted person's conduct. Both of these acts were hailed by the handful of professional criminologists throughout the nation. The state also terminated its contract-lease system under which convict labor was sold to private employers. Thenceforward convicts could work for the state only. These laws resulted from a widespread scandal unearthed first by newspapers in 1908–1909 and then uncovered more thoroughly by a legislative joint investigating committee. The combined findings revealed that convicts had been shot or whipped to death for trivial offenses, given unreasonable duties, fed and clothed inadequately, and housed in some instances without sanitation. The prison system was placed under the direction of three commissioners, while the attorney general, state treasurer, and comptroller were to name a prison auditor. Stripes were abolished, sanitation and medical service improved, and each convict was paid 10 cents a day for his labors.

The state continued its antitrust action, its biggest case being the already noted one against the Waters-Pierce Oil Company. Students of antitrust policies hold that the Texas policy was con-

siderably more severe than that of the United States, even with
the old trust-buster Theodore Roosevelt in office for seven
years. Texas brought 119 prosecutions against trusts up to 1915,
settling 84 by compromise. Of these, 74 carried money penal-
ties totaling $3,324,766. At the federal level the Department of
Justice brought 187 prosecutions, collected fines in only 33
cases, and received $548,881. In some corporate board rooms
the directors looked on Texas as a no-man's land in which to do
business, but in reform circles Texas was hailed. Both groups
have long since changed their opinions.

For years the statewide elections each biennium featured the
various candidates aligning on one side or the other with the
Prohibition issue. But then in 1914 along came a man of the
people, from a bank no less, named James E. Ferguson, who
vowed to lay the Prohibition issue to rest by ignoring it. He
would not take either side. In his opinion Texas had other press-
ing needs. Ferguson and his wife, Miriam A., would be the
biggest names in Texas state politics for the next quarter of a
century. And Farmer Jim, as he was known, would become
something of a national figure.

Although Ferguson ran as a businessman's candidate, he
made his principal appeal to tenant farmers, who for generations
had been suffering. Tenancy had increased from 37 percent of
all operating farms in 1880 to 52.6 percent in 1910. Not only
did the degree of tenancy increase, but the lot of the tenants
themselves deteriorated both comparably and actually. Tradi-
tionally the landlord took a rental of one-fourth of the cotton
and one-third of most other crops, but Texas was not a traditional state. Not only did Texas landlords take the prescribed
percentages, but they often demanded a money bonus.

Ferguson promised that if elected he would fix the one-fourth,
one-third formula by law. To prove his sincerity, he opened his
campaign for governor in 1914 at the tenant community of
Blum. Of the 155 speeches which he delivered before the primary, only ten were made in recognized towns and cities. He
won with little difficulty. He ran a constructive administration
and was easily re-elected in 1916. Almost any governor's or
president's popularity declines during his second administration,

but Ferguson's descent was, in the cliché of the times, Texas-sized. His popularity disappeared.

Ferguson was defeated by a university, which might happen in England or on the European continent but surely not in the United States of America. He started his feud with the University of Texas when he tried to dictate to acting president William J. Battle how the university's appropriation law should be interpreted. Battle, a wealthy man with the stubbornness and other matching attributes of a mule, told the governor he would make his own interpretations. When in the next year the regents of the university named a president without clearing it with Ferguson, the governor demanded that President Robert E. Vinson and several other faculty members be fired. The regents refused.

In June 1917, with the legislature adjourned, the governor vetoed the university's appropriation, outraging its huge claque of ex-students. Two regents, Major George W. Littlefield and George W. Brackenridge, offered independently of each other to underwrite the entire university budget until the governor returned to his senses. In Brackenridge's case, such an underwriting would have cleaned him out. But the fight was joined, with these two men showing a rare sense of public service. In the midst of it the fire was taken out of the fight temporarily when the attorney general declared Ferguson's veto void on a technicality.

Meanwhile, as if Ferguson didn't have enough of a battle on his hands, the House of Representatives Investigating Committee charged that the governor had been somewhat less than ethical in some of his business relationships. At first the legislature dropped the charges, but after the state's ire rose over his high-handed treatment toward the University, demand for reopening the case and for Ferguson's possible impeachment grew. Although he had no constitutional authority to do so, the Speaker of the House called a special session of the legislature. Seeing that the legislature was going to convene regardless, Ferguson helped the Speaker by issuing his own call.

Convened, the House impeached the governor on twenty-one articles. The Senate convicted him on ten of them on September

24, 1917. Charges included that Ferguson had appropriated certain state funds to his own use, that he had committed certain irregularities in depositing public funds in the Temple State Bank, of which he was a stockholder, and that he had received from unknown sources $156,500 for his campaign in 1916. Later investigation revealed that Ferguson had borrowed most of this sum from brewery interests of the state and that he had never repaid the amount. Ferguson was both removed from office and barred from holding office again in Texas. He was succeeded by Lieutenant Governor William P. Hobby.

Meanwhile Texas settled up, moving steadily northward and westward. But what happened to the nation as it moved westward failed to happen in Texas. When gold was discovered in California, the process of settlement leapfrogged across the Great Plains to the Pacific Coast, leaving a vast tract to be pinched in and filled up later. But Texas had only one area that settled ahead of the natural movement, that being El Paso in the far west corner on the border of Mexico. In an area whose density ran virtually zero per square mile, El Paso had a population of 10,000 in 1890 and just under 40,000 in 1910.

As West Texas settled, the disposition of Texas public domain became a matter of continuing controversy attended by scandal and undoubtedly fraud. Even though the state tried to tighten its land laws, the feeling continued that the state made more sales than it had settlers. Most of the land went into the hands of ranchers—not at all surprising, since that was what land was suited for at that period.

Throughout the history of western settlement legislators at both state and federal levels have tried to make laws to fit the farmers whom they knew and represented, but the laws for farmers didn't fit the land. While obviating the law is reprehensible under any conditions, laws made without understanding of needs or processes invite violation, and local enforcement becomes impossible. Thus Texas ranchers might be considered lawless, but they would consider themselves simply practical.

Finally in 1895 West Texans received a law which reflected their needs instead of the preconceptions of men who farmed in the piney woods and in the black waxy. A man could buy a sec-

tion of land in West Texas at $2 an acre for agricultural pur-
poses and three additional sections for grazing at $1 per acre,
which translates as 2,560 acres for $3,200. The state offered
liberal credit—one-fortieth down, and the remainder to be carried for forty years at 3 percent interest. The act gave former
purchasers a break. If they had forfeited their lands for non-
payment of interest, they were now given preference for ninety
days to repurchase under the new law. This meant that the state
invited previous purchasers under less liberal laws to forfeit, so
that they could then repurchase under more generous terms.
Commissioners' courts, as was their right, classified most of the
land as grazing land. Probably the public school funds of Texas
lost between eight and twelve million dollars by this change, but
the reclassification permitted Texas to be settled much more
quickly and fully. The school's loss became the poor man's
gain. Any less generous law would undoubtedly have resulted in
poor people remaining poor as they settled on uselessly small
tracts in a semiarid land.

By 1901 one person could purchase four sections of land regardless of whether it was agricultural or grazing. As land became available, ranchers and farmers contended at county court-
houses for right to purchase. Fights naturally resulted in some
chicanery, as in Howard County, where cowboys built a chute
to the window of the county clerk's office, beat off farmers,
lived in the chute for 60 days, and when the time for filing arrived slid through the window. After 1905 sealed bids had to be
submitted, eliminating such head-to-head contests.

Under competitive bidding, land brought as high as $22 an
acre. In two years Texans bought six and one-third million acres
of school land. The public school fund received nearly
$72,000,000 for its lands, and the state retained mineral rights
on more than 7,000,000 acres.

As in the remainder of the nation the railroads played a val-
iant if somewhat selfish role as colonizers. They spread advertising material all over the East, ran exhibition trains, established demonstration farms, and gave special rates to
immigrants. Once on the land, the newcomers further advertised
and persuaded by sending home enthusiastic reports, despite the

handicaps of the region, just as in Minnesota, Nebraska, and elsewhere men wrote extravagant reports back to Bohemia and Norway rather than relate their miseries, which they hoped were transitory.

As the plains of West Texas filled up, both farmers and ranchers discovered that crops could grow in the area. Some of the ranchers, particularly those with British backgrounds, refused to believe that the land was unsuited for a plow. Consequently they raised sorghum as a feed as early as 1880 and in 1886 began to raise kaffir corn, which had proved successful on the Kansas prairie. Milo maize supplanted kaffir corn, so that by the 1890s Texas ranchers had an excellent substitute for corn. Johnson grass was introduced and did well, even to the point of becoming the bane of a farmer's existence with its proliferation. Again the farmer replaced it with Sudan grass, which has remained popular. These crops were utilized, of course, for feed. Wheat was grown as well; its greatest year was 1910, when 117,040,000 bushels were raised. Average value of the crop has run consistently more than $100,000,000, an important part of the Texas economy.

Cotton did not move west until the mid-twentieth century. According to folklore, the first farmer on Texas's South Plains who planted cotton was forced by cowboys to plow it up. Not only did the ranchers feel that the plains were not suited for cotton, but they felt that its development would change West Texas from a white man's country to one dotted with blacks. Although tradition places racism with its ordinary connotations in the eastern portion of Texas, as late as the 1930s a number of West Texas towns still had signs just beyond their city limits sign saying in effect, "Negro: Don't let the sun set on you in this town." As machinery took over, the historic association of cotton with the black diminished, and cotton came to West Texas without the accompanying black man.

The last great land boom in Texas, for once not attributable to discovery of petroleum deposits, occurred in the Lower Rio Grande Valley and to a great extent was stimulated by the speculator-developer. This area, the cradle of the Texas cattle industry, was considered a brush desert, but water for irrigation was found to lie in quantity fairly close to the land surface. After the St. Louis, Brownsville, and Mexico Railroad built into the area in 1904, the need to produce intensified. The land, which reminds one of the citrus country of California—desert till irrigated—was looked on as a potential winter garden for vegetables and fruits, below the Texas frost line except in extreme years. In 1914 men discovered that by budding grapefruit and oranges into the native stock, the grower could produce a tree especially adapted to the Rio Grande soil and climate.

Speculators saw the potentialities and scoured areas like Minnesota and Iowa, inducing farmers to come to Texas with promises of mild winters and bonanza profits. In chugged the usual special trains, while speculators talked up the scrub land as if it were Eden. Theirs was a gull job from start to finish, with a happier ending than even the most optimistic anticipated. Although developers poured out bagsful of money transporting guests without charge, land sales on a single excursion sometimes totaled more than a million dollars. Many a gullible purchaser was made more ill when he had to show his wife where their life savings had been sunk, but the land did yield to hard work and water. And the developers, con men or not, had been selective—they had sold only to reasonably wealthy people and had pegged prices at a level which the poor could not afford.

Gradually the Rio Grande Valley zoomed as a producer of vegetables and fruits. It has also proved important for cotton, now its chief crop. Texas ranks behind only California and Florida in acreage, production, and value of fresh-market vegetables, and the valley is responsible for a considerable portion of the more than $100,000,000 worth of such produce sold annually by Texas.

Considered overall, Texas land may not be quite so fertile as lands in some other states, for with 13.2 percent of harvested acreage in the United States, Texas provides only 8.1 percent of production, and 7.3 percent of total value of fresh vegetables. Meanwhile the number of farms reporting vegetables for sale dropped 28 percent in the five years between 1959 and 1964, while acreage dropped 9 percent. The future of Texas vegetable growing is not likely to follow a consistent upward curve. Hay, forage, and silage crops consume ten times as much acreage as vegetables, although their crop value totals about the same.

Texas succumbed to the national wave of patriotism that marked its participation in the "war to end all wars," and its spirit carried over right into the 1920s. As late as 1923 Texas passed a law requiring that the Constitution of the United States and the constitution of Texas be taught in all public schools and that all teachers be citizens of the United States. During World War I Texas made it punishable by fine and imprisonment to criticize the United States government, its flag, its officers, or its uniform; to question the wisdom of being in the war; to have books in libraries which pictured Germany in a favorable light; to permit naturalized foreign-born persons to vote; or to teach German in the public schools (this in a state whose center core was heavily Teutonic). Regular roundups of suspected draft dodgers were held, and men of the right age were hustled to recruiting stations long before the service planned to call them in the draft. Men with German names were told publicly how much money they had in the bank and threatened with having their shops closed or destroyed if they did not contribute specified percentages.

With the exception of the study of foreign languages, all classes had to be conducted in English, a rule aimed at the Germans but continued against chicano youth in the decades ahead. Schools had to devote at least ten minutes each day to teaching patriotism. On the other hand, Texas provided partial suffrage for women ahead of the federal government, permitting women to vote in its primaries in 1918. A patriotic woman voter was superior to a treason-inclined hyphenated-American male voter any day, even though his liberty-seeking family might have come to Texas three-quarters of a century before.

Although Governor Hobby might challenge the legislature in 1919 to deal with the problems of a new age, and his successor, Governor Pat M. Neff, pious to the extreme, might warn of the uncertainties of the financial world, Texas would pay little attention to either the promise of Hobby or the warning of Neff. Hobby was right, of course. Texas shared the synthetic prosperity of the 1920s, turned ever more urban, opened up new oil fields with almost ho-hum regularity, discovered the Wall Street securities market, built a superb highway system, and almost as casually founded and built new colleges, each of them a potential university.

The farmer missed this upsurge, so that every politician from public weigher to governor included a plank in his platform for "farm-to-market roads." The farmer felt isolated, except for his rural free delivery, his semiweekly farm journal, and his catalogs from Sears and "Monkey" Ward's. The new era looked just like the old era to him, as he lagged relatively farther behind his town cousin.

The one-room, one-teacher school was disappearing as school consolidation came into vogue. By 1930 school trustees had effected 1,530 consolidations. On the higher education scene the Agricultural and Mechanical College of Texas was separated from its bitter rival, the University of Texas. Both schools became physically rich while remaining poor in spirit when the Santa Rita well, named for the Saint of the Impossible, opened up a new field on the public land given to the two schools, with the income now divided two-thirds to the University of Texas and one-third to A&M. By 1976 the University of Texas endowment ran second only to Harvard, somewhere in the neighborhood of $1,000,000,000, enabling its regents to build a magnificent and sometimes extravagant plant and lifting the school out of the class of its sister state universities in nearby states. Also in the 1920s the state normal schools were made teachers' colleges en route to their eventual status as universities, and Texas Technological College was established at Lubbock.

Mostly the issues faced by the state were local, with some national overtones. A strike of longshoremen at Galveston in March 1920 caused the Texas legislature to pass an open-port law authorizing the governor to assume special police jurisdiction over any region where persons interfered with the transportation of goods. When in July 1922 railway shopmen struck in seventeen communities in North Texas, Governor Neff maintained a police force for a period. In 1926 the federal court ruled that the enabling law violated both state and federal constitutions.

The citizenry became tremendously exercised over the use or nonuse of pardons. From January 1915 to September 1917 Governor Ferguson granted 1,774 pardons and 479 conditional pardons; his successor, Governor Hobby, granted 1,319 pardons and 199 conditional pardons during his administration; and from January 1925 to September 1926 Governor Miriam A. Ferguson granted 384 pardons and 777 conditional pardons. In between, Governor Pat M. Neff granted only 92 pardons and 107 conditional pardons and did his utmost to get the legislature to repeal the suspended-sentence law. Neff disbanded the Board of Pardons and made his own investigation in person to determine who should receive clemency. If he had but known, the most flagrant use of pardons would come in a later administration of Governor Miriam A. Ferguson, who displayed a motherly solicitude admirable for its humanity and questionable in its effectiveness for rehabilitation and keeping down crime. In one period she granted 2,000 acts of executive clemency within twenty months, prompting formation of an investigating committee which found that her husband had recommended most of the pardons, some of them before the recipients even reached prison.

As a post-World War I crime wave hit Texas, the Ku Klux Klan spoke out for strong measures to preserve law and order, which ranged it on the side of the angels insofar as many Texans were concerned. In 1922 the Klan was making itself felt in Texas politics, electing local officers and pushing towards state control. Its progress was part of the phenomenon that spread beyond the South into such industrial areas as Detroit.

Since he was prohibited only from running for state office, James E. Ferguson was eligible to run for the U.S. Senate. Although he had defected from the Democrats to run for president in 1920 on the American Party ticket (no relationship to a later American Party but simply one of his own creation), the pragmatic Ferguson returned to the Democratic fold to run on that party's ticket in 1922. His strongest opponent in the primary was Earle B. Mayfield, member of the Texas Railroad Commission and an admitted Klansman. Ferguson bitterly opposed the Ku Klux Klan. When Mayfield won the primary, many disturbed Democrats joined with the Republicans behind George E. B. Peddy, a Houston attorney and the Republican candidate. Again Mayfield won. The question became one of how much farther the Klan could spread its influence.

By 1924 the Klan was an even hotter issue, particularly with Miriam A.—or Ma—Ferguson, as she was now called, being a contestant for governor against Judge Felix D. Robertson of Dallas, who had Klan support. By now Texans were tiring of the Klan's excesses, of hooded men at midnight serving as extraterritorial and extralegal police, judge, and court. How Mrs. Ferguson would have fared without the Klan as an issue cannot be determined, because this gubernatorial fight took on the overtones of a fight for and against the Klan. If she had done nothing else for Texas politics, she would deserve the voters' lasting thanks for having so severely blunted the power of the Klan that it never came back. In the primary she defeated Judge Robertson by nearly 100,000 votes. This time conservative Democrats voted with the Republicans to support George C. Butte, dean of the University of Texas Law School and a later attorney general, acting governor of Puerto Rico, and governor general of the Philippine Islands. Although Butte was a considerably superior gubernatorial candidate to most of those offered by the Republicans during these years, he lost by about the same margin as Robertson.

Texas had thus elected its only woman governor and the second in the United States. Throughout her term of office Mrs. Ferguson's enemies subjected her to continual derision and abuse, undoubtedly out of hate for Farmer Jim, presumably the puppeteer pulling her strings, and from leftover antifeminist sentiment. Through no fault of her own, except that she cherished her husband, hers was not a particularly good administration, marked more by humane concerns than by any progressive legislation. She was a quiet woman, petite and shy, who would have been better suited to being a banker's wife as she started out to be than on display in the maelstrom of politics.

Besides her excessive pardon record, Governor Ferguson also was a target for charges of scandal in the Highway Commission, which at that time had retained its political flavor. When she ran for re-election in 1926 against the aggressive and attractive young attorney general, Dan Moody, she lost rather decisively.

In 1930, with the Depression beginning, Mrs. Ferguson tried again and was defeated. When the Depression deepened in 1932, she was again elected. She ran one more time, in 1940; but by then Pa Ferguson's sun had set, and both Ma and Pa Ferguson lost in a campaign in which they seemed more weary than anything else.

While governor, Moody ran a moderately successful administration which led to his easy re-election. He reformed the prison system, tried to reform the judicial and executive branches of the government with mixed success, and pushed through an act which provided for a state auditor and efficiency expert.

Probably the biggest political event of the 1920s was Texas's defection from the Democratic ranks when Democrats nominated Governor Alfred E. Smith, a Catholic, an antiprohibitionist, and the first completely urban candidate from cradle to sidewalk to grave. All the doubts raised in other states about a Catholic being president were echoed in Texas. School children fought each other over accusations that one child's father was going to jump the Democratic party or was going to vote for the Pope's candidate. Charges that Smith would put a saloon next door to every church were widespread, and many Protestants were certain that his election would mean the end of moral and religious life as they had known it.

Smith had received the nomination in Texas, supported by a big number of Texas Democrats. The convention had been placed in Houston at the request of Jesse H. Jones, a rising power in Texas and on the national scene because of the financial interests he controlled. Uptown a few blocks from the convention hall where it appeared that Smith might be nominated, the First Baptist Church sponsored a wild scene of Protestants who held an around-the-clock prayer meeting and singing to keep such an awful thing from happening. Neither Houston nor any other place had air conditioning in those days, the time was midsummer, and the delegates came in from the cool hills of Vermont and the Cascades of Washington State after several days' train ride, detraining in Houston into heat that could be cut and layered with a putty knife.

Physically and spiritually the Houston convention was a debacle. Even if the body could have stood it, the Baptists up the street gave no surcease. Many a delegate left Houston determined never to return, and despite air-conditioned Astrodomes and six tons of air conditioning for every man, woman, and child, no national political convention has been held there since. The fact that Hoover carried Texas by 26,000 votes, the first Republican to receive an electoral vote in the state, didn't help their feelings. The chief issues in the campaign of 1928 were "the three P's—Prosperity, Prohibition, and Prejudice." Texas voted for all three, partially redeeming itself by electing Tom Connally over the Klansman incumbent, Senator Mayfield.

Otherwise, Texas just lived along, somehow surviving from one year to the next. The Chautauqua came through the small towns, giving "folks" a taste of the "Quartet" from *Rigoletto* and a powerful address delivered for the ninety-seventh time by some name politician or orator. Frequently you could hear a revivalist—Mordecai Ham, Gypsy Smith, or some Texas minister. The best crowd-pleaser and the most controversial was the fundamentalist pastor of the First Baptist Church in Fort Worth, J. Frank Norris, who had his church burned (or burned it, according to his enemies), shot a man who assaulted him (or shot him in cold blood), filled his congregation with a choir of hundreds, and hired first an Englishman and then the director of the Fort Worth Symphony as his choir director, as the 5,000 people in his congregation every Sunday morning and night clapped after every number and Norris entertained them with attacks on Fort Worth business leaders who opposed him and hapless Baptist ministers whom he branded "modernists"—an allegation which undoubtedly surprised most of them.

Other profound issues perturbed communities, such as whether the local Episcopalian minister was sneaking off to Fort Worth to attend Sunday shows; the attempt of the local theater owner to introduce Sunday picture shows beginning at 10 o'clock at night, after all church-going folk should have been out of church; the problem of bootleggers; and who was settin' up illicitly with whom.

In short, Texas was just like the remainder of the nation, drifting toward an economic abyss without any particular rudder, mildly dissatisfied about some things but generally taking life on its terms. The Texas League was more important than the major leagues in baseball, and in football the Southwest Conference was just beginning to be recognized in the North and East as playing a better game than cowlot pool. The politicians were adequate, just adequate, both in Texas and in Washington. Blacks had no problems, because God had made them a happy people; while the chicanos were dismissed because you could never tell what one was thinking and hardly ever knew one personally. Life was as insular for Texans as it was for Vermonters, who undoubtedly thought that all Texans rode horses and forted up against Indians every night. Texans were undergoing their last years of innocence, admixed with outbreaks of deviltry here and there, content to go to debates in which the Rev. Mr. Norris debated the touring agnostic evangelist, Clarence Darrow, returning home more confirmed in their beliefs than ever. Small towns tolerated atheists teaching in the third grade, and little white boys played with little black boys because no one was aware that one race was disadvantaged and the other received all the breaks.

While the more knowledgeable and more sophisticated got arrested for making speeches against the Ku Klux Klan on the street corners in Houston or wrote from New York and Paris about the frustration and narrowness of life on the main streets of Minnesota and by implication Texas, most Texans simply followed the current, unaware that they were frustrated or pinched in.

15

Intimations of Maturity

URING the 1930s Texas finally arrived as a national factor—or threat, depending on one's side of the aisle—in national politics. This surge onto the national political scene had little to do with the Depression; Texas politicians had at last come of age and begun to assert influence and leadership commensurate with Texas's growing population.

When Franklin D. Roosevelt chose him as running mate in 1932, John Nance Garner of Uvalde was already Speaker of the House of Representatives. It could be questioned whether Garner brought any affirmative qualities to either the speakership or the vice-presidency except a certain wiliness and the ability to keep his mouth shut; in the latter office, he became a focal point for conservative Democratic opposition to Roosevelt and served only two terms.

Other Texans held positions of leadership and influence in Congress as well. Morris Sheppard, who had been a congressman until elected to fill the unexpired Senate term of Joseph Weldon Bailey, helped write the Volstead Act and introduced the law which became the Eighteenth Amendment. Even after Repeal he continued to favor another Prohibition amendment. In 1932 he became chairman of the Military Affairs Committee, and at his death in office in 1941 he was recognized as one of Congress's elder statesmen.

Two Texans took the lead in fighting Roosevelt's court-pack-ing plan: Tom Connally in the Senate and Hatton W. Sumners in the House. In addition to Sumners, who was chairman of the House Judiciary Committee, five other Texans chaired major House committees in 1933: James P. Buchanan, Appropriations (the first Texan in the twentieth century to hold that assignment); Marvin Jones, Agriculture; Fritz G. Lanham, Public Buildings and Grounds; Joseph J. Mansfield, Rivers and Harbors; and Sam Rayburn—who would wield his greatest power twenty years later—Interstate and Foreign Commerce.

Jesse Jones held several significant posts through the Depression: director of the Reconstruction Finance Corporation from 1933 to 1939, administrator of the Federal Loan Agency for a year, then secretary of commerce—in which position he was in continual disagreement with Vice-President Henry A. Wallace.

Such clout in Washington could not, of course, protect Texas from being hurt by international depression. Although petroleum production helped the pain, farmers had been suffering since 1921. Consequently Texas embraced Roosevelt like a savior, but support drifted into placid acceptance and then downright dislike among more conservative Democrats. At the gubernatorial level, the voters threw out businessman Ross Sterling of Houston after just one term and resumed their old love affair with the Fergusons. Farmer Jim always knew how to talk to his constituents, and in 1932 he told the voters that he would "be on hand picking up chips and bringing in water for mama." The voters bought the bargain opportunity, though by only a few hundred votes out of nearly a million cast.

Under Governor Ferguson the state set up an employment relief agency, ratified the Twenty-First Amendment, repealed the state prohibition law; and the governor attempted to establish a state sales tax of 3 percent. The legislature resisted that regressive idea, as it continued to do for twenty-four years more. In 1933, an estimated 267,000 persons—breadwinners for a million—were unemployed, and 7.1 percent of the population (well under the national average of 10.3 percent) were on relief. Despite federal aid in 1933–1934 of $50,000,000, there were still 246,849 relief cases in Texas. The state began old-age assistance in 1936 and a program for handicapped children and public health services in 1937 (though neither of the latter was funded until 1941), and Texas shared in the various work-relief programs of the federal government which not only provided an income for citizens in the programs but also resulted in physical improvements to the state. Texas needed World War II for recovery as much as did the remainder of the nation.

Meanwhile Texas began to discover both amateur and professional sports, and the country began to notice Texas sports figures. Texans won the National Collegiate Athletic Association tennis singles championships in 1927 (Wilmer Allison) and 1929 (Berkeley Bell); Jim Reese, in 1925, was the first NCAA individual track champion from the Southwest Conference. Texas Christian University, which gave Slingin' Sammy Baugh to the pros, was the first Southwest team to finish first in national football rankings but by no means the last.

The Texas League, a Class A and AA professional baseball league, had its heyday in the 1920s and 1930s. Such eventual major-league stars as Dizzy Dean, Carl Hubbell, Joe Medwick, and Hank Greenberg followed early stars like Tris Speaker and Rogers Hornsby. The Texas League, now spread beyond the borders of the state, still exists; but frequent moves of players and teams have diminished interest in Texas as in other states.

Out of Depression-era Port Arthur and Beaumont came probably the greatest woman athlete of the first half of the twentieth century, Mildred (Babe) Didriksen Zaharias. In 1932, at eighteen, she singlehandedly won the national Amateur Athletic Union's women's track and field meet, defeating the runner-up (a whole team of Illinois girls) 30–22. She won two gold medals in the 1932 Olympics, and after turning to professional golf she won every major women's title from 1940 to 1950. Once more singlehandedly, she lifted women's professional golf from an almost quaint to a competitive sport, and she became an enormously popular figure.

Texas found another means of entertainment when an apostate Kansas flour salesman, W. Lee (Pappy) O'Daniel, who doubled as a radio entertainer to sell his flour, complained about the quality of leadership in Texas. He told his listeners, largely farm folk, that if they agreed with his views they should send in a postcard. When he had received 54,999 postcards he announced for governor in 1938—dumping two more logical candidates, Attorney General William McCraw and Railroad Commissioner Ernest O. Thompson, in the primary. At first opponents and newspapers treated his candidacy as a joke and attributed the huge crowds he drew to people's interest in hearing a band for free. But O'Daniel always passed the hat, and soon it became evident that everyone who dropped in a dime was likely to vote for O'Daniel at the ballot box. Against twelve other candidates he won a majority of primary votes for the first time since the Texas primary law had been adopted.

Among other promises O'Daniel agreed to give a pension to every old person, which didn't hurt with the sixty-five-year-old vote. After his election, financial reality caused him to pare down his proposal to needy persons and set the upper limit at $30 a month. He made good on little else and fought the legislature with unaccustomed venom. Although his popularity dropped somewhat, he still was re-elected for a second term in 1940. With his showman tactics and his western band, he didn't improve the Texas political image.

When Morris Sheppard died in 1941, O'Daniel was rescued from an increasingly untenable position as governor. O'Daniel announced for and won Sheppard's Senate seat, defeating by only 1,100 votes thirty-two-year-old Congressman Lyndon B. Johnson, making his first statewide race as an "old friend" of President Roosevelt. When O'Daniel ran in the regular Senate election of 1942, he defeated former Governor Dan Moody and James V. Allred.

Once Texas recovered from the doldrums of the Depression, business activity rose steadily. Time, Inc. began to use paper from Texas lumber in the late 1930s, textile manufacturing showed an upsurge, and the petrochemical industry arose alongside the oil and gas industry. Southern and national and even international concerns (especially chemicals and metals) moved into Texas, attracted by climate, petroleum, and Gulf of Mexico availability. In particular, the aircraft industry expanded into Texas: North American Aviation at Grand Prairie; Consolidated Vultee (Convair, now General Dynamics) outside Fort Worth;

Chance-Vought at Grand Prairie; Bell Aircraft's helicopter division at Hurst. These moves had a political as well as economic impact, for they brought in people of attainment and education who didn't associate being Republican with being defeatist or social pariahs.

Meanwhile more oil fields continued to be discovered. In parts of West Texas one could drive one hundred and fifty miles without ever losing sight of oil derricks, and before conservation measures were established, one could almost drive the breadth of East Texas without lights because of the giant flares from waste gas burning in the oil fields. In 1928 Texas became the leading oil-producing state with an output of 257,320,000 barrels. The growth of production continued, until it reached a billion barrels in 1951.

One day in September 1930 Columbus Marion (Dad) Joiner, a wildcatter who had worked East Texas fields for years, brought in a well that splattered oil all over East Texas. The field turned out to be forty-two miles long and between four and eight miles wide, at least 200 square miles of territory whose every acre oozed oil. By 1953 the field had already produced three billion barrels of oil and in 1976 it is still pumping. East Texas, which had been threatening to become the Appalachia of the state, began to pave its roads, raise roses, buy Cadillacs, and build mansions and country clubs. Other fields continued to come in, and in the decade from 1946 to 1955 Texas produced more than nine billion barrels of crude oil—nearly equal to its production for the half-century preceding. For 1956 alone the value of oil produced was more than three billion dollars, making production of petroleum the greatest industry in the state.

Much of the wealth produced was new wealth, insofar as the individual was concerned. Families grubbing along on thin topsoil suddenly found themselves rich off royalties and leases, and the old sourdough of the petroleum industry, the wildcatter, came in out of the mud and ooze to get rich until he sank it all in the next series of dry holes. About one in five wells drilled were wildcats—exploratory wells, and of them 88 percent were dry. Independent producers, again often people of small means, made about 80 percent of the discoveries.

Undoubtedly the quick wealth of oil has produced an audacious effect on the Texas psyche. Affluent financiers from the State Street trust companies in Boston, accustomed to slow but inexorable accretion of wealth over the centuries, are taken aback when they run into the free-swinging confidence of the Houston entrepreneur. Nothing seems out of reach—that is, out of business reach—to many Texas businessmen. Wealth is not a commodity to conserve, and the Texas business leader disdains being a custodian to a bunch of money. Wealth is meant to be used in calculated risks, and if it's lost, so what? The once-wealthy entrepreneur who is broke knows he will rise again, and (uniquely) his acquaintances also think he will rise again and consequently don't turn their backs on him. He may own them next month.

The city of Houston provides a good example of this faith. Its leaders decided it should become a major port. But how do you become a major port fifty miles inland on sinuous Buffalo Bayou, little more than a rambling mud hole? So Houston began to push for a channel and in 1899 persuaded Congress to appropriate enough money to dig a channel of eighteen and one-half feet. This effort represented a start, but only a start. A Harris County Navigation District raised funds, obtained a federal appropriation, and spent about fourteen million dollars ($10,600,000 of it federal) to complete a channel thirty feet deep and fifty-five miles to the outer bar along the Texas coast. In 1935 work began to deepen the channel to thirty-six feet, and Houston became the second largest port in the nation. Either side of its channel is lighted by huge plants, and Houston may well be the most polluted city in the United States and its Houston Ship Channel the thickest seepage this side of the LaBrea tar pits. And as much as it brags about the Astrodome—first of the great indoor stadiums and the origin of Astroturf—Houston remains the largest city in the United States without zoning.

Dallas, which now fixes the same wary eye on Houston that it once used to stare balefully at Fort Worth, couldn't begin to match the Astrodome without seeming to establish a sort of civic "me-too-ism." Instead, Dallas took the unfamiliar step of joining hands with Fort Worth to build the Greater Dallas–Fort

Worth International Airport halfway between the two cities, the current record-holder of the title of world's largest airport, "larger than all of Manhattan Island." The purpose was to make the so-called metroplex of Dallas and Fort Worth an instant international depot and entrepôt for the world's traffic, with big jet engines taking off nonstop for everywhere from Stuttgart to Spitsbergen. The airport is a maze of roads and automatic devices which have given metroplex citizens enormous pride in outsize gadgetry, harried engineers because of intermittent breakdowns, and concerned men of the spirit because it seems the ultimate word in the depersonalization of life.

While Texans take inordinate pride in such achievements, they are sophisticated enough to realize that records are made to be broken, and that New Orleans and Buffalo will build larger and grander indoor sports arenas, while Paris and Tokyo, and maybe eventually Narvik and Archangel will build larger and more gorgeously gadgeted airports. But Texans will always feel proud that they showed the way, even though social critics may point out how much more beneficially the huge sums could have been utilized for cleaning up poverty pockets within their area.

On the other hand, San Antonio with its mixed population of Mexican pecan shellers, German flautists, and active and retired militarists has developed into a city with a certain *joie de vivre,* to use a French term for a Mexican town. Since 1930 the home of Randolph Field, which characterized itself as "the West Point of the air" until the Air Force Academy was established, and clustered by Kelly Field, Brooks Field, and Lackland, San Antonio took time to improve the open sewer which meandered through its town masquerading as the San Antonio River and built an in-town river walkway that even the most evangelically critical anti-Texan finds delightful. San Antonio possesses just enough of the Latin fiesta feeling that even its brewers and generals will drop their duties to come down to the river and have a ball.

During World War II Texas became the greatest training region for airmen anywhere in the United States and probably on earth. This was only natural for a state in which the Air Force had its origins before World War I. In 1910 an aviation section of the United States Army's Signal Corps was formed at Fort Sam Houston in San Antonio, consisting of eight enlisted men and Lieutenant Benjamin D. Foulois, who was given the Army's sole airplane, a Wright Pusher, and told to teach himself to fly. Later Foulois set up an aviation post with a six-plane squadron. On the entrance of the United States into World War I, Kelly Field became the nation's training camp for pilots and grew into one of the largest aviation training centers in the world. It has never closed, and until 1938 all army pilots were trained in Texas.

Airfields were also either rebuilt or created outside Houston, Austin, Wichita Falls, San Angelo, Lubbock, Midland, and San Marcos. The American Air Force Training Command was headquartered at Fort Worth and the Women in the United States Air Force at Sweetwater. In a little more than two years after January 1, 1942, more than 200,000 airmen were trained in Texas: about 45,000 pilots, more than 12,000 bombardiers, and about 12,000 navigators. Altogether the state had more than 50 airfields and stations. The Navy had air training installations at Corpus Christi, Beeville, and Kingsville.

Not surprisingly Texas ranks fourth among the states in enplaned passengers and in airmail and sixth in air cargo. Dallas, Houston, and San Antonio are the only three cities which carry international traffic. In such prime border towns as Laredo, the first city in the nation in number of international crossings, and El Paso, which with its Mexican sister city of Juárez has a million inhabitants, a passenger has to get off on the Texas side, take a taxi across the river to the Mexican side, and enplane from there.

Texas became a major military center in World War II. About one in every ten members of the armed services trained in the state. (With twenty-one prisoner-of-war centers, the Germans, Italians, and Japanese might also feel that they trained in Texas.) About 750,000 Texans joined the services—about 6 percent of all those serving in the several branches of the armed forces. By birth or long residence Texas claimed 155 army generals and 12 admirals, including two of the highest ranking— General of the Army Dwight D. Eisenhower, born in Denison, and Admiral of the Fleet Chester W. Nimitz of Fredericksburg. General Douglas MacArthur had been in and out of Texas so much that he was considered an ex officio native son by everyone except politicians. Audie Murphy, the most decorated hero of World War II, came from Farmersville. Twenty-nine other Texans received the Congressional Medal of Honor and six Texans received the Navy Medal of Honor, among them Commander Samuel D. Dealey, killed in action and Murphy's counterpart as the "most decorated man in the Navy." Altogether Texas surrendered 23,022 to the list of the war dead.

Naturally Texas could not come through World War II without its share of attention and hassling. For one thing, too many outsiders were stationed there, homesick and uprooted from familiar routine. On the day after Pearl Harbor, Lyndon B. Johnson took a leave from his House post to become the first congressman to go on active duty in the armed services as a lieutenant commander in the Naval Air Force. The Thirty-Sixth Division became the first division to enter Europe when it landed at Salerno and in 400 days of combat advanced through Italy, France, and Germany, and into Austria. Everywhere that Texans seemed to go in the armed services, they tended to make their presence known if not felt. Europeans spoke of the Thirty-Sixth Division as the Texas Army, and some Texan was always planting a Texas flag over a conquest on Luzon or Eniwetok or Anzio or Remagen. And on the home front Texas finally got its general revenue fund out of debt, which was hailed by Governor Coke Stevenson and his adherents as a triumph for gubernatorial fiscal responsibility but in reality reflected the fact that the federal government was picking up the tab for nearly everything.

Toward the close of the war the University of Texas made unseemly headlines again with the firing of its president, Homer Price Rainey, by an ultraconservative board of regents bent on silencing him. Instead of skulking off into the badlands, Rainey remained to run for governor against Beauford Jester and an easily forgotten group of other opponents. One of them insulted—and undoubtedly titillated—the voters of Texas by holding "For Men Only" campaign sessions during which he read lurid passages from books in the University of Texas Library with the intimation that Rainey must have either written or read and approved all of them. Texas chose Jester, a railroad commissioner and a middle-of-the-roader who had the support of the anti-Truman element of the party.

The main excitement of the otherwise placid Jester administration was an organized march on Austin by teachers intent on establishing a salary floor of $2,700. Although Jester sided with them, the legislature did not. In 1975, 35,000 teachers were still marching on Austin, this time asking for $10,000. Again, they were turned back by the legislature. The legislature did finally recognize that the Civil War era was ending by submitting a constitutional amendment, subsequently ratified by the voters, appropriating 5 cents of the Confederate Veterans' pension tax to a fund for constructing buildings for the fourteen state colleges.

The political event that attracted national attention was the race for the vacated Senate seat of W. Lee O'Daniel, who did not seek re-election in 1948. Congressman Lyndon B. Johnson, defeated by O'Daniel in 1941, ran against former Governor Stevenson, who looked even more like a stereotype of a Texan than Johnson, being tall, lean, meditative, and conservative. While others talked, he puffed on his pipe, breaking silence occasionally to point to the fact that he had made public money for the State of Texas while he was governor. The race attracted national attention because Johnson, although only thirty-nine years old, was already a national figure as a congressman and to the nation's press represented the post-war world against Stevenson's throwback tendencies. The race was won on the very last ballots by a figure popularly accepted as 87 votes. Actually the figure was closer to 150, but the "87-vote landslide' became an identifying catchword whenever Senator Johnson was later introduced, and he learned to use the figure with considerable relish and affection. Stevenson threw the contest into court, and only at the last minute did Johnson receive certification by Justice Hugo Black of the Supreme Court of the United States.

When on July 11, 1949, Governor Jester died of a heart attack, Lieutenant Governor Allan Shivers, only forty-one but in training for the post at least since his college days, succeeded him. With the possible exception of John Connally, Texas has had no other governor so powerful in the twentieth century. Both governors, operating twenty years apart, would have to be considered good governors for what they accomplished, but both can be faulted for having had the power to push Texas into the progressive forefront of the nation and failing to utilize that power to the utmost good. Each became increasingly careful as he continued in office, and inclined more toward business interests than toward the general welfare of the state. In short, they chose to run good administrations with orderliness and some progressivism when they had the clout to be truly "the greatest governor since James Stephen Hogg."

Shivers, who did not lack courage, called for additional taxes because he said the state needed additional expenditures. With the fractious legislature reasonably in his pocket, he pushed through relatively generous appropriations for state hospitals; a gathering tax on natural-gas pipelines which was later declared unconstitutional, enabling the natural-gas interests to avoid their equitable share of taxation; the first redistricting law in thirty years, which brought into the Texas legislature a somewhat more nearly fair representation; a safety inspection and driver responsibility law; a state building commission; modernization of the state prison system; reorganization of the state public school system through the so-called Gilmer-Aiken school laws; and a commission on higher education with supervisory powers over curricula and budgets of state-supported colleges and universities.

On the other hand Shivers's administration attained national attention by getting sidetracked on an anti-Truman and tidelands byroad. One reason that Texas was ready to dislike Truman was his veto of a law of Congress giving Texas title to her tidelands, believed to be rich in oil deposits. It was generally held that a state owned the land beneath the marginal sea, or tidelands, until Secretary of the Interior Harold Ickes challenged the claim in 1937. In August 1947, the Supreme Court of the United States held that the State of California lacked the right to exploit its tidelands because the federal government had "paramount right and power" over this domain. In 1950 the Supreme Court in a four-to-three decision decided against Texas. The oil men of Texas made the tidelands fight a hallmark for Texas patriotism, claiming that Truman by his veto and the Supreme Court by its decision were robbing the children of Texas of their natural heritage.

Texans, who like their issues simple, could see the justice of the tidelands fight by the state's leaders. Since education consumed ever more money and a portion of the lease and royalty rights was dedicated to support of the public schools, then taking away the tidelands was indeed tantamount to robbing one's grandchildren of the right to a first-class education. The royalties were still largely potential, for the tidelands were in the exploratory stage, but already nearly $10,000,000 in lease bonuses had been received. By mid-1974 the tidelands receipts totalled $230,766,851.15; obviously important money is concerned here. All petroleum industry payments to the permanent school fund through August 31, 1972, totalled $857,553,691, while the same industry's payments to the Permanent University Fund of Texas totalled $598,514,979. The petroleum industry deserves to be treated with some tenderness for its largesse and its potential. But the inevitable question arises, with that sort of income, why does Texas have such a comparatively poor school record and why isn't the University of Texas the best in the land? The answer has to go back to the state's governance and to its citizens who accept it.

Truman compounded the insult to Texas by vetoing a Tidelands Act not once but twice. In 1946 he vetoed an act which would have recognized the right of states with tidelands to lease such lands. Texas argued that even admitting the paramount right of the federal government to the tidelands did not pertain in Texas, because Texas had entered the Union by negotiation which gave it a right to its own public lands and to a marginal shore for three Spanish leagues (ten and a half miles) from the littoral. Of course, the fact that Texas probably abrogated any rights to the original contract by leaving the Union to join the Confederacy was not mentioned by Texans. Four months after he became president, Dwight Eisenhower won Texas's eternal gratitude by signing a quitclaim bill restoring the tidelands to state ownership within its historic limits. Four and a half years later Texas lost its three-league concession when Attorney General Herbert Brownell persuaded the United States Supreme Court to limit Texas and West Florida tidelands to three miles.

When the Democrats nominated Governor Adlai Stevenson of Illinois as their candidate for president in 1952, Shivers made a much-trumpeted trip to see where Stevenson stood on tidelands. When Stevenson sided with the federal view, Shivers returned to Texas with a nationally noted announcement that he could no longer support the Democratic candidate. The conservatives formed into a "Democrats for Eisenhower" group, while the liberals bolted for the millionth time or so. The Texas Republicans weren't much better off, for the conservatives supported Senator Robert A. Taft as their party's nominee for president, and Texas moderates, if any, supported General Eisenhower, who had been seriously considered as the Democratic candidate in 1948.

Since Eisenhower was nominated, was a native Texan, had married Mamie after a courtship in San Antonio, was not a Catholic, and did not have to declare himself on the wet-dry issue, conservative Democrats joined with the Republicans to carry Eisenhower to victory in Texas by more than 100,000 votes. But the Republicans, then a clubby group in Texas really interested only in national issues, did not field candidates for the local offices, and the state as usual elected Democrats (although some critics argued whether most were Democrats at heart or just in name only).

The election of 1952 brought to the fore the Texas counterpart of Henry Clay or William Jennings Bryan, Ralph W. Yarborough. Yarborough would be that loneliest of all Texas creatures, a liberal, if he weren't so everlastingly hard-working, vociferous, emotional, intellectual, and persistent in causes in which he believes. He ran against Shivers in 1952, lost badly; ran again in 1954 as Shivers campaigned for his third full term, and carried the governor into a runoff; and in the presidential year of 1956, when Shivers again refused to support Adlai Stevenson and Senator Price Daniel joined the governor, Yarborough ran against Daniel in a bitter campaign helped along by the fact that public Texas was once again rife with scandal. Daniel barely nosed out Yarborough. When Daniel's victory vacated his Senate seat, Yarborough ran for it and in a sweepstake race was elected. He would continue in office through two regularly elected terms, widely respected on the national scene but controversial in the extreme within Texas. Yarborough's single-minded focusing on issues was responsible for passage of the Cold War GI bill and for the establishment of the Padre Island National Seashore and the Big Thicket Biological Preserve, the latter two among Texas's chief treasures. In addition he was a standard bearer for the Great Society's social advances.

Two scandals occurred during the 1950s, one connected with insurance and the other with land. In 1907 the Robertson insurance law had required life insurance companies to invest in Texas securities at least 75 percent of the reserves set aside for insurance policies on the lives of Texas citizens, causing twenty-one insurance companies to withdraw from the state for its being "harsh and unreasonable." Seeing a steadily growing population and wealth, companies had drifted back in, others had been formed within the state, and by 1954 Texas had 1,875 insurance companies, two-thirds of them Texas-based. Of the 793 legal reserve life insurance companies in the nation in 1953, 215 were in Texas. Other than the Robertson law, insurance regulation was lax and tended to favor the wildcat company. Insurance company stock received no official supervision and was exempted under the terms of the Texas Securities Act.

So insurance companies were formed frequently, and failures occurred often enough that only investors and policyholders noticed them. In 1955 Lieutenant Governor Ben Ramsey, no firebrand reformer, reminded the legislature that eighty-six insurance companies had failed within the past decade, and that most of these failures were due to inadequate laws. The legislature responded by enacting twenty-two laws on the subject, strengthening the insurance code but still not making it sufficiently taut.

Failures continued almost unnoticed until United Services Trust and Guaranty Company (with 128,000 depositors and stockholders) and the ICT Corporation (a holding company controlling seventy-four insurance and finance companies in twenty-two states and Alaska) went under, taking along the life savings of many Texans. Governor Daniel received permission to name an entire new insurance commission, pushed through sixteen more insurance laws, and caused an audit of Texas insurance companies, after which more than a hundred companies were denied permits to continue in business. Investigation showed that nine of thirty-one members, or 29 percent, of the state senate had received legal fees or other income from United Services Trust and Guaranty alone.

While the insurance scandal was blowing in the Texas breeze, a new scandal erupted around the veterans land board, of which Shivers and Daniel had been ex officio members when Daniel was attorney general. The state had authorized a $100,000,000 program to purchase land for resale to veterans of World War II and had increased the fund by another $100,000,000 in 1956. When rumors of irregularities led to investigations, Bascom Giles, just elected to his ninth successive term as commissioner of the General Land Office and a man supposed to represent everything fine in public service, refused to qualify for his new term. In the stepped-up probe, more than 300 indictments were handed down, a continuing stream of good names were convicted in criminal charges, and Giles himself received a six-year sentence in the penitentiary—which proved a long-range benefit for the state, since with his vast administrative experience he reorganized internal procedures of the prison to its benefit during his sojourn there. Yarborough tried to fasten guilt on Shivers, Daniel, and later Attorney General John Ben Shepperd, but succeeded only in persuading Shepperd that he would be happier in private life.

By the end of the 1950s Sam Rayburn was running the national House of Representatives as its longest-term Speaker in history, Lyndon Johnson was proving the most dynamic Senate majority leader in United States history, and together they were leading the Republican Eisenhower administration down a reasonably moderate path. Most of the state was satisfied with itself, long on energetic friendliness, but a bit deficient in spiritual qualities.

16

Texas Now

$\mathcal{T}$HE 1960s catapulted Texas into the forefront of the nation's thinking. Political pundits conceded Lyndon B. Johnson a chance to be nominated as the Democratic candidate for president in case the party's national convention should get past one or two ballots without nominating Senator John F. Kennedy. When Kennedy won, Johnson caused more than a little static on the Texas political scene by joining the ticket, and a number of former supporters treated him for a while as a leper for having accepted the vice-presidential nomination on a ticket with a man whom they abominated. Many liberal Democrats were equally displeased; but when Johnson helped to hold the South in the Democratic Party and possibly made the difference in Kennedy's being elected, Johnson's support drew praise.

Also, 1960 was the year when Johnson's Senate term came up for renewal, and he somewhat naturally desired the best of both worlds—to be vice-president if the national electorate so decided, or to return as senator and presumably majority leader if Kennedy failed to get elected. So Johnson ran for both offices in Texas, which led to more intense opposition by anti-Johnson Democrats and by Republicans, who fielded a relatively unknown college political-science professor, John G. Tower of Wichita Falls, as their candidate. Tower turned out to be an unusually articulate candidate who can talk conservative sense without sputtering, a rare quality among Texas Republicans.

Johnson won both races, holding Texas in the Democratic camp for the national ticket and necessitating a special election for his vacated seat in the Senate. Since Tower received 900,000 votes in the senatorial election, he entered the special election with the bonus of having become known throughout the state through a respectable losing effort.

The special election brought out a field of seventy-one candidates, six of whom were serious and qualified, but the race evolved into a two-way fight between the interim senator, William Blakley, and Tower, both conservative.

If the cause had not been so serious, the race would have reached a new high in low comedy, for Tower and Blakley each made repeated claims that his opponent was Communist-tinged. Tower called Blakley a left-winger for the simple reason that he was a Democrat, and the Democrats were the party who had opposed Senator Joseph McCarthy and housed Walter Reuther and Hubert H. Humphrey. Blakley pointed out regularly that Tower had done graduate work at the London School of Economics and had undoubtedly been tainted by the leftist views of Professor Harold Laski.

Blakley, reputed to be worth some two hundred million dollars but a cowboy in his early adulthood, plastered the state with larger-than-life posters showing him in cowboy regalia—Dallas cowboy, not working cowboy. When Blakley's advertising proclaimed that he stood for the Constitution, J. Frank Dobie took large ads in the state's major newspapers to retort, "Who the hell *ain't* for the Constitution!" Tower's election made him the first Republican senator from Texas since Reconstruction. He is now serving his third term, in the upper half of Senate seniority and in the upper reaches of Republican councils.

The period saw the passing of Sam Rayburn, leaving a void in Texas and Democratic leadership which has since gone unfilled. Rayburn served from 1912 until his death in 1961, nearly a half-century. In 1937 he was named House majority leader, and three years later became Speaker of the House, in which position he served until his death except for two terms of Republican control. He was a decisive leader who knew how to compromise and how to control a meeting.

Lyndon Johnson had been a particular protégé of Rayburn's, although the Speaker had originally opposed Johnson's accepting the nomination for vice-president. But Texans would pick up the slack elsewhere, as with Congressman Wright Patman, chairman of Banking and Currency; George Mahon, chairman of Appropriations; Albert Thomas, who preceded Mahon as Appropriations chairman; Omar Burleson, chairman of House Administration; Olin E. Teague, chairman of Veterans Affairs; Robert Poage, chairman of Agriculture; and a team of younger comers like Jack Brooks, Jim Wright, Henry Gonzalez, and J. J. "Jake" Pickle.

Kennedy added to Texas prestige by naming a former Johnson administrative assistant, John Bowden Connally, as secretary of the navy. In 1962 Connally resigned this position to return to Texas to run successfully for governor, and Fred Korth, a banker-lawyer from Fort Worth, succeeded him as secretary of the navy. Meanwhile the liberal and moderate-conservative wing of the Texas Democrats personalized their fight in the persons of Senator Ralph Yarborough and Governor Connally.

With the election of 1964 on the horizon, President Kennedy decided to visit Texas to try to salve whatever wounds Yarborough and Connally had inflicted on each other. The trip was well advanced and was proceeding splendidly in Dallas when shots rang out, evidently from the Texas School Depository, killing President Kennedy and seriously wounding the governor. The fact that the assassination of a president took place in Lyndon Johnson's Texas backyard and that it occurred in a town already derided as politically Neanderthal loosed such a national outpouring of hate against Texas in general and Dallas in particular that a lynch spirit against Texas seemed to pervade the nation and undoubtedly handicapped Johnson in his years as president.

The explosive rise and subsequent steady decline of Lyndon Johnson's presidency are too well known to repeat here. Certainly Texans dotted the Johnson administration, because these were the people he knew best. Although many of the appointments were regularly denigrated, political scientists generally concede that Johnson ran the tightest administration in memory.

Ramsey Clark (whose Texas father, Tom Clark, had been named to the Supreme Court by President Truman) became almost a cultish attorney general, despite his being from Texas. Bill Moyers was another Johnson appointee who was admitted spiritually into circles of national admiration, and his handicaps were even greater than Clark's—he was not only a Texan but an ordained Baptist minister.

The victory of John Tower in 1961 had encouraged Republicans to put up local candidates in 1962, and the subsequent election sent eight Republican legislators to Austin and Ed Foreman of Odessa to Washington as a Republican congressman. Otherwise political life continued as always, with the Democrats in control and forever threatening to fall apart. Governor Connally joined Allan Shivers and Price Daniel in holding the governorship for three full elective terms. Connally worked diligently to push through educational reforms, maneuvered higher education so that the University of Texas would carry more political power, and raised salaries for schoolteachers through the age-old device of a sin tax, this time on cigarettes. By 1966 the complexion of representation began to change as a number of Negroes and Republicans were elected to Texas offices. In that year the legislature put out sixteen amendments to the Texas constitution, such a profusion that only the experts could grasp all of them. Obediently Texas voted for fifteen of the sixteen. Texas abolished the poll tax as a condition for voting and legalized annual registration of voters.

During the next legislature Texas redistricted congressional and legislative districts to comply with court orders, again raised salaries of teachers and state officials, and authorized a city sales tax. The federal government created Padre Island National Seashore, a lovely, lonely stretch of island beach outside Corpus Christi that runs for sixty miles almost without human interruption, and the Big Thicket National Biological Preserve, a unique region characterized by its fauna and flora, indicative of a biological and cultural crossroads.

Before President Kennedy was killed, he had designated Harris County southeast of Houston as the site for the United States Manned Spacecraft Center for space flights, particularly to the moon. The choosing of Texas for this NASA installation was credited or blamed on Vice-President Johnson, although probably Congressman Albert Thomas exerted even more influence on Kennedy than did his vice-president. The center is now known as the Lyndon B. Johnson Space Center.

President Kennedy also began and Johnson completed a settlement over a disputed area on the edge of El Paso and Juárez caused by the change in channel of the Rio Grande. The argument reached back a century and had seemed to be settled during President Taft's administration, but the United States had refused to accept the adjudication. Since the Rio Grande's alteration had favored Texas, the United States had showed no eagerness to settle, but the unsettled Chamizal issue rankled with the Mexicans. Its final disposition pleased both nations and Texans accepted it as long overdue, even though they lost some land in the process. The Department of the Interior has cooperated with the government of Mexico in erecting a suitable park to commemorate the peaceful if drawn-out settlement of an international border problem.

Governor Connally unnecessarily called down opprobrium on his head from labor unions, chicanos, and liberals when he refused to treat with Rio Grande Valley workers marching on Austin seeking a minimum-wage law. He met them about sixty miles south of Austin at New Braunfels, where like a kindly but fatherly *patrón* he turned them back. He was, of course, only delaying the inevitable, and under his successor, Preston Smith, Texas passed its first minimum-wage law during the 1970–1971 biennium.

Texas also moved up to date with passage of a constitutional amendment authorizing the legislature to legalize sale of liquor by the drink. Even many drys agreed that the privilege, if that's what it is, was overdue. For the first time in fifty-two years mixed drinks were sold legally in Texas bars. Loopholes had been found in previous laws permitting private clubs which could serve liquor, some of them so private that anyone could walk off the street, pay fifty cents, and become a member. Once the shock of buying a legal drink diminished, Texans noted little difference in drinking after the law had gone into effect, except for the disappearance of the brown paper sack in both posher and cheaper nightclubs.

Another scandal of historic proportions hit Texas in 1971 and 1972, this one centered on the distribution of bank stock among public officials. Speaker of the House Gus Mutscher, his aide, and a state representative were found guilty of conspiring to accept a bribe and given five-year probated sentences. Although Governor Preston Smith made a considerable profit on the sale of stock, his sin seems to have been more ethical than legal.

Texas worried a lot about the role of Lyndon Johnson when he returned to the state at the end of January 1969. Knowing his hyperactive metabolism, his opponents with near hysteria foresaw Johnson's hand in every activity of which they disapproved. He was going to be chancellor of the university, president of the university, own all the banks in the state, control all the land, run the state government, and on and on and on. When his Lyndon B. Johnson Library was dedicated in Austin in 1971, Washington depopulated to attend the dedication ceremonies, including President Richard Nixon and Vice-President Spiro Agnew. But Texas fears were considerably overblown.

The political love affair with women which began with Ma Ferguson has continued. The state came close to electing a woman liberal, Frances (Cissy) Fahrenthold, as governor in 1972, admiring her courage as she went about the state blithely committing political suicide almost everywhere she turned up. Houston sent Barbara Jordan to the state Senate, unaccustomed either to women or blacks, much less a combination in one body. At first Texas senators observed Miss Jordan warily, but they soon learned that usually she was the best prepared among them. So they showed their recognition for quality by electing her president *pro tempore* of the Senate and giving her customary ''Governor for a Day'' honors.

When Houston elected Miss Jordan to Congress as the first black House member from the South, she not only received national attention but performed so capably that many Texans, liberal and conservative alike, are making tentative predictions that she will be not only the first woman president but also the first black president of the United States. After the Judiciary Committee hearings regarding impeachment of President Nixon in the summer of 1974, one advertising executive in Houston, no liberal, took space on a number of large signboards dotted over Houston with the simple message: "Thank you, Barbara Jordan, for teaching me about the Constitution."

Despite his identification with the Democratic Party and Lyndon B. Johnson, John Connally returned to Washington as a regular adviser to President Richard M. Nixon and eventually as his secretary of the treasury. Many noted similarities between Connally and Johnson, both big men with restless energy and a ready recall and grasp of details. When in 1972 the Democrats chose George McGovern as their presidential standard bearer, Connally decided that his interest lay nearer the tenets of the Republican Party and moved over. Most Texans privately predicted that he would become another Wendell Willkie and stand in the line of succession when Nixon finished his administration. But events, both national and personal, got somewhat out of hand.

The polite resurgence of the Republican Party in Texas represents a heartening development in Texas politics. Democrats need their challenge. As indicated many chapters ago, Republicans in Texas suffered unfairly through identification with alleged carpetbag and black excesses following the Civil War, and whites fled the party. For a period Negroes provided the only glue.

In February 1868 Negroes voted in Texas for the first time, electing nine delegates to a constitutional convention. In 1869 two Negroes were elected to the state Senate and nine to the state House of Representatives. Gradually blacks moved into the power vacuum of the Republican Party. G. T. Ruby, a New York mulatto by way of Maine and Haiti, and Matthew Gaines, former slave and minister, influenced party policy in late Reconstruction days and provided most of the Republican votes. Although many black Republicans held local office, even counties with large Negro majorities never enjoyed a majority of black officials.

With Texas under the grip of the white establishment after 1874, five Negroes still were chosen as delegates to the constitutional convention of 1875 which wrote Texas's present organic law. Norris Wright Cuney, a native Texas black, was a delegate to the Republican national conventions from 1872 through 1896, one of the longer attendance records white or black, and served on the Republican national executive committee in 1891 and 1892. In reward for his exceptional services he was appointed inspector of customs at Galveston in 1872, chief inspector in 1881, and collector of customs in 1889. He also served as alderman for Galveston and as a water commissioner for that port city from 1887 to 1889.

As remarkable as Cuney was William Madison (Gooseneck Bill) McDonald, a native Texan son of a slave and a free woman and college educated. In 1892 McDonald, then twenty-six, was elected to the Republican Party's state executive committee. For thirty years he would remain a party power in company with Edward Howland Robinson Green, the somewhat bewitched son of Hetty Green, the "witch of Wall Street." The pair ran the Republican Party in Texas and were a growing force on the national scene until 1912, when the Bull Moose schism split the party. McDonald's star dimmed when he and Green supported General Leonard Wood for the G.O.P. nomination for president in 1920, only to see R. B. Creager of Brownsville move to the front by backing Warren G. Harding. Creager then ran the party for three decades, but under him it developed an exclusive club complexion that handicapped its growth in Texas.

Between 1890 and 1896 Republicans began to copy Democrats with their Lily-White Movement, an attempt to purge the party of its black majority. The conflict dated back to 1870, broke open in 1884 when Cuney seized control of the party's state convention, and became truly serious when blacks refused to seat delegates from white Republican clubs in 1890. In retaliation the whites urged an all-white primary, only to have their fangs drawn when the blacks nominated only whites for their 1890 ticket. Two years later white Republicans sent a completely white rival delegation to the Republican national convention and nominated Andrew Jackson Houston, Old Sam's son, for governor. Boycotted by the blacks, Houston received 0.3 percent of the vote.

Again in 1896 the party split, sending a "black and tan" as well as an all-white delegation to the national convention in St. Louis. The Lily-Whites were not seated. Later in the year the Lily-Whites adopted the strategy of joining what you can't beat, moved in on the black Republicans, utilized the institution of the poll tax and white primary to dominate and eliminate, and the black voice in the Republican Party began to grow silent. Since he had nowhere else to go, the black remained a political nothing until 1944, when the Texas case of Smith *v.* Allwright opened primaries to blacks. On his return as a citizen the Negro turned to the once-hated Democrats as the party holding the best hope for his improvement. Gooseneck McDonald, for instance, supported Al Smith and Franklin Roosevelt before rejoining the Republican fold for Thomas E. Dewey in 1944 and 1948.

Since 1960 Republicans have returned as a loyal opposition. While they don't dominate the state, they influence it—and once in a while they join with disaffected liberals to scare the daylights out of regular Democrats. Their threat represents a healthy political situation for the state, another signpost along its highway to maturity. In 1972 the Republicans nearly pulled an upset in the gubernatorial race, as their candidate Henry C. Grover, a personable former teacher of history, polled 1,534,000 votes to 1,633,000 for Democratic nominee Dolph Briscoe. Probably the only reason that Grover did not win is that old-line Republicans did not feel that he belonged to the club.

A separate force arising in Texas has been Raza Unida (United Race), an independent political party organized in 1970 to make the town of Crystal City a model for chicano self-determination. José Angel Gutiérrez and his wife, Luz, led the group from the start and by 1973 had organized in twenty-three states. The party endeavors to bring dignity and power to all disfranchised groups, whether chicano, black, women, the poor, or the voiceless Anglo.

Raza Unida hit the political ground at full stride when in

April 1970 its slate swept school-board elections in Crystal City (population 8,104). It followed up with victories in city-council elections in Crystal City, Carrizo Springs, and Cotulla. In each instance reforms instituted included bilingual-bicultural education at elementary levels; hiring of teachers, principals, and counselors of Mexican descent; free breakfast programs for elementary schools; housing projects; street improvements; summer recreation programs; and elimination of rules prohibiting speaking of Spanish on school grounds. Since 1972 the party has entered statewide contests, won nothing, but looked good as Ramsey Muñiz polled 214,118 votes for governor in his first attempt. Crystal City, where the chicanos had first won in 1963 with another organization but had been unable to sustain themselves, has been studied in California, Colorado, Illinois, Wisconsin, Arizona—anywhere that a local majority of disfranchised people wonder how to exercise majority rights currently denied. Crystal City may well become a generic name for takeovers by the politically underprivileged.

Texas has avoided that entrapment that often appears in other states—emotional entrancement with a family name. No Kennedys, no Roosevelts that crop up in succeeding political generations. Governor Jester's father was a lieutenant governor in the 1890s, while the incumbent lieutenant governor, William P. Hobby, is the son of the W. P. Hobby who succeeded Jim Ferguson as governor. But that was fifty years ago, and very few repeater voters are around to remember. Evidently Texans believe that public office should be passed around, or that political sagacity is not an inherited trait. Or perhaps the periodic fresh face loses too much of its bloom while in office, and no one wants to be reminded of it again.

Texas is in no way lacking cultural amenities and other aspects of the "good life": it has nearly 300 registered museums, three major symphonies and a small horde of lesser ones, lakes, mostly dammed but representing enormous acreage in expanse, regattas, 130 or so institutions of higher learning, and pleasant tree-lined neighborhoods.

On the negative side, Texas has yet to turn out a novelist or poet of certified international reputation, but that is no sign that it is not a well-adjusted state. Texas has produced any number of good entertainers—Mary Martin for musical comedy; Harvey Schmidt and Tom Jones as producers (their *The Fantastiks* apparently will run till the Second Coming); producers like Joshua Logan; movie directors like King Vidor; classical performers like Van Cliburn; an endless spate of popular performers (black, Teddy Wilson; white, Jack Teagarden; brown, Trini Lopez and Johnny Rodriguez); historians, Walter Prescott Webb; sociologists, C. Wright Mills; folklorists, John A. Lomax and J. Frank Dobie; composers, Scott Joplin; dancers, Alvin Ailey; short story writers, O. Henry and Katherine Anne Porter (who has rejected yet drawn upon her East Texas heritage);—an endless list that runs on and on and on. Fred Gipson's *Old Yeller* has all the appearance of a minor classic for adolescents, a latter-day *Huckleberry Finn* that rivals *The Fantastiks* in number of performances.

The University of Texas may be a cow-country college (albeit heavily financed by oil royalties), but its Humanities Research Collection provides a mecca for scholars all over the world, while Latin Americanists from Latin America find that they can work more satisfactorily in Texas's Latin American Collection than they can in any other library in the world including their own countries'. The Margo Jones Theatre in Dallas, Paul Baker's theaters in San Antonio and Dallas, and Nina Vance's Alley Theater in Houston produce innovative shows that Broadway lacks the courage and support to produce and that rank alongside what Tyrone Guthrie is producing in Minnesota. A San Antonian, Robert Tobin, virtually underwrites the experimental Santa Fe opera season each year and for San Antonio's HemisFair produced the only complete version of Verdi's *Don Carlo* in the history of the United States. And a Texan would drive a hundred miles for such performances.

On the popular side Texans pioneered in country and western swing, producing their own sort of folk music apart from an extension of Appalachia with Bob Wills and his Texas Playboys. Now musicians from throughout the nation are clustering around the hills of Austin and a raffish establishment called the Armadillo World Headquarters to found a counter-school to the

country commercialism of Nashville. Naturally some local musicians are involved, and their lyrics point toward a harsh Texas
sentiment that doesn't fit the more careful Nashville version.
Entertainment as culture? Certainly. But entertainment that has
sprung up, rather than having been transplanted from another
clime. Uncontrived.

Notably, when the Hermitage sent its art exhibit to the United
States, the Leningrad group chose Fort Worth's Kimball Museum as one of its three stops in the United States. The Amon
Carter Museum of Western Art in the same city spent half of
1973–1974 displaying its Remingtons and Russells behind the
Iron Curtain to a stampeding crowd. Some hold that western art
should be denigrated, but how much more parochial is Reming-
ton than Winslow Homer; or Porfirio Salinas and his bluebon-
nets; or José Cisneros and his conquistadores; or Tom Lea,
who can't be categorized as a western artist any more than his
The Brave Bulls can be called a Mexican book?

In the 1890s the little town of Waco had a fire-eating editor-
publisher named William Cowper Brann, whose *The Iconoclast*
de-hided all sorts of pseudo-religious cant and hypocrisy. At his
peak he had an international subscription of 96,000 in a town of
15,000. In a later day the *Texas Observer* shows just as much
courage as *The Iconoclast* and a lot more balance and liberality
of spirit as it takes apart the Texas Establishment. Run now by
two remarkable girls, Kaye Northcott and Molly Ivins, but
nursed for years by Ronnie Dugger and cigar-smoking Frankie
Randolph, a Houston banker's wife, the *Observer* uncovers
stories that more wealthy newspapers overlook, twits erring politicians, lambasts wrong-headed legislators, and generally turns
the state topsy-turvy. Probably it is read most carefully by its
detractors, who want to know what the opposition (whose paths
they seldom cross) is thinking.

Taken in an absolute sense, Texas's attitude toward race has
not been a cause for Texas pride. On the other hand, Texas observed *de jure* integration with a reasonably good attitude, and
followed the same deliberate *de facto* segregation path that practically everyone else trod. When the time came for Houston
schools to integrate, the city fathers asked Governor Daniel to

assist them with troops, not so much to open up white schools to blacks as to keep blacks away "to avoid trouble." Governor Daniel wisely told Houston that the school board had its orders and that keeping blacks out of Houston white schools was not part of the governor's prerogative. Houston integrated with relatively little incident. Seeing what had happened at Little Rock, Oxford, New Orleans, and Charlotte, for instance, where economic progress had stalled, the Dallas business establishment resolved that this slowdown of business activity would not happen to Dallas. For good business reasons, Dallas integrated schools without incident.

In the matter of union labor Texas can be faulted. Although the Screwman's Benevolent Association became an effective union in Galveston more than a century ago and Texas became accustomed to unions on railroads and on docks, by and large union development in Texas proceeded slowly. The political and social climate was not propitious. In particular, Texas remains a battleground for organization of agricultural workers by the United Farm Workers, especially in the Rio Grande Valley. With the third largest farm-worker population in the United States, Texas nationally ranks third in priority in organizing drives among migrant and seasonal farm workers. But the long, generally unguarded border with Mexico gives growers immediate access to a pliant strikebreaking force, and UFW leaders have been reluctant to go all out in trying to organize. Success looks more likely for the farm workers than it did in 1966, when they lost the strike, only to prove in a suit against the Rangers that violence and repression were practiced. Since then, Rangers and other law-enforcement officers handle the pickets with more care.

Where does all of this leave Texas? Mainly, striving. Its people get up in the morning, try to endure their jobs and their bosses, go home in the evening, perhaps by way of a *cantina,* enjoy their families or kick their children, worry about inflation, try to pay some of their bills, and hope that somehow the Lord will provide. Washington is a long way off, but not so far as it once was, while to many the state capital seems almost as far away.

Texas has turned into an urban state with an outside image
that is still rural. Yet Texas is more urban than most of the
remainder of the nation. Only New York, California, and Illinois have more citizens living in urban areas than does Texas:
80 percent of all Texans, according to the census of 1970, compared with 73.5 percent of the nation. And the movement to
town is accelerating. Only Houston oil men and Dallas bankers
are turning rural, as they irrigate and plant grass on rocky hill-
sides.

This transformation has happened recently enough to be in-
toxicating and confusing, or even to go unnoticed, especially by
state legislators who still view mass transit as something for
Boston and Cincinnati. After all, fifty years ago two out of
every three Texans lived outside the cities; you can't breed out
country attitudes that quickly. More than half the population
lived in rural areas at the close of World War II and reveled in
the western image portrayed in movies and fiction. But now
Texas has five cities listed among the forty-five leading cities in
the United States—Houston, Dallas, San Antonio, El Paso, and
Fort Worth. And cities like Austin and Corpus Christi are
knocking at the gate.

Texas is getting younger, and all age groups below fifty-five
are increasing. The proportion of women is likewise increasing,
and a state which sometimes has recognized women as people
already has begun to see women grow in business and political
clout. Austin's legislative delegation, for example, consists of
two women, one of them black; one chicano; and one white
male—all of them reasonably liberal. By 1980 Texas will likely
have 100 females for every 93.8 males. How does that square
with the long-legged, be-Stetsoned, *macho* Texas stereotype?

In the middle of all this change, one more statistic should be
considered for balance: despite its rapid and nearly complete ur-
banization, Texas retains a larger rural population than the *total*
populations of twenty-five other states. If you're looking for
country ham with red-eye gravy, you can still find it.

Sometimes Texans try a little self-improvement, sometimes
they get a little excited about public scandals, and sometimes
they think they perceive opportunity. The impatient chafe be-

cause its public officials won't live up to the possibility of Texas, don't seem to realize they could fashion a state which could be a showpiece for the nation. But since most Texans are ordinary people, their leaders are about as ordinary, with the exception of a now-and-again Sam Houston or Lyndon Johnson who wants to drag them along faster and farther than they want to go.

To generalize about Texas is tantamount to asking foreign visitors what they think about the United States when the only places they have seen are New York and Washington. Which is the American university, Harvard or Sul Ross? Neither. Who is the typical Texan, Ramsey Clark or Bonnie and Clyde or Lee Trevino? None of them. Who represents Texas culture—Van Cliburn or Ornette Coleman, Bob Wills and his "New San Antonio Rose" or Leadbelly or that good ol' Dallas boy, Terry Southern, who wrote the outrageously funny *Candy,* the screenplay for *Dr. Strangelove,* the novel *The Magic Christian,* and the collection known as *Red-Dirt Marijuana?* Or Janis Joplin, who used Southern Comfort and a microphone for her growing pains, and an exploitive public for her psychiatrist and confessional?

Texas is sliced neatly from Del Rio on the Rio Grande for several hundred miles northeastward through San Antonio on to Austin and eventually to the Red River by the Balcones Fault, an escarpment formed during the Tertiary time when a downwarping occurred near the Gulf Coast along with a moderate uplift inland. The Balcones forms more than a geological zone; it is also a cultural fault line. To the east of Balcones lies the farthest west extension of the Old South, the fertile wellwatered agricultural valley that forms part of the broader Mississippi River trough and Gulf of Mexico plain. That portion of Texas is southern culturally—heavily black and evangelical, with a poor-white cotton mentality that barrels of oil won't quite wash away. To the north and west of the Balcones Fault the land belongs to sheep, goats, and cattle and is the easternmost-southernmost extension of the Rocky Mountains and the semiarid desert. Here people talk louder, are more casual about religion, and learn to live with chicanos.

In East Texas lives the largest concentration of Negro millionaires in the world. Eighty percent of the state's blacks live in East Texas. Most are not millionaires. Meanwhile the proportion of blacks to whites dwindles from 30 percent in 1870 to 11 percent nearly a century later, though the net population increases.

To the east rainfall is plentiful. To the west the citizens hold prayer meetings for rain, which God answers only when the wind is right. Not infrequently the western areas seem to get their yearly average in one weekend. Houston wallows in water; Lubbock thirsts and rations. When integration of whites and blacks was a problem, every town west of the Balcones line integrated automatically, while the eastern portion uttered a quavery "Never!" before backing down. East Texas is George Wallace country; West Texas belongs to Barry Goldwater. Two decades ago a rigid conservative and a mild liberal contended for speakership of the state house. The conservative, somewhere in another century economically and socially, came from the Rio Grande Valley, where it would have been political suicide to oppose integration, and he didn't; the liberal came from Gober, near Bug Tussle, in northeast Texas, where it would have been political suicide to favor integration, and he didn't. The division in Texas is that distinct, that inflexible.

Most Texas cities lie below the Balcones line. Only El Paso, Lubbock, and Amarillo among the larger cities reside behind. The latter three towns, as well as the remainder of West Texas, possess a strong booster drive. West Texas is alive; Central and East Texas are more sophisticated, which translates as somewhere between cynical and tired.

On the negative side Houston for years required special social-science textbooks which did not mention the *verboten* United Nations nor social security. Once Houston banned Plato from a local junior high school, which led its resident pundit, Hubert Mewhinney, to muse in print his surprise, not that the book was banned but that any school in Houston had a copy of Plato's works in the first place. At one period recently the Houston school board meetings were so abusive that they were telecast locally, and people turned down dinner invitations to stay home to watch the school board. Locally it outranked "I Love Lucy." On the other hand, the University of Houston established the first educational TV station in the nation. In that same community the *Houston Post,* Lieutenant Governor Hobby's paper, for years endured Mewhinney, a most erratic character with probably as much raw brainpower as anyone in Texas, when any other newspaper would have fired him for absenteeism, stabbing sacred cows, and preferring to listen to a honky-tonk pianist in a Negro holy roller church over turning in this or last week's copy.

And from that same "intellectual desert" have emerged Barbara Jordan and Denton Cooley and Michael DeBakey, the latter two among the foremost open-heart surgeons in the world. Impossible cases are flown in from all over the world to be renewed in Houston. In the 1930s and 1940s jazz musicians from all over the United States came to Houston to be renewed also—not by a surgeon's skillful hands but by the firm fingers of Peck Kelley, who played the blues on the piano like no other white man. The visitors would play their gig at some country club or posh party and then take off for whatever club Kelley was playing in, to sit and blow and listen and jam the remainder of the night, and then go away to praise his taste and talent to other musicians.

Also out of Houston plays Lightnin' Hopkins, a black man whose blues are real; while over in Navasota lives Mance Lipscomb, another black belter whose records are prized by Harvard undergraduates while generally ignored in Texas. Like Peck, neither has ever turned commercial; both remain as genuine as the soil which nurtured them. When Lightnin' sings those "Long Gone Blues," you know he's been where he's shouting about.

In Temple in Central Texas (a town a bit smaller than Mayo's Rochester, Minnesota) Dr. Arthur C. Scott and Dr. R. R. White pooled their medical talents three-quarters of a century ago to found a hospital which grew into Scott and White Hospital, not only the most noted private hospital in the Southwest but internationally recognized for its diagnosis and treatment of malignant diseases. And in a recent poll the Southwestern Medical

College of the University of Texas was named one of the ten best hospitals in the United States in the field of diagnosis.

Rivalry between Dallas and Houston has replaced the old-time contention between Dallas and Fort Worth. The two cities are unlike—Dallas is a white-collar town that faces east; Houston is a blue-collar, big-dealer town that faces—anywhere. Dallas feels like a city; Houston, like Los Angeles, is a country town with more than a million people in it. Dallas is contained, assured, a bit defensive; Houston is brash, aggressive, full of frontier exaggeration and excess. Houston may not be Texan at all but "standard American," a buzz of continual motion. Hubert Mewhinney also capsuled the two cities by observing that Dallas is a piccolo and soufflé town, while Houston—"Houston is a steak and trombone town."

The lesser cities and towns move on, too: Fort Worth gradually shucking its cowtown image as it becomes an art center; San Antonio and El Paso regularly building their special Latin ambience; Corpus Christi growing into a kind of Nice of Texas, not quite a Riviera but next door; and Austin, pleasantly civilized except when the legislature's in town, an oasis and every Texan's second city.

As you enter the state from the northeast, you are invariably impressed with the rawness, the unkempt quality. Farmers don't button up their landscapes. You miss the white fences and mowed verdancy of Kentucky, the gardenlike greenery of Vermont, the hedgerows of Illinois, the gentility of Virginia. But travel from Austin to Corpus Christi in late June—the old brush country where the range-cattle industry originated, and watch the variegations of green fields with the topaz heads of milo maize; or drive from San Angelo to the eastward and see the unfolding light green of mesquites blending with the dark green of the hated ubiquitous cedars, the broad scapes dotted with Herefords and Angus and Brahmas; or visit the Big Bend at any season. It wasn't so long ago that Pancho Villa's Mexicans invaded the Big Bend at Glenn Springs, several hundred of them, to sack the town, kill a boy, set fire to the brush roof of a United States barracks, and shoot three of the garrison as they rushed from the burning building. Some sons of homesteaders still expect them to return. You can almost feel the tension.

Texas is a land of contradictions, capable of expanding the soul and equally capable of being mean and petty. Texas raises a breed of religious zealots whose piety masks a poverty of spirit akin to meanness. Unlike the eastern Kentucky fundamentalist who gets drunk on Saturday night, cuts up his best friend, maybe "sets a spell" in county jail, and then dominates the mourner's bench the next time he is free to go to church, his Texan equivalent looks on all merriment as sternly as the old Puritan Congregationalist and then ruins his neighbor on Monday almost "for the good of his soul." Thus Billy Sol Estes was a lay minister who neither drank nor smoked nor took the Lord's name in vain, and did not permit even his children to indulge in mixed bathing in the swimming pool of his luxurious home, all the while milking the federal government of an estimated $40 million in one of the biggest swindles in history.

If the state were suddenly to withdraw from the world, the world would still carry its name along. With a growing world conscience that makes it forever more difficult to defame groups and promote stereotypes, Texans may well at times be the last whipping boy—the last minority group—safe to attack. If Texans should outgrow their usefulness as objects of detestation, they will continue as commercial objects. Texas Bucks, Texas-size jiggers, ten-gallon hats—most Texans don't buy them—people from other states do. The largest order for Texas Bucks, according to George Fuermann, came out of Kansas City. And Chrysler puts out a Dodge that insults every Texan with its advertising—giving it a Texas name and throwing in every claim except that Santa Anna drove it at the Alamo. Seventy years ago Richard Sears hit Dallas the same way with a special Texas edition of the Sears Roebuck catalog. He buttered Texas pride on every page—no wonder the catalog was the buttress of every Texas privy.

Hubert Mewhinney probably summed it up as well as anyone. In 1955, before Alaska displaced Texas as the largest state, he wrote as follows:

Texas is the biggest state in area but the biggest and best of any single thing will be found somewhere else. . . . Texans ought to be content with the variety of loveliness, the picturesqueness of what they actually do have.[1]

AMEN!

1. Quoted in Fuermann, *Reluctant Empire*, p. 231.

Suggestions for Further Reading

The history of Texas is recorded in an appropriately vast array of literature, and there are numerous bibliographies to guide the interested reader. A good unspecialized listing was made by William M. Morrison in *Texas Book Prices* (Waco, 1963). The most useful bibliography for the general reader in a recent state history is in Seymour V. Connor's *Texas: A History* (New York: Thomas Y. Crowell, 1971). It is organized topically and chronologically, and key works are annotated.

The best straightforward, one-volume texts are Rupert N. Richardson, et al., *Texas: The Lone Star State*, 3rd ed. (Englewood Cliffs, N.J.: Prentice Hall, 1970); T. R. Fehrenbach, *Lone Star: A History of Texas and the Texans* (New York: Macmillan, 1968); and Connor. George Fuermann offers a more interpretive treatment of the Texas past in *The Reluctant Empire* (Garden City, N.Y.: Doubleday & Co., 1957). The most recent comprehensive series history is *The Saga of Texas* (Austin: Steck-Vaughn, 1965), edited by Seymour V. Connor, in six volumes: Odie B. Faulk, *A Successful Failure, 1519–1810;* David M. Vigness, *The Revolutionary Decades, 1810–1836;* Seymour V. Connor, *Adventure in Glory, 1836–1849;* Ernest Wallace, *Texas in Turmoil, 1849–1875;* Billy Mac Jones, *The Search for Maturity, 1875–1900;* and Seth Shepard McKay and Odie B. Faulk, *Texas After Spindletop, 1901–1965*. *The Handbook of Texas* (Austin: Texas State Historical Association, 1952), edited by Walter Prescott Webb and H. Bailey Carroll, is an invaluable two-volume encyclopedia of Texas history; and the journal of the Texas State Historical Association, the *Southwestern Historical Quarterly,* is an unequaled source of fine articles on all aspects of Texas history.

Various topics in Texas history have been well treated in books of interest to the nonspecialist. A good survey of Texas's aboriginal inhabitants is W. W. Newcomb, Jr., *The Indians of Texas: From Prehistoric to Modern Times* (Austin: University of Texas Press, 1969).

213

The 1830s, one of the more myth-encrusted eras of the Texas past, are treated judiciously in William C. Binkley's short interpretive work *The Texas Revolution* (Baton Rouge: Louisiana State University Press, 1952), and that most sanctified of Texas battles, the Alamo, receives its lively narrative due in Lon Tinkle's *Thirteen Days to Glory* (New York: McGraw-Hill, 1958). While most action in the Civil War bypassed Texas, the aftermath did not; Charles W. Ramsdell's *Reconstruction in Texas* (New York: Columbia University Press, 1910), an early classic state study of that aftermath, understandably embodies some interpretations since revised in work on other states, as does W. C. Nunn's more recent *Texas Under the Carpetbaggers* (Austin: University of Texas Press, 1962).

The history of change in Texas over the last century has been written in part in three letters; *Oil! Titan of the Southwest* (Norman: University of Oklahoma Press, 1949), by Carl C. Rister, tells that story. A broader economic study, more sharply focused on Texas, is John S. Spratt's fine *The Road to Spindletop: Economic Change in Texas, 1875–1901* (Austin: University of Texas Press, 1970). Cattle, fence, and open spaces speak of another Texas—and another Texan. *The American Cowboy* (Norman: University of Oklahoma Press, 1955), by Joe B. Frantz and Julian E. Choate, Jr., separates what he was from what he wasn't, while in *6000 Miles of Fence: Life on the XIT Ranch of Texas* (Austin: University of Texas Press, 1961), by Cordia Sloan Duke and Joe B. Frantz, the principals themselves tell what it was like on Texas's—and the world's—largest ranch. Another fine study of the XIT and the great Staked Plain is J. Evetts Haley, *XIT Ranch of Texas and the Early Days of the Llano Estacado* (Norman: University of Oklahoma Press, 1953). In a slightly different key, J. Frank Dobie's *Cow People* (Boston: Little, Brown, 1964) is an evocative rendering of the life of soil and saddle. The creatures who made that life possible are described in Dobie's *The Mustangs* (Boston: Little, Brown, 1952) and *The Longhorns* (Boston: Little, Brown, 1941); and one of his earliest works on the lure of the Southwest, *Coronado's Children* (New York: Grosset & Dunlap, 1963), has remained in print in one edition or another for nearly half a century. Dobie is as much subject as he is student of that which truly shapes the Texas spirit. The ups and downs of law and order begin to emerge in Walter Prescott Webb's scholarly and largely admiring account of *The Texas Rangers* (Boston: Houghton Mifflin, 1935). A newer, urban Texas is beginning to find a voice in state history; as with astrodomes and ersatz turf, Houston seems in the lead with Marilyn McAdams Sibley, *The Port of Houston: A History* (Austin: University of Texas Press, 1968), and David G. McComb, *Houston: The Bayou City* (Austin: University of Texas Press, 1969).

Connoisseurs of biography will find a number of good accounts of major Texas figures. Eugene C. Barker's *Life of Stephen F. Austin, Founder of Texas, 1793–1836* (Nashville: Cokesbury Press, 1925) is still useful. In *Sam Houston, the Great Designer* (Austin: University of Texas Press, 1954) Llerena Friend portrays a practical leader and politician worthy of the admiration that made him a symbol of both independence and statehood. Herbert Gambrell's *Anson Jones: The Last President of Texas* (Austin: University of Texas Press, 1964) is probably the best biography ever written of a Texan. Ben H. Procter offers a favorable study of the postmaster general and secretary of the treasury in the Confederacy (and later coauthor of the Interstate Commerce Act) in *Not Without Honor: The Life of John H. Reagan* (Austin: University of Texas Press, 1962). James Hogg, who left such a mark of quality on Texas public and political life, is presented in Robert C. Cotner's *James Stephen Hogg* (Austin: University of Texas Press, 1959). J. Evetts Haley has written two excellent biographies of Texans, *Charles Goodnight: Cowman and Plainsman* (Norman: University of Oklahoma Press, 1970), and *George W. Littlefield, Texan* (Norman: University of Oklahoma Press, 1972). In the very recent past, the life of Texas's most famous native son has already generated several (and varied) interpretations. A good place to start might be William C. Pool, Emmie Craddock, and David E. Conrad, *Lyndon Baines Johnson: The Formative Years* (San Marcos: Southwest Texas State College Press, 1965), and Alfred Steinberg, *Sam Johnson's Boy: A Close-Up of the President from Texas* (New York: Macmillan, 1968).

Two works of fiction have captured significant segments of the Texas population with great grace: Andy Adams, *The Log of a Cowboy: A Narrative of the Old Trail Days* (Lincoln: University of Nebraska Press, 1964), the best book on cattle trails ever written, and John Houghton Allen's *Southwest* (Philadelphia: Lippincott, 1952), a superb evocation of the Mexican-American in Texas and a gorgeous work.

Finally, for those who prefer rivers to people, the only required reading is Paul Horgan's lovely *Great River: The Rio Grande in North American History* (New York: Holt, Rinehart & Winston, 1954), which well deserves the Pulitzer and Bancroft prizes it received.

Index

Adams, John Quincy, 37, 38, 44, 71
Adams-Onís Treaty, 38, 44
Aguayo, Marqués, 30–31
Air Force Academy, 184–185
Aircraft industry, 181–182, 184–185
Airport, Dallas-Fort Worth: world's largest, 184
Alamo, 63–70
Alarcón, Don Martín de, 30
Antitrust movement, 150–152, 158
Arredondo, Joaquín de, 43, 50
Artists, Texan. *See* Entertainers and artists, Texan
Austin, Stephen F.: colonizes Anglo-Americans in Texas, 48, 51–52; organization of settlers, 53–55, 59–61; imprisoned by Mexicans, 61; fights at Gonzales, 62; elected president of Texas, 75
Austin, Moses, father of Stephen, 50–51
Avavares, Indians, 17–18

Bailey, Joseph W., 147, 152–153, 178
Balcones fault, 207–208
Banks: wildcat, 76–77; insurance on, 161
Barbed wire: and open range, 133–134
Baylor, John R.: in Civil War, 105
Bell, Gov. Peter H., 96–97
Bexar settlement, 30
Bonavia y Zapata, free trade and immigration, 39
Bowie, Col. James: at Alamo, 64–70
Bowie knife, 65
Buchanan, James P., 95, 179
Burleson, A. S., 157, 195
Burnet, David G., 73–74, 78–79
Bustamente, Gov. A., 60
Bryan, William J., 152, 157

Cabeza de Vaca, Alvar Nuñez: explorer, writer, 16–18, 24, 48; first describes

buffalo, 17; skilled medicine man, 18; exaggerated reports, 24
Cabrera, Juan Márques: at St. Augustine, 24
Caddo Indians: give Texas (Tejas) name, 9–10; role of women, 11; agriculture, 11
Calhoun, John C., 85, 93, 96
Camargo, Diego de: expedition against Cortés, 15
Camargo, Francisco: expedition of, 15
Carranza, A. Dorantes de, 16
Castillo Maldanado, Alonso de, 16–18
Cattle industry, 126–135
Chicanos, 139, 143, 171, 202, 206–207
Chiles, John, 118–119
Christianity: among Indians, 28, 32
Cíbola, Seven Cities of, 5
Civil War: secession convention, 103–104, 118; Confederate Congress, 104; the war in Texas, 105–114; privations resulting from, 112–113
Cleveland, Grover, 148, 151
Coahuiltecan Indians, 8
Compromise of 1850, 97
Connally, John B., 188, 195–197, 199
Connally, Tom, 176, 178–179
Constitution of Texas: of 1824, 61; of 1836, 75; of 1845, 92–93, 124; of 1866, 115–116; of 1869, 118, 144; of 1875, 116, 124
Coronado, Francisco Vásquez de, 127
Cortés, Hernando: first Spanish landing, 15; host to Narvaez, 16; receives survivors of Narvaez expedition, 18; introduces horses to New World, 127
Cortina, Juan Nepomuceno (Cheno): Chicano hero, 139; cattle stealer, 139
Cós, Gen. Martín Perfecto de: brother-in-law of Santa Anna, 62; surrenders San Antonio, 63
Cotton industry, 5, 129, 134, 137, 145, 169

217

Index